ENERGY FUTURE
FOSSILS AND BEYOND

MOTY KUPERBERG

ENERGY FUTURE

FOSSILS AND BEYOND

MOTY KUPERBERG

SAMUEL WACHTMAN'S SONS   DEKEL PUBLISHING HOUSE

ENERGY FUTURE: FOSSILS AND BEYOND

MOTY KUPERBERG
Copyright © 2017

Dekel Publishing House
www.dekelpublishing.com

North American rights by
Samuel Wachtman's Sons, Inc.
ISBN 978-1-941905-16-6

Editor:	Zvi Morik
Language editing:	Richard Reinprecht
Proofreading:	Dory Morik
Cover photography:	Moty Kuperberg

Open chapter fleuron images from
@Truemitra - FreeVector.com

Cover design and typesetting by
DesignPeaks@gmail.com

For information contact:

Dekel Publishing House
P.O. Box 6430
Tel Aviv 6106301, Israel
Tel: +972 3506-3235
Fax: +972 6044-627
Email: info@dekelpublishing.com

Samuel Wachtman's Sons, Inc.
2460 Garden Road, Suite C
Monterey, CA 93940, U.S.A.
Tel: 831 649-0669
Fax: 831 649-8007
Email: samuelwachtman@gmail.com

Acknowledgment

I would like to express my deep and sincere thanks and appreciation to the Joint Managing Directors of Dynamic Shipping Services Ltd., Captain Yaron Karmi and Mr. Zimi Cohen, who have supported me throughout this journey in history, geopolitics, oil price, and supply.

This could only happen through the energy-related projects we have been carrying on since 2003. From travels all over the world to so many business trips, energy conferences, and events that gave me the opportunity to meet outstanding professionals from the top league of the industry; major oil and gas companies, related shipping, and other field and subsea service companies.

My publisher, Zvi Morik, Managing Director of Dekel Publishing Group, and his expert team of language editors, Ms. Kathleen Roman and Mr. Richard Reinprecht, and the graphic studio, Design Peaks.

I am grateful for the professional assistance of Prof. Ofira Ayalon, from the University of Haifa and S. Neaman Institute, Technion, Haifa; Mr. Ron Kessary, from the gas industry; Dr Yaron Wolfsthal, an industrial computer security expert, who has pointed out the complementarity between cyber security and energy security as key ingredients of national security; and my friend Dr. Emile Nakhleh, from the University of New Mexico, whose knowledge of the Middle East is second to none, as expressed in the 2016 NSCJ conference where he spoke on the energy security session that I chaired, and his contribution to chapter 8, especially on current events in the Persian Gulf.

Much appreciated is the encouragement from Dr Henry Tan of the University of Aberdeen, Chairman of the International Symposium on Energy, and Editor of the Journal of Energy Challenges and Mechanics. He and the Director of the North Sea Conference and Journal, Mrs.

Ronda Chen, gave me an excellent opportunity to introduce the topic of this book as a result of their successful energy symposium series, which has been held since 2014.

Furthermore, this work could not have been completed without the assistance of the four American internship students of summer 2015-2016: Simon Spector, from Northeastern University, CA, USA, who was a great help and recourse; Jordan Angel, University of Connecticut, Storrs, CT, USA; Aline Gonicman, Brandeis University, Waltham, MA, USA; and Mara Tazartus, Northeastern University, Boston, MA, USA, who significantly contributed to this book.

Last but not least, my wife Shosh and our children Alon, Shira, Tal and Guy—see them on page 257 (playing *Team Work* and a *Different Tune*), were always there for me with the right push and help to continue this three-year-long journey.

Thank you all!

Moty Kuperberg
Haifa, December 2017

TABLE OF CONTENTS

II. GEOPOLITICS

III. PRICING

IV. SUPPLY

FOREWORD

We need energy. We depend on energy. Our dependence on energy is dictating the economic policies of each country but also foreign policy, security, transportation and environmental policies, and more.

Energy is defined as the "ability of a system to perform work." When it comes to "work," we mean electricity, heat (and cold), as well as transportation. Since our world is constantly developing, the need for energy is increasing constantly as well.

Given the above paradigm, the question that needs to be asked is: should this growth in demand remain "conventional," based on fossil, polluting fuels, or should we aim at decoupling our growth from this dependency? The latter, of course, is the answer.

The challenges of supplying sustainable energy are huge.

The path to these challenges is suggested in this book, "Energy Future," by Moty Kuperberg. The book draws the line along more than 100 years of history of the human race through the lens of energy supply, including wars, geopolitics and conflicts affecting oil availability and prices.

The world of energy today, and in the coming decades, will and should include a very high diversity of resources:

- Conventional sources— mainly coal, natural gas, and oil
- Renewable energy—mainly solar, wind and hydro
- Alternative energy, such as nuclear.

We need to protect the planet and ensure prosperity for all; therefore, the energy systems should be diverse, economic, environmental, and socially efficient.

This book enables the reader to understand the long history of oil and proposes new ways to achieve energy security and sustainability.

Ofira Ayalon, Professor. Senior Researcher and Head of Environment Cluster, Samuel Neaman Institute, Technion, Haifa. Director of the Natural Resources and Environmental Research Center (NRERC) at the University of Haifa. Professor at the Department of Natural Resources and Environmental Management, Faculty of Management, University of Haifa.

PROLOGUE:

HOUSTON, SPRING 2002; ABERDEEN, SUMMER 2017

---◆---

Warning Signs

The accumulation of events over nearly a decade drove me to write this book. In March of 2002, only six months after the September 11 terror attacks on the United States, a *Houston Chronicle* article quoted an OPEC official calling to raise oil prices, saying that OPEC "gave the world enough time to recover." In September of 2004, for the first time in the history of the oil industry, oil prices crossed the $50 per barrel threshold. By May of 2008, oil prices reached $130 per barrel, while Goldman-Sachs, a leading global investment banking firm, predicted that oil prices could reach $200 a barrel. At the same time, the *Oil and Gas Journal* (OGJ) wrote that a price level of $150 a barrel was imminent.

Among these milestones, one cannot disregard the threat made in July of 2008 by the late Venezuelan president, Hugo Chavez, asserting that oil might even reach $300 a barrel if Exxon, an American oil company, froze Venezuelan assets in a financial dispute. One must also acknowledge the words of the mythological Saudi Arabian minister of oil, Ahmed Zaki Yamani, who was quoted in April of 2011 saying that the price of oil could hit $300 a barrel as a result of the increasing unrest in his country.

Stories like these contribute to the growing consensus that the age of cheap oil is coming to an end. For years, we've been well trained to consider oil and other energy products as expensive commodities, luxuries even, whose price is written in stone. From oil kingdoms in the desert to giant oil companies rooted in the first days of the oil industry, it seems someone always expects consumers to pay any price, no questions asked, simply because it's oil.

Have all of the entities and organizations to whom we entrust control over our energy security—governments, media, and industry—truly forgotten how prices are affected by inflation, and particularly speculation? It seems that all have put aside their aversion to OPEC and chosen to forget the direct connection of energy price with very basic world commodities such as grains and livestock. While they bask in the scent of gas and the fragrance of oil, it seems everyone is ignoring the immediate need to stop the greed, foolishness, and deception surrounding us. It is time to break the vicious cycle of this great Ponzi scheme.

An Insatiable Thirst

In his defining book, *The Prize: The Epic Quest for Oil, Money and Power* (a highly recommended source for those wishing to further their knowledge of oil and fossil fuels' rich and fascinating history), Daniel Yergin coined the term "the Hydrocarbon Man." This refers to human society's insatiable thirst for oil and other fossil fuel products and byproducts, with which all of our lives are irreversibly intertwined. Industrialized human society is powered by fossil fuels: from industry and power production; through air conditioning, refrigeration and lighting our homes and cities; to medicine, military and agriculture.

As industrialization, urbanization, and motorization all expand and grow, they are inseparably accompanied by the devastating pollution of land, air, and sea. Natural gas, the new rising star shining above the global energy horizon, is quickly becoming a cleaner, cost-effective, and abundant energy source. At a time in which the power we produce and consume affects the very air we breathe, natural gas offers a great relief to environmental pollution. Of course, at the same time we must keep striving toward increasing the efficacy and usability of all fuel types through technological advancements, better preservation, and further development of renewable, alternative, and sustainable energy sources.

The American Petroleum Institute lists an abundance of oil's seemingly endless uses and applications. First and foremost is power production and transportation, followed closely by the petrochemical industry, which utilizes oil products and by-products in numerous versatile fields. Some examples include agricultural fertilizers; food preservation and storage; sealants, adhesives, and paints; nylon bags and ropes; cleaning supplies, care products, and toiletries; tapes, cassettes, computers, and digital hardware; candles, balloons, baby strollers, and toys; bandages, medical supplies, artificial heart valves, drug capsules, and pills.

To better understand oil's vast history, it is first necessary to introduce an important basic term: *the oil barrel*. A standard barrel holds 42 gallons, which equals 159 liters, and is counted in units of *Bbl* or *Blue Barrel*. Alluding to Standard Oil's signature drum color, the blue barrel became world renowned in times when oil trade and marketing expanded across the American, European, and Southeast Asian markets. The barrel remains the unit by which oil is measured, quantified, and priced. It was the first mode of transporting the newly drawn crude oil from early, primitive wells to the forming markets in which it fulfilled a growing demand for an affordable and efficient source of lighting.

Our journey along oil's history takes us to the near past and present, an age in which oil has become a speculative instrument, which is only used to raise prices. Such increases are always explained away "professionally," and for such politically and economically grounded reasons.

When prices decrease, however, the explanation is always so infuriatingly simple: *profit taking*. Repeating itself with every price decrease, this reasoning can only mean one thing: traders, having pushed oil prices as high as they can, are withdrawing their investments, riding the oil tanker all the way to the bank. Traders do not need to purchase a single *real* oil barrel, but nevertheless, by buying *positions*, they can push future demand up, up, and away.

Yet Another Energy Crisis

Did the vertiginous oil price climb that began in 2003 carry with it a rise in food prices? What is the connection between the two, if such a connection even exists? In the end, consumers always pay the price, whether they are private end users or entire economies of the world, all consumers fold under the burden of energy prices. So can we regain control? Is it even possible anymore? We argue that the traditional economic fundamentals must be reapplied to the oil trade and industry since many claim that there is no economic fundamental reason or cause for such a price rampage. On the other hand, many others call for simply allowing the market to run its course. Some wave the green banner of environmental protection to justify high oil prices to reduce consumption. And of course, there are the followers of "the end of the fossil energy era"—those who seem to spot the *peak oil* of the famous Hubbert curve in every corner, awaiting it year after year for over four decades.

Why is it that any local, specific incident in some remote oil pipeline or small refinery in the central United States, or perhaps on the fringes of Europe, disrupts the sleep of Wall Street dwellers? Why is it that any terror-related event taking place in any oil facility anywhere on the globe makes every single capital trustee's heart skip a beat? After all, for some years now, it has been agreed that oil prices contain some terror risk premium.

Reserve quotes are reported in an enviable transparency by American authorities, including the Energy Information Administration (EIA) and the American Petroleum Institute. Each and every weekly report reawakens these sleeping financial lions, while the ordinary person, fueling his or her car or paying the electricity bill, really doesn't care if the crude oil reserve in the United States is 300 million barrels or 304 million; that person wouldn't even care if reserves suddenly plummeted that week to below 300 million barrels.

Often some analysts and Wall Street traders will have already announced the previous week that they foresee a rise in reserves; however, if in reality reserves drop, even just a little beneath the analysts' prediction, the decline is blown completely out of proportion to the degree of yet another energy crisis and vice versa.

Other important questions remain to be raised and answered. How do these giant oil companies report equally giant revenues year after year? Where do these monster earnings come from? What's the precise source of the revenue, and can it be channeled back to the consumers? Such a mutually beneficial notion sounds almost bizarre when looking at real gasoline consumer price history in the United States, which rose higher and higher up to an all-time peak in the summer of 2008, when gasoline reached $4.00 a gallon—a whopping 300 to 400 percent increase from $1.50 per gallon in early 2004, and under $1.00 in 1999. While the situation has changed since 2015, there is still a lack of assurance for stability.

Fears and Concerns

Throughout the following chapters, my message is clear: stability has to be reached, both in *security of supply* and in the strong and solid economic price base for this supply.

When prices are being imposed in sophisticated global stock exchange markets, and always for the benefit of the producing countries (both OPEC and non-OPEC members), one should bear in mind that it takes two to tango. Just as OPEC has instituted its own *floor and cap* prices and enforced them for decades, such top and bottom oil price levels should be equally set by consumers. Fair and stable energy prices and supply for the market are the true meaning of global energy security.

As oil prices fell at the end of 2008 and beginning of 2009, the world economy faced its most severe crisis since the 1930s, and voices began to emerge calling for a tight collaboration between producing and consuming countries, between buyers and sellers. At that time, the word *traders* was hardly being used anymore; could it be that it had become a derogatory term, a metaphor for a *market failure*? The beginning of the twenty-first century brought with it the greediness of the NYMEX traders, thus enhancing the long-standing political sluggishness of OPEC.

Capital market "evildoers," such as the many traders, different analysts, and financial consultants, have contributed their share to the chaos that peaked in 2008. We cannot live without them, but we can definitely live with fewer of them.

The recent years' wild oil market, exceeding the bounds of classical economics and its conservative rules, is bound to return to a normal pattern behavior of reliable supply and demand forecasts. Only then can we truly recover from the decades of crises and welcome *The New Energy Era*, an era that will last and be our **Energy Future**.

OPEC and other international organizations such as the International Energy Agency (IEA) failed to maintain control over the market from 2002–2015. In a self-perpetuating cycle, prices rose as concerns and claims of global oil shortage were raised, which caused fingers to be pointed mainly at OPEC since it is a cartel that only benefits from rising prices. Although having admitted at the peak of the crisis that it had lost control over oil prices, OPEC has also gone out of its way to assert that there was no oil shortage whatsoever. We can definitely agree with the latter assertion. Many other entities, such as large investment banks, research institutes, and governments that were supposed to be responsible for stabilization and control over the market, failed as well and were swept away by the rising tide of oil prices.

We are the market. You, the readers of this book, are part of the largest consumer community worldwide. The market is not NYMEX traders or OPEC officials. Realizing this simple and basic truth, we are not terrified anymore by the magic words *fear* and *concern*. These words are thrust upon us by the media and the industry, with reports that open with phrases like *"traders fear . . ."* or *"analysts are concerned. . . ."*

In fact, we never had any reason to be afraid or concerned in the first place. An encouraging confirmation for this is found in an *Oil and Gas Journal* (OGJ) online edition headline from October 29, 2008: "Prices Fall as Market Ignores OPEC." For the first time, a major news medium in the industry stated loud and clear that the market can in fact do without OPEC's price dictation.

The question remains as to how can we maintain and enforce market fairness. Moreover, can an oil price limit be achieved? Would that be the answer for an affordable and secure energy supply? For example, what if back in early 2008 the George W. Bush administration had set a ceiling price on gasoline at $3.00 per gallon, representing $75 per barrel, just as OPEC set its floor price? What if the US government had imposed a 100% tax on oil companies who charged even a cent above this cap price? Could it have had any effect on the rising oil price crisis of that year? Alternatively, imagine ExxonMobil, an energy giant, setting a ceiling price of $2.99 per gallon in its gas stations across the United States and Europe during the spring of 2008; could it have stopped the oil price surge? It stands to reason that the answer to both questions is yes.

The Century of Oil

Throughout the following four parts of this book, we travel along the exceptional chronicles of energy: from the discovery of petroleum and its early use for illumination, through the invention of the internal combustion engine, generating electric power from oil, and to the mass production and distribution of oil and gas. In these chapters, we witness the birth of the first large corporations—the Majors—and see the formation of great powers and cartels, from Rockefeller's Standard Oil and the Salomon brothers' Shell to the Seven Sisters (the top seven oil companies that had the most influence on the oil industry during the 1960s and early 1970s—Shell, Texaco, Mobil, Esso, BP, Gulf Oil, Chevron). We examine Russia and the United States, and the wars for territories and wealth that are intertwined with the development of the oil and gas industry. The analysis takes us all the way to our contemporary times, when modern lust and thirst for black gold raise concerns regarding the future of oil and our environment.

As this bleak, grim future will come to pass within several decades, is there really any justification for the present panic and soaring prices, such as those we faced in the first decade of this century? Are we doomed to pay today the price of tomorrow's energy?

Could a better approach to energy preservation delay the end of this current energy era? What other options and alternatives do we have? And what might be their economic, environmental, and social effects? Does the use of more nuclear power delay the end of the fossil fuel age and leave sufficient time to develop reliable and sustainable new energy sources? Could hydrogen fuel cells, nuclear fission/fusion, and renewable technologies reach economic viability and mass distribution in time to allow a smooth transition to the next evolution of energy?

Not all the answers to these numerous questions can be found in this book, but there is a simple and clear guideline that runs through them all: Neither human society nor global economy can accept paying extravagant prices for the energy that is currently available. We should never agree to be extorted or blackmailed by cartels and terrorists, speculators and traders, whose sole interest is to keep money and power flowing straight their way, into their pockets.

In early 2012, as we published the first edition of this book, it seemed that history was about to repeat itself, with the price of a barrel of oil soaring to $100 for the first time in two years, and staying at that level for almost four years. Only by late 2014 had oil prices dropped to end the year at $56 per barrel, and continued to drop below the $50 mark, to hover there through 2015 to 2017, as we prepared to publish this book. This, in a way, reflects the pattern seen in 2008 when prices rose to a peak of $147 per barrel, only to free-fall down to $44 by year's end. As we are in the midst of yet another energy price crisis, we have the obligation to make sure this one will be the last.

The winter of 2014 through the summer of 2016 brought a sharp price drop to below $50 per barrel, finally allowing the opportunity for the oil and gas market to settle and adjust. In the winter of 2016–2017, as we prepared to publish this edition, prices were hovering at the $40 to $50 per barrel range, to stabilize at the low-mid $50s. A price we believe should be the floor-level benchmark.

Now is precisely the right time to initiate a global energy price regime, founded on the basis of a sufficient supply to meet demands worldwide, free of any foreign influence, interest, and manipulation. This is a crucial period in time for the energy industry, as twenty-first century technologies mature to better create suitable substitutes while diminishing and controlling the dangerous environmental effects of today's fossil fuel consumption.

In his book, published more than two decades ago, Daniel Yergin ended the prologue with the following words: ". . . The twentieth century rightly deserves the title 'the century of oil'. . . . This is a story of individual people, of powerful economic forces, of technological change, of political struggles, of international conflict and, indeed, of epic change."

But what really changed when we entered the twenty-first century? Far too little.

Furthermore, we should do our utmost to promote energy conservation and efficiency, as well as further technological development to allow for suitable substitutes. This will result in other, more sustainable energy sources, which will utilize advanced twenty-first-century technologies, in order to add to, complement, and ultimately phase out or reduce the use of fossil fuels.

To better understand the present, and to attempt to see the future, one must first study the past. What is the history of oil and gas, their trade and industry, their peaks and crises? Where are they heading now, and what does the future hold for them? All issues and answers clearly covered in this book: *ENERGY FUTURE – FOSSILS AND BEYOND.*

I. HISTORY

1. BIRTH OF AN INDUSTRY

———————◆———————

Black Gold: "Rock Oil"

So what is the elusive and mysterious *black gold*? Why does the black gold rush that started in the mid-nineteenth century drive traders, speculators, giant companies, governments, and entire economies oil-crazy?

Requiring nearly no introduction, the origin of oil is well known. This organic substance, which formed hundreds of millions of years ago, is the end product of the natural recycling of many species of organisms whose remains sank, buried beneath both land and sea. As countless years passed, the ground layers and bodies of water grew higher and denser, pressing down against the ancient remains with enormous physical powers. Temperature and pressure changes, among other factors, turned these deposits of animal and plant remains into what we now call *fossil fuels*: coal, oil, natural gas, and their by-products.

Most of the earth's oil is hidden deep beneath land and sea and remained inaccessible to mankind for thousands of years. However, a sparse fraction of it, which has accumulated close to the earth's crust, has been slowly diffusing for millennia, flowing upwards and out onto the surface.

The name for oil, *petroleum*, comes from the Latin words for rock, *petra,* and oil, *oleum*. This derives from ancient times when oil was known as the greasy substance seen oozing and flowing from cracks in the Earth's surface.

In the nineteenth century, it was coal that first drove the racing wheels of the Industrial Revolution. But by the turn of the twentieth century, coal was partially disowned by the other members of the fossil fuel family, oil and natural gas. The latter two have quickly gained their place as the prominent energy sources for power production, transportation, and industry. Finally, the worldwide mobilization and motorization of vast armies in the world wars of the twentieth century proved these energy sources to be crucial and indisputably important for both mankind and its machines.

Let There Be Light

The very first black gold rush began in the state of Pennsylvania in the mid-nineteenth century with a passionate entrepreneur, George Henry Bissell. Considered the father of the oil industry, it was he who brought about the oil revolution by investing in the first oil well in 1859, located in Titusville. This was the beginning of the century of oil as it was produced for lighting and household use, available for the improvement of mankind's quality of life.

Along the Stream

In the mid-nineteenth century, the oil industry developed beyond oil supply for household lighting. Large companies were founded, and high investment in exploration licenses as well as in infrastructure for the budding oil industry became common. As new market forces emerged, so began the constant competition for market control. New, vertically integrated companies aimed to achieve full control over the petroleum supply chain. They coined the terms *upstream*, *midstream*, and *downstream*, referring to the main links of the supply chain: exportation and production, transportation and refinement, and distribution.

Standard Oil was one of the prominent companies among these emerging oil producers. In 1911, antitrust laws were passed in the United States, restricting the formation of cartels and prohibiting the creation of monopolies. These laws outlined a new economic and regulatory framework, which is still enforced to this day. Standard Oil's aggressive grasp for control of the market came to a halt with the implementation of these antitrust laws.

The growth of the American market brought about the expansion of oil discoveries, first in Texas in 1901, then in California in 1910, and later in Oklahoma and several neighboring states. The Gulf of Mexico, as well as the Venezuelan area of the Caribbean Sea, became well known for huge oil potential when the Gulf Oil company discovered oil in Mexico in 1914.

At the same time, European demand for oil for lighting was expanding. The American companies, mainly Standard Oil, searched for markets in Europe, Russia, and the Far East. While American Standard Oil was becoming increasingly powerful, the two emerging European companies, the British Shell and the Swedish-French Nobel-Rothschild partnership, were striving to become major forces in the global industry.

Fossil Power

By the end of the nineteenth century, the oil lamp was the most common method of illumination. While it had its limitations, including smoke, soot, bad odors, and the danger of open fire, its use had become of great significance to mankind. Therefore, the invention of the electric light in 1882 almost came as a surprise to the oil industry, shocking it by causing falling demand and resulting in the very first oil price collapse—

the first *oil crisis* in the history of black gold. The public soon embraced this new, risk-free, and cheaper electrical lighting solution, leaving the oil lamp a relic of darker times.

The oil industry's loss of its original market for lighting meant new and far greater markets for power production. In 1882, the first fossil fueled central power plant in the United States started generating electricity in New York City, and very soon thereafter, electricity was generated across the Atlantic in London as well.

The Internal Combustion Engine

The oil market soon recovered, as the invention of the internal combustion engine and the birth of the motor vehicle proved oil to be the only widespread source of energy for everyday transportation. Within three decades, what started as an accessible and inexpensive solution for lighting and heating became the most prominent energy source for society's next giant technological leap—the motorized vehicle.

In 1896, Henry Ford, an American businessman, produced his first car. European automobile producers, such as Germany's Mercedes-Benz, also contributed to the development of global motorization. At the same time, various industries and shipping companies started using fuel oil instead of coal.

In 1891, Henry Ford started his career as an engineer with the Edison Illuminating Company in Detroit. Soon he became a car producer, also introducing major improvements in mass production to lower vehicles' prices. In 1903, the year that the Ford Motor Company was founded, the Wright brothers, Ohio bicycle builders Orville and Wilbur, made the first motorized heavier-than-air flight—how very symbolic. The newly formed oil industry was now about to embrace far greater markets and demands, spanning across the globe. Oil would soon take to skies.

The cost of the first Ford Model T in 1908 was $850, which would be approximately $17,000 today. In the beginning of the twentieth century the price dropped below $300. Ford also paid his workers remarkably well, encouraging them to buy cars themselves.

The number of vehicles on register increased from 8,000 during the first decade of the twentieth century to more than 80,000 by 1910. The demand for new vehicles significantly outnumbered the supply, and the Ford Motor Company installed a moving assembly line for the mass production of an entire automobile. This innovation increased the company's annual production from 10,000 vehicles in 1909 to 300,000 within five years, creating new records in the demand for oil.

Rise of the "Majors"

The battle for control over global oil markets commenced in the United States, spread to Europe, expanded as far as the Tsardom of Russia, and eventually reached the Far East. As the American Civil War came to an end in 1865, so began a global struggle for market control between the world oil powers of the time. This intercontinental battle for supremacy led to another price crisis. By the turn of the century, this ruthless skirmish was put to rest with the various rulings of American courts, echoing the public campaign against monopolies and trusts, focusing on the largest oil company at the time, Standard Oil, which wielded tremendous power. This eventually resulted in the passage of American antitrust legislation of the early twentieth century.

In the United States, John D. Rockefeller's Standard Oil emerged as the dominant oil company, and would remain so for quite some time. The company was founded in January 1870 in order to bring standardization of product quality during a time when oil was used for lighting. Eventually, this goal of standardization would lead Rockefeller and his company to become the dominant power in the oil market. The company purchased its first refinery in 1863, which became highly profitable within a year, encouraging Rockefeller to purchase more and more refineries.

Rockefeller was the first to realize the strength of a vertically integrated company, one that controls all aspects of production and supply. Drilling, production, refining, transportation, and supply were all under sole ownership and at the disposal of a single massive company. This gave Standard Oil complete control over its oil price. This strategy became a standard methodology in the developing oil industry and soon led to the creation of the major oil companies that to this day continue to gain massive strength and profits.

Rockefeller gradually gained complete control over his competitors in the market, first in the United States and later on in the developing global markets of Europe and the Far East. The oil price crisis of the early 1870s presented Standard Oil with a golden opportunity to commence its takeover campaign, aggressively pursuing mergers with its American competitors to consolidate power within the industry. Rockefeller and his company were engaged in a determined and persistent pursuit of absolute control of the industry, eliminating most competitors along the way. By 1879, the company's nearly two-decade-long quest for power finally ended as Standard Oil came to control about 90 percent of the refining capacity of the United States.

In his triumphal voyage to the top of the industry, Rockefeller gained some enemies: the American public, as well as competitors and independent producers. It became clear that eliminating competition, allegedly to create a stronger market and stabilize prices, can only mean one thing: a monopoly that controls the market and dictates prices.

Russian Oil on the Rise

In the global battle for market control, the European front, including the Russian Empire, was just as aggressive. By the 1870s and 1880s, Standard Oil had gained control over oil export to Europe, which at the time accounted for about one half of the oil production capacity in the United States. Export began with slow and hesitant steps; the first oil shipment to Europe safely reached London in 1861. This marked an exceptional milestone for an industry that had emerged less than a decade earlier. This very first shipment of refined kerosene barrels opened the era of international oil trade.

Although oil was new in Europe, it easily penetrated the European market, and demand increased by the end of the century. The daily oil production in the United States increased from less than 7,000 barrels in 1865 to nearly 33,000 just one decade later. By 1885, the volume doubled only to be met by large-scale Russian oil production. Russian production would keep growing and later compete with Standard Oil in the Asian markets.

During the early years of the oil industry, the general opinion was that oil could be found solely in Pennsylvania, at least for the foreseeable future. However, during those same years, the first oil wells outside of the United States were drilled in the region of Baku. In the early 1870s, American oil was already in vast use with great success in western Russia, where it had first arrived in 1862. The Russian oil producers' main problem was geographic location, which required a seemingly impossible transportation solution across the Caucasus to Western European markets. Thus, American oil from across the ocean turned out to be cheaper and more accessible than local Russian oil, which originated in the Caspian Sea.

The Nobel's Prize

A turning point came about with the Swedish Nobel family, the Nobel brothers, whose main business was firearm and ammunition production. In 1873, Robert Nobel was sent to the Caucasus to procure Russian walnut trees that were needed for the production of rifles. When Robert arrived in Baku, in 1873, he was fascinated by the flourishing oil industry and decided to purchase a local refinery. With this foray into the forming industry, the Nobel brothers became oil men.

The brothers immediately identified the bottleneck in the oil distribution chain: transportation. At the time, oil was still transported in barrels, making transport the main hurdle in expanding and gaining a larger market share. Recognizing this, the brothers started to transport their oil in liquid bulk wagons and sea tankers, drawing from Ludwig's pioneering work in designing marine oil tankers. Their oil could now be transported six hundred miles across the Caspian Sea to Astrakhan and along Russia's inner waterways.

Their innovative solution was later adopted by the oil industry for transatlantic oil transport. Within a decade, the Nobel's company became the largest oil company in the Russian Empire, producing 50 percent of the oil for illumination in Russia. They were also a vertically integrated company with control of drilling, production, refining, and transportation, which only made their growing position in the Russian market even stronger.

By the late 1870s, the Nobel brothers had already realized that the Russian market was limited, and they sought larger markets outside of the Russian Empire. Within one decade, total oil production in Russia grew rapidly, from 0.6 million barrels in 1874 to a staggering 23 million barrels in 1888, just 5 million barrels less than the American production.

Seeking new markets, the Nobel brothers once more found that transportation was the bottleneck in their expansion plans. As it turned out, it was one thing to transport oil across the Caspian Sea and up the Volga into central Russia, but it was an entirely different story to transport it across the Caucasus to the Black Sea for export to global markets.

The Caucasus Challenge

For Russian oil to be exported, it needed to reach the city of Batumi on the eastern shore of the Black Sea. Here, a more complex solution for inland transportation was required, but such infrastructure was not yet in existence. A railroad across the Caucasus Mountains, connecting the Caspian Sea to the Black Sea, was just a matter of initiative, funds, and time. The challenge was met by two independent entrepreneurs from

Baku, who were looking to compete with the Nobel distribution chain in Russia. By the early 1880s, the two started working on the railway thanks to loans granted by the famous French bankers, the Rothschild family. The Rothschild brothers, Alphonse and Edmund, already owned railway and oil enterprises across Europe. In return for the loans they were assured a regular supply of Russian oil at a competitive price. And so a new competitor, well financed and highly ambitious, entered the scene, challenging the Nobel brothers' dominance in the Russian and European markets. Yet the real challenge was waiting overseas.

Standard Oil's dominance was threatened by the emerging competition, which brought it to lower its oil prices in 1885. It was not enough to stave off competitors like the Nobels and Rothschilds. Russian oil export volumes through the Black Sea increased to a point that a new impediment arose—the Greater Caucasus mountain range. In order to bypass the rough terrain of the Caucasus, the Nobel brothers, using their expertise in dynamite, laid a pipeline running through the mountains, thus allowing them to increase the supply of Russian oil to export from the Black Sea.

At this early stage of the industry's development, the United States and Russia were the only two oil-producing countries. The Americans' share of the export oil market fell from 78 percent in 1888 to 71 percent in 1891, while the Russian share rose from 22 percent to 29 percent. Untapped markets in the Far East remained the most attractive potential for growth.

Flowing Eastward

The breakthrough to the markets in the East started when three Frenchmen, two Jews, and a Briton sat down together. The men involved were the Samuel brothers, who were well connected in the East; the Rothschilds, with their oil expertise; and Fred Lane, a British shipping broker. These men were major players behind the global revolution that posed the most serious competition and challenge to Standard Oil thus far—shipping oil in tankers east of the Suez.

The maiden voyage of the first liquid bulk oil tanker through the Suez Canal, which marked the revolution in oil transportation and supply, came to be known as the Coup of 1892. On August 23, 1892, the first oil tanker, the *Murex* (a kind of seashell), crossed the Suez Canal loaded with Russian oil bound for Singapore and Bangkok.

The Murex

This voyage was the peak of combined technological, political, and commercial efforts. The Samuel brothers, facing difficulties in receiving official approval from the Suez Canal Company, had to overcome domestic political hurdles as well as somewhat hostile British press coverage and public opinion; this negative coverage may have resulted from the influence of Standard Oil itself. The exclusive contract to distribute the Rothschilds' Russian oil in the East was signed in 1891, while the first oil tanker to carry this oil was built in Britain. Official approval from the Suez Canal authorities was received in January of 1892. The Suez Canal was partly under the control of Britain per the 1875 agreement between Benjamin Disraeli, the British prime minister at the time, and Ismail Pasha, his Egyptian counterpart. Yet, in practice, Egypt had been under British occupancy since 1882.

Having lagged behind in the Far East race, Standard Oil came up with another solution to reach eastern markets. If they couldn't ship their European oil eastward, they would gain control over oil sources in the East, thus supplying the main eastern markets of Singapore and Hong Kong with local oil.

In the East, just a few hours away from Singapore, a new industry player, the Royal Dutch Petroleum Company, was investing heavily in exploring for oil in the Dutch East Indies near Sumatra (now part of Indonesia).

American Competition

By the turn of the century, new companies had emerged in the United States and posed increasing challenges to Standard Oil's dominance. A breakthrough finally came in January of 1901 with a huge oil field discovery in Texas. This would prove to be a key element in breaking the hegemony of Standard Oil, and would provide a new production base for expanding the American oil industry. In 1905 a major oil discovery in Tulsa, Oklahoma, added to the developing oil industry in the United States. Oil produced in Oklahoma was piped to refineries in Texas, and within two years the Gulf Oil Corporation was established through the merger of a number of oil businesses, principally the J.M. Guffey Petroleum and Gulf Refining companies of Texas. Later on, Gulf Oil became one of the so-called Seven Sisters. The "Seven Sisters" was a term coined to describe the seven largest integrated oil companies that dominated the global petroleum industry for decades.

Other US-based companies emerged to take advantage of the growing market due to the motorization era that swept through the

United States in the early twentieth century. Some Americans began to invest in Mexican oil fields, which proved to be prolific. In 1914, the Tampico oil discovery gave Gulf Oil its first international activity. The Tampico discovery established the Gulf of Mexico as a rich area of oil and gas. Other companies such as Sun Oil and Texaco emerged during that time.

The Monopoly Collapse

Standard Oil, which controlled 90 percent of American refining capacity in 1880, saw a dramatic decrease of its market share to 65 percent by 1911.

The most significant measures taken to fight the monopoly of Standard Oil were constitutional, establishing a precedent on how to deal with monopolies and cartels. The public and commercial campaign of Standard Oil's competitors also deserves credit for this development. The monopoly of Standard Oil was taken over by the hegemony of the Seven Sisters.

The public campaign against Standard Oil's monopoly peaked during the early twentieth century. It was the journalist Ida Tarbell—together with the determined Roosevelt administration—that exposed Standard Oil's conduct. Tarbell's research resulted in the book *The History of the Standard Oil Company*, which she published in 1904. The detailed information she exposed attracted the attention of the wider public. Interestingly enough, the "trusts" system had a history in the American business system, so Standard Oil was not the first company to act as a trust, but it was the first to register as such. Other leading trusts existed in the meat industry, drugs, and food, but the oil trust somehow attracted more public attention.

By 1882 the Standard Oil Company structure became a trust. The term *trust* very soon became derogatory in American economy and commerce. At this stage, the public and legal activities against Standard Oil hardly caused the company any damage, though it promoted

Rockefeller's increase in philanthropic activity, which reached $500 million by 1910.

The trust, which could ignore public criticism in its early days, faced more difficult and determined opposition in the early twentieth century. President Roosevelt had the power and determination to fight the trust. By his second presidential term, a lawsuit against Standard Oil in St. Louis, paired with massive media and public campaigns, exposed Standard Oil and its management as public enemies. Other states followed, and, in 1909, a federal court found Standard Oil in violation of the Antitrust Act and ordered the dissolution of the company.

After two years of appeals, the trust broke up in 1911. Thus, Standard Oil split into several companies, some larger than others, but together these new entities would eventually surpass the size of the original company.

From the Ruins

Some of the top brands of the oil industry emerged in 1911. Standard Oil of New Jersey became Exxon, Standard Oil of New York became Mobil, Standard Oil of California became Chevron as well as Amoco and Conoco.

It took about ninety more years for the next transformation of those Majors. In the 1990s there was another round of industry mergers, when Chevron merged with Texaco to form ChevronTexaco, Exxon merged with Mobil to form ExxonMobil, and Conoco merged with Phillips Petroleum to form ConocoPhillips.

This wave of mergers reached Europe as well, with the great French merger of TotalFinaElf. Later in 2007 it was the GDF merger with SUEZ that formed the €74 billion energy giant GDFSUEZ. Yet again, in early April of 2015, another merger occurred when Shell acquired BG in a multibillion-dollar deal.

Was it the result of some stress and unrest due to the latest decline in energy prices or the quest for more power by these giants?

The End or the Beginning?

In 1903, after two years of intense negotiation between the Shell Transport and Trading Company, the Royal Dutch Petroleum Company, and the Rothschild brothers, the Asiatic Petroleum Company was founded based on three equal parts between Royal Dutch (that was already British Dutch), Shell, and the Rothschilds. Royal Dutch took the lead. It took them another four years to conclude a full merger that created Royal Dutch Shell. The fall of the Russian oil supply started with the Russo-Japanese War and the social and labor unrest surrounding the 1905 Russian Revolution, destroying the oil industry in Baku.

The decline of Russian oil supply after the 1905 revolution, from 31 percent to 9 percent of the world international oil trade, was about to be offset by the recently discovered Persian oil. The first discoveries in 1901 resulted in the formation of the Anglo-Persian Oil Company, in 1909, under British hegemony.

Demand for oil increased as the world discovered that oil would be crucial for civilian and military use in the conflict to come. A worldwide global supply chain developed, yet the major catalysts were the geopolitical changes that occurred toward the Great War in 1914 and the large expansion of transportation by land, air, and sea brought about by the war.

2. OIL INDUSTRY TAKES TO THE SEA AND SKY

———————◆———————

A. Era of Manned Flight

By the late nineteenth century, aerodynamic physics was known and understood well enough to support a heavier-than-air aircraft flight. The internal combustion engine, which consumed gasoline to produce mechanical energy, was smaller and lighter than the steam engines that preceded it, making it highly suitable for airplane propulsion. The missing piece, however, was a proper power unit—an engine that was light and small, yet capable of sufficient power output to be married to an aircraft body.

Though Germany and France already had vast knowledge and experience with aerodynamics and flight, it was two American brothers, Wilbur and Orville Wright, who claimed their place in history with the first heavier-than-air manned flight. To do so, the brothers designed and built their own specific internal combustion engine. Their first engine produced thirteen horsepower, revolving a thousand times per minute. Their breakthrough triggered a surge in development and manufacturing of lighter aero engines, and within less than two years, engines produced as much as fifty horsepower, and continued to increase in power thereafter. By 1914, as World War I began, several airplane engine manufacturing companies existed worldwide, and in the United States and Britain, engines producing 400 HP were already available for flight.

———

The emergence of new growing energy markets was but one of the results of the new era of manned flight. The millennia-old dream of imitating birds' flight was realized with manmade aircraft—propelled, controlled, and manned, they revolutionized human societies and economies, won wars, and even conquered space and the moon.

During the second half of the nineteenth century, aviation knowledge was still limited to building and flying air gliders. The ever-renewing and expanding theories of aerodynamics and physics were constantly tested and improved. Starting in 1871, a prominent aviation pioneer named Otto Lilienthal began conducting aerodynamic studies by observing birds in flight. It took the German engineer twenty years to study, develop, and compile the aerodynamic theories required for human flight, as it was then dubbed. In 1891, he built his first glider and dedicated the following five years to improving and perfecting his models; Lilienthal completed more than two thousand flights with his technology. In August of 1896, Lilienthal perished in an unfortunate crash while testing his latest glider.

Having received wide press coverage at the time, Lilienthal's fatal air crash might have sparked the Wright brothers' interest in aviation. The two bicycle builders from Ohio were surprised to learn that although dreams of human flight had ignited the imagination of man since the dawn of history, few contemporary scientists and engineers paid any attention to the new field of aeronautics.

After reviewing and studying the available material, the brothers concluded that manned flight faced three major challenges: an efficient system to produce enough lift (wings), a control and balance system for the aircraft in flight, and suitable propulsion—an engine that was both lightweight and efficient to produce enough power to take off and keep the airplane in the air.

The Wright brothers were confident that overcoming these aerodynamic and propulsion challenges was a matter of designing proper lift surfaces and suitable wings, as well as finding the right engine. Thus, they concentrated on solving what they believed was the most crucial challenge: a system to control and balance the airplane while in flight. Within a short while, they made significant progress in their design, which was key to manned aircraft becoming a reality. Their inspiration came from a surprising source, one close to their area of expertise—bicycle building.

Their innovation took shape as *ailerons*, a system that produces more lift in one wing with coordinated drag in the other wing, which allows for better controlled balance, roll, and turns of the gliders. In 1900, they built a better controlled glider only to find out that some lift was still missing, a problem easily solved by increasing the wing area. After solving several other problems with the control systems, the brothers built their first maneuverable glider in 1902; one year later it was used for their first powered airplane.

Relatively efficient internal combustion engines were already available in the United States from dozens of producers, but none could fit the Wright brothers' advanced design characteristics. They had calculated a requirement for an 8 HP engine, weighing two hundred pounds and producing ninety pounds of thrust, thus allowing their airplane to fly at a speed of twenty-three miles per hour. Alas, no available producer could build and supply this engine, forcing the brothers to build it themselves. They built their propelling unit out of aluminum, which allowed their homemade engine to be much lighter and produce enough power to lift them off the ground at 12 HP.

Beginning with their first successful flight in 1903, they went on to complete a circular flight within ten months, and by late 1905, they managed to stay airborne for a full thirty-nine minutes. They invested in public relations and marketing, for potential sales, and sure enough, in July of 1909, they sold their first airplane to the United States Army for $30,000. It was the world's first military aircraft. The United States Navy was also interested in aerial operation, so it purchased a Wright airplane in 1911 to start naval flight tests. Soon the Navy would also start to use Curtiss company's aircrafts, starting a fiery competition in the airplane industry.

The Sky Is the Limit

As the aircraft industry started to develop, civil aviation became the second largest market after military aviation. The first commercial flight in the United States took off in November of 1910 from Dayton to Columbus, Ohio, and it was one of the Wright brothers' aircrafts. During the 1920s and early 1930s, civil aviation took off with airmail and commercial passenger services in the United States. A great achievement was the Dakota C-47. This was the first transport airplane to offer significant payload, range, comfort, and speed for the time. Its civilian version, the DC-3, was introduced in 1935. The C-47 went on to become the main workhorse for military operations and transportation during World War II, and it continued to serve decades later.

Aviation became of great importance for commercial services of cargo and passengers, military purposes, and for technological inspiration, which eventually led man to outer space.

During the twentieth century, hundreds of thousands of aircraft were built for different armed forces worldwide. The first military application of aircraft was for reconnaissance flights as early as World War I; these military aircraft did not require significant technological advancement.

Such a development came with Nazi Germany's arms race of the 1930s for the war to come. Germany's neighbors, now fearing the aggressive growth of the Nazi military power, followed suit in an air force arms race, creating increasingly sophisticated military aircrafts. Yet the German aviation industry remained far superior to that of its enemies.

World War II brought about major leaps in technology, with aviation technology in particular seeing the most rapid and drastic changes. Massive aircraft production broke any record with large numbers of aircraft to be built. Among them 12,748 units of the Dakota C-47, and 12,085 units of the enormous American bomber B-17, known as the flying fortress, were built. And so were many Boeing B-29 bombers, the same type of plane as the *Enola Gay,* which dropped the first-ever nuclear bomb on Hiroshima.

Hundreds of thousands of military aircraft were also built by nations under siege in an unbelievable achievement of production. A total of 20,351 Spitfire fighters were built in England under massive Nazi airstrikes. At the same time in Germany, some 33,000 Messerschmitt Bf 109 fighters were built; this was the main fighter among tens of thousands of other German airplanes produced during the war. In comparison, during World War I, France, Great Britain, Germany, Italy, and the United States used a combined total of just 12,130 frontline combat aircraft. One can only imagine the enormity of the volumes of fuel required to fly these various air fleets across the globe.

During World War II, aviation firmly established itself as a crucial component of modern warfare. By the end of the war, jet engines had been introduced, first with the Nazi V-1 and V-2 jet missiles, then in jet plane prototypes. These were now the forefront of aviation technology.

Jet Age: 'All over the World Boeing Jetliners Are Getting People Together'

It only took another decade for commercial intercontinental jet flights to become a reality. The jet age enabled millions of people to fly from one side of the world to the other in a matter of hours and at relatively low costs. The new jet engines were far more powerful than piston engines and allowed aircraft to travel faster, higher, and farther. In 1958 a Pan American Airways Boeing 707 inaugurated a transatlantic jet service between New York and London. It took half the time and was more comfortable and safe than earlier technology. In 1969, the first Concorde supersonic aircraft took off, cutting the flight time from New York to London in half once again.

In this fossil fuel energy era, aviation brought about an amazing surge in fuel demand and consumption. Today, over twenty thousand commercial airplanes are in service worldwide. Jet fuel, refined high-grade kerosene, which was once a rudimentary and early source of illumination, is now in ever-growing demand for jet airliners and military aircraft all across the world. It has been widely accepted that as long as there is no appropriate alternative, kerosene (in its jet fuel form) will continue to power the roaring and bustling engines of aviation. Whereas alternative fuels may have already been found and used for land and sea travel, fossil fuels will continue to be used for aviation for years to come.

B. Across the Seven Seas: The Transition from Coal to Oil

Energy Transition

While the internal combustion engine was a great feat in the history of energy, its predecessor, the steam engine, proved to be the earliest sign of the Industrial Revolution. James Watt, a Scottish engineer, improved the original steam engine and allowed for its widespread use. His steam engine, which used to burn coal to heat water and create steam, also brought coal into use for power generation. The name *Watt* later became the standard unit of measurement for energy output.

The new electricity industry brought coal consumption to new peaks. By the late nineteenth century, the developing oil industry merged with the dominant industries of the time, leading to an increased usage of oil in power production at coal's expense.

Oil was well-suited for the shipping industry, as shipping played a significant role in the international balance of power in the early twentieth century. As the saying by Alfred Thayer Mahan goes, "Never has a nation that ruled the seas been beaten." Churchill, who also served as first lord of the Admiralty, contributed greatly to the introduction of oil to the British Royal Navy. For this transition, he took the required steps to build an oil supply chain throughout the entire British Empire.

The transition to oil as fuel gave a huge advantage to shipping, mostly for military fleets, which at the time constituted the backbone of any great power. Such a transition, from coal-burning boilers used to produce steam, to *mazut*, a heavy and low-grade oil derivative, meant ship engine operation became simpler and more efficient. Having greater calorific value, mazut gave vessels greater range and speed, making any fleet faster and stronger.

Ease of operation manifested in very basic logistics; loading and storing of fuel, a strenuous and difficult job when it came to coal, became relatively easy with oil, which could now be stored in tanks located in different compartments of a ship. Oil could then be piped using simple pumps and pipelines—a great improvement compared to the hard labor required to feed coal to steam furnaces.

Oil for War

While Britain had the world's largest fleet in the early twentieth century, there were no oil resources in its territories. This was in contrast to the virtually endless supply of coal resources throughout Britain. Thus, the British Admiralty had to present a strong opposition to coal supporters in the debate within the British government on the issue of fuel oil.

Throughout the empire, British officials were already in pursuit of gaining control over oil resources for the benefit of the British Royal Navy's fleet. By then, the Royal Navy had already begun to consume oil in small quantities.

Another intense debate took place in the British government concerning the nature and size of the fleet. Some wanted to allocate more budget to domestic, internal, and social affairs; others asserted that the Germans were in an ongoing arms race, claiming that a clash between the two powers was imminent.

A young member of parliament, Winston Churchill, was appointed home secretary in 1910 at the age of thirty-five. He soon assumed a prominent role in the development of the British Royal Navy and its transition from coal to oil. As home secretary, he opposed the military's expansion plans, which were intended to compete with the

German arms race. Together with the treasury secretary, David Lloyd George—who would later become prime minister during the Great War—they advocated for constraining the Royal Navy's budget, along with a diplomatic German-British agreement for the reduction of arms. Churchill reiterated that the widespread belief that war between Britain and Germany was inevitable was "nonsense."

This conciliatory tone, however, was soon replaced by disillusionment following a military and diplomatic clash as a result of German provocation. In July of 1911, a German gunboat named *Panther* entered the port of Agadir, in Morocco, located in a strategic position on the coast of the Atlantic Ocean some 500 kilometers south of Casablanca. Agadir is a dominant position across from the Canary Islands and shipping routes leading from the Mediterranean Sea and Northern Europe to western and southern Africa. This crisis came to a diplomatic resolution in September mainly due to Churchill's involvement. Soon Churchill would be appointed first lord of the Admiralty.

Churchill now turned to examining the Royal Navy's readiness for a possible confrontation with Germany. Three years before the Great War broke out, Britain was fortunate to have a first lord of the Admiralty who prioritized readiness for a possible war with Germany, quoted as saying that Britain must prepare as if such an attack were expected the very next day.

"Secure and Sustainable"

Returning to the ongoing fuel debate, a decision had to be made in regards to the type of fuel to be used. This issue now became a top priority in preparing the Royal Navy for war. On the agenda was the use of coal versus liquid fuel. As a former home secretary, Churchill understood the contribution of coal to the domestic economy. For example, Welsh coal was highly favored by military and merchant fleets worldwide, and Britain had already spread a supply network for coal loading throughout the empire. On the other hand, the immediate benefits of oil were clear and significant. Moreover, the Royal Navy already had submarines and destroyers running on liquid fuel. However, the majority of the naval force consisted of large coal-fueled battleships, and it was clear that their role in warfare of any kind was crucial. The debate now revolved around the transition of this heavy fleet to oil.

In his book on World War I titled *The World Crisis,* published between 1923 and 1931, Churchill wrote that there was no question of the superiority of liquid fuel over coal. But implementing such a fundamental change would be a highly difficult task, partly because of the new challenge it posed—identifying and securing reliable and sustainable sources of this fuel. Churchill wrote, "The world's oil supply is in the hands of the large oil trusts that are under foreign control. . . . If we can overcome the difficulties and risks, we will be able to increase the power and efficiency of the fleet." Better ships, better crews, and lower cost would lead to a stronger and effective naval force. "Mastery itself was the prize of the venture," he wrote; in other words, those who dare and turn to oil and support its supply sources, win complete control over the battlefield.

As politicians often do, Churchill appointed a committee to study all aspects of the possible transition to oil in 1912. Admiral Sir John Fisher, who preceded Churchill as secretary of the Royal Navy, headed the committee. Since the late nineteenth century, Admiral Fisher had been considered an advocate of oil, having recognized its potential and importance for the fleet. By 1910, at the end of Fisher's term, the British fleet already had fifty-six warships and seventy-four submarines powered by liquid fuel. In addition, oil was already utilized in other naval ships to some extent to spray on the coal in the furnaces in order to raise the coal's heat value and produce more steam and engine power.

The Fisher Committee recommended transition to oil. Churchill was now provided with a much-needed seal of approval to make the final decision of general transition from coal to oil. Oil also carried a strategic contribution to naval warfare by securing the element of speed necessary for deciding the naval battlefield. These were the missing four knots admirals had said their vessels lacked in speed, on top of the twenty-one knots produced by coal.

In April of 1912, five new oil-fueled Queen Elizabeth class battleships were ordered, bringing an end to the coal era for the British Royal Navy. Churchill wrote in his book, "The fate of our lives depends on these ships." All the massive efforts aimed to make this oil revolution a reality were now redirected into finding and securing oil resources for the British Royal Navy wherever it may sail.

For the Right Price

At the time, there were only two candidates with the capacity to supply oil for the Royal Navy: the Royal Dutch Shell company, already a major world supplier, and the Anglo-Persian Oil Company, a new company established for the recently discovered oil in Persia. As these two companies fought over a hefty prize, the British government commendably and consistently adhered to its national interests by resisting to blindly accept the highest, or lowest, bid. Largely thanks to the influence of Churchill, the British government chose to work with both suppliers, maintaining a steady competition between the two. This proved to be beneficial for the newer and smaller company, Anglo-Persian Oil, as the government acquired 51 percent of the company's shares. This purchase came with a capital injection by the government and the appointment of two directors on its behalf. Undoubtedly the most important result was a secret agreement signed between the British government and its newly acquired oil company to supply the Royal Navy with oil for twenty years on preferential terms.

At a session held in the House of Commons on June 17, 1914, Churchill spoke harsh words against trusts and monopolies. Churchill's speech focused on securing a long-term oil supply under contractual prices. He spoke out against both of the world's largest oil corporations, which were eliminating all competition and thus denying consumers the freedom of choice. These monopolies were the well-established Standard Oil and Royal Dutch Shell. Churchill accused the two majors of a long and constant extortion of all consumers, including the Admiralty. In reality, this served to justify the takeover of a private oil company by the government, which was almost unprecedented, just as the exception had been made to purchase Suez Canal Company shares several decades earlier. The purchases marked a strategic necessity.

The Samuel brothers of Shell Oil Company, who were present at the session, loudly confronted Churchill during parts of his speech, specifically those that were accompanied by a blatant, mocking tone directed toward the Samuel brothers and their company. As Churchill pointed out, although their company had always been courteous and considerate, and eager to meet the demands of the Admiralty, they had always made sure to do so for a high price. A law was passed by an overwhelming majority, which some attribute to Churchill's aggressive tone against foreign interests.

However, this did not prevent the government from signing a supply contract with Royal Dutch Shell as well, thus assuring that the Anglo-Persian Oil Company would not become a sole supplier for the British Royal Navy.

The transition from coal to oil, while encountering much criticism and opposition, mainly from local parties in Britain, was nevertheless accomplished at a critical point in time, by the eve of the Great War.

3. THE WORLD WARS 1914–1945

A. The Great War, the First Motorized Warfare

When discussing the Great War of the early twentieth century, our focus is not on the battles and fronts, which spread across the world, but on how this war differed from previous wars by the substantial changes brought about by motorization. In contrast to the horses, steam powered vehicles, and trains of past wars, new advancements multiplied tenfold the power of destruction, battle range, and mobility of the sparring enemies.

More important than the contribution of oil to the course of the war was the conduct of the victors to assure their future oil sources and supply. More prevalent than in any past war, this proved that control over oil sources and their regular supply and flow to the battlefield and logistic operations is the key factor separating victory from defeat.

Victory or Defeat

The first of the "people's mass wars," as it is called in German historian John Grenville's book *Europe Reshaped, 1848–1878*, was the Franco-Prussian War, which raged between 1870 and 1871. This war ended in French defeat by the Germans and marked the climax of Germany's unification and its rise to become a prominent military power in Europe, together with the formation and reshaping of the nationally oriented Europe.

The Franco-Prussian War ended with peace treaties imposed on the French by the Germans, causing a crisis across Europe. Following the end of the war, imperialist Germany became the most powerful nation in Europe. Yet, as Germany continued to grow and dominate in both economic and military respects, it still suffered from an inept political system.

With the onset of the Great War in the autumn of 1914, the deployment of forces was reliant on existing railways, which resulted in ground campaigns still lagging far behind. It would be a long stalemate before utilization of the internal combustion engine could bring its much needed and awaited influence to the battlefields. The development of airplanes and tanks provided both mobility and power that were unprecedented in the history of warfare.

Oil-Fueled Warfare

Once motorized arms entered the campaign on a massive scale, the need to secure strategic oil resources arose due to the need for secured supplies for fighting forces. In order to understand the scope of the military forces involved, we should note that in 1914 the British had fewer than 1,000 military vehicles in Europe, whereas by the end of the war they had more than 100,000. When the United States entered the war in 1917, it brought with it an additional 50,000 vehicles to the European front. Other significant change occurred in aerial warfare. Initially used for surveillance and reconnaissance, many aircrafts were converted to bombers and fighters, resulting in the production of tens of thousands of new aircraft. The Royal Air Force had only 63 aircraft when the war began, but the number rapidly grew to an astonishing 22,000 by the end of the war. This wide array of military equipment created a huge demand for fuel, which no one had anticipated in the early days of the war.

By the summer of 1916, lack of gasoline became apparent, and during the following year, as German submarine attacks on American supply convoys increased, the shortage became ever more pressing.

The crisis that emerged from the growing demand of oil resulted in the establishment of the Inter-Allied Petroleum Conference. France and Britain realized that only collaboration with the United States could save them from imminent defeat. French Premier Georges Clemenceau and British Prime Minister David Lloyd George appealed to American President Woodrow Wilson, emphasizing that oil was the blood flowing through the veins of the war. Such urgent appeals resulted in an increase of oil supply supported by expedited shipbuilding of tankers in American shipyards. A joint committee within the Inter-Allied Petroleum Conference was established at the beginning of the winter of 1918. Its objective was to coordinate and control fuel supplies in real time, assuring a constant flow of oil to the fronts for the remainder of the war. These logistic strategies were significantly improved over the course of the war and were reinstated during World War II.

The Cost of Victory

The Germans, who were relying on their own coal and oil resources at the beginning of the war, were forced to look elsewhere for oil sources to fuel their motorized armies. Possible sources could be either in Azerbaijan or in Romania, and the latter proved to be an easier target. By the winter of 1916, the Germans had captured the Romanian oil fields and refineries. The Allies' response was decisive and violent; the destruction of Romanian storage and refining capacities was completed within a few weeks of German occupation. Annihilation of the Romanian oil industry turned out to be a crucial strategic loss to the German war machine. Restoration and reconstruction attempts by the Germans were only partially successful. By late 1917, Romanian oil production reached only 30 percent of its original volume, and it took another six months to achieve an 80 percent restoration in production. At that period in time, it became clear to the Germans that their current oil reserve could fuel their armies for only a few more months, standing to reason that oil shortage played a crucial role in Germany's official surrender in November of 1918.

The Battle of Amiens in August of 1918 proved to be the most decisive battle against the Germans on the Western Front. It was the first arena in which tanks were introduced to the battlefield by the British army; this breached an almost four-year-long stagnated status quo in the European trenches. Wilson, Lloyd George, and Clemenceau, the leaders of the victorious nations, knew that ensuring fuel sources, while using tactics to prevent the Germans' access to oil, would be critical to final victory over Germany. Oil dramatically changed the course of the war and the balance of power in favor of the better-supplied armies.

B. The Inter-War Years: Oil and Politics New Order

The Great Depression

The aftermath of the Great War brought a drastic change across Europe, Africa, and the Middle East. A new world order emerged: the Ottoman Empire was ripped apart and European powers established new Arab states while keeping the majority of the Middle East under a new iteration of French and British mandates.

As it became increasingly clear that oil was the key to power, this new world order was now focused on oil sources and supply. The winning nations planned well how to take over the oil in Mesopotamia (more specifically, in Iraq) and other former Ottoman Empire territories. Both Iraq and Saudi Arabia were founded by the British as a reward to the Hussein family and the Sharif of Mecca for their support of the British in the war against the Turks. Yet oil had not yet been discovered in Saudi Arabia; that reward was waiting beneath the sand. In Europe, the Treaty of Versailles gave rise to other crucial problems for the coming near future of the world.

The post-war world suffered an economic depression fueled by millions of unemployed soldiers returning home to devastated infrastructure. The situation escalated to the Great Depression of 1929 and the birth of the dictators.

The Birth of the Dictators

Yet, while nations' economies plummeted during the 1930s, Japan occupied China (1931), Italy invaded Ethiopia (1935), the Spanish Civil War broke out (1936–1939), and in Germany, Hitler prepared to take over the Czech Sudetenland and announced the Anschluss—"unification" with Austria. All these required huge capital in terms of manpower, economic resources, and energy. Under these circumstances, Nazi Germany commenced forming a powerful, modernized army in violation of World War I's Treaty of Versailles, signed in 1919. In the aftermath of World War I, monarchies and dictatorships seemed like the best solution to the crisis, at least according to the people who lived in these struggling regions.

The emergence of communism in the USSR was considered to be a threat to the other European nations. By 1922, Joseph Stalin was the general secretary of the Communist Party of the Soviet Union's Central Committee. Following Lenin's death in 1924, he became the leader of the Soviet Union. As of 1935, a campaign of political oppression—known as the Great Purge—began in the Soviet Union, sending about 1.2 million people to death in a series of brutal executions. Stalin's aim was to "clean" any potential rivalries. That same year, Stalin commenced his second revolution, destroying the autonomy of Russian peasants, and leading an industrialization initiative. Neighboring countries feared potential penetration and influence of this communism into their nations.

In Italy, Benito Mussolini came to power in 1922, becoming the dictator of fascist Italy. Mussolini's dictatorship was dangerous to the political stability of the neighboring countries.

In 1933 Adolf Hitler, leader of the National Socialist Party in Germany, took power. He promised to restore Germany to its original power with the backing of the formation of a strong military force needed to realize his war ambitions. Under the Treaty of Versailles, Germany was not allowed to form a military force. But Hitler's Nazi racial ideology dominated.

Far away in Japan, a similar political process occurred in 1936 when army officers seized power and overruled the emperor.

Nazism in Germany, fascism in Italy, and militarism in Japan resulted in a broad mobilization of people, technology, logistic infrastructure, and any available resources to build up a combination of circumstances what would explode by the onset of World War II.

Germany, rich with coal, managed to produce synthetic fuel. Italy and Japan, lacking energy resources, managed to build up reserves that enabled their war efforts. The United States supplied Japan with most of its fuel demands until 1941.

During those years, as the three dictatorships built up their huge armed forces, European democracies were struggling through a severe economic crisis. A depression had resulted from the Great War, now known as World War I.

C. World War II

Fall of the Dictators and the Nuclear Dawn

The victory of the Allies over the three dictatorships could happen initially due to the major difference between the dictatorships and the democracies. The democracies mobilized almost overnight to defend their freedom and did not build armies to threaten their neighbors. They had had enough of these tactics during World War I. It is interesting to note how the massive industrialization, recourses, and logistics of the war led to peak energy production and supply, and drove the democratic countries to victory.

Darkest Hour

In logistics, economics, and industry, oil continued to play a key role. Fueling the hundreds of thousands of airplanes, vehicles, and ships in all arenas and fronts would not have been possible without a secure oil supply. A clear example is the logistics behind the most crucial maneuver of the war in Europe: the landing operations in Normandy in June of 1944.

In 1939, Stalin signed a non-aggression pact with Nazi Germany, known as the Molotov-Ribbentrop Pact. Yet this agreement did not save the Russians from the Germans, as they invaded the Soviet Union in 1941, during Operation Barbarossa, one of the largest military operations in history.

In 1941, the United States, along with Britain, boycotted Japan and cut off Japan's oil supply. At this point, Japan's planned aggression could not be curtailed, and its attack on Pearl Harbor surprised the world. Richard Overy's book *Why the Allies Won* calls the Pearl Harbor attack "Japanese treachery." However, it brought about Roosevelt's decision to join the war. The war in the Pacific became a long and bitter naval, air, and land bloodshed that continued months after victory in Europe due to the militant Japanese regime's determination to fight to the last man rather than surrender to superior forces.

Why Did the Allies Win?

An immense military industry rapidly arose, and demand for energy and logistics to support it increased drastically. An additional challenge was the coordination between the Allies' supply and distribution of resources, which, at times, were limited, blocked, or destroyed.

One of the first Allied successes was in the summer of 1942 in the North African western desert. The southern arm of the German Wehrmacht was blocked from reaching the Suez Canal and advancing into British mandated territories in the Middle East, where they could access important oil treasures that were so essential to the Nazi war machine.

In his book, Overy describes the logistical effort during the war. The use of the term "logistical effort" does not do justice to all those who worked and contributed so much to work it out. Much to Germany and Japan's surprise, it took the Americans, motivated by vengeance for Pearl Harbor, only one year to transform from a state of peace and welfare to an incredible war machine. So successful were these efforts that American production managed to exceed the Japanese and German military industries in volume, technological innovation, and quality.

Recruited Industries

Until the end of the war in 1945, and in fact within less than four years, the United States supplied over two-thirds of all military equipment for the Allied Forces. The sheer numbers are staggering: The United States produced 297,000 airplanes, 193,000 cannons, 86,000 tanks, 2 million military trucks and vehicles, 8,800 merchant and supply ships, and 87,000 landing craft.

The key to these incredible numbers lies in the conversion of civilian industries into military application. Examples include the production of the Liberty Ship, a standard merchant ship that was built in mass production to supply convoys mainly sailing the Atlantic routes to England. The automotive industry was converted to mass-produce aircrafts. The American military industries also provided over half a million military vehicles, as well as other military supplies, to the Soviets. This, along with massive Soviet industrial efforts, proved to be an industrial miracle.

The Importance of Oil

Oil was the main driver behind these military maneuvers. By late 1941, it seemed that Germany would soon secure control over the major oil sources on the fronts. Romanian oil fields were taken, and the next target was the Caucasus. Once the Germans were stopped on the

Russian front and in North Africa, it was well understood that their oil supply was in danger.

For the Allies on the European and Mediterranean fronts, they relied mostly on imported oil from the United States. These shipments were subject to attacks by German U-boats, which terrorized ships sailing in the Atlantic Ocean and the Mediterranean Sea. During the crucial year of 1942, 1,662 ships were sunk by the Germans, including many tankers. As a result, by early 1943, the British fleet was left with a supply of fuel that would last only two months. Huge efforts were made to secure more supplies.

Escort of a vital oil tanker approaching Britain in WW2

It is also interesting to examine the lack of natural rubber, a resource that was so important to the war machine. During the Japanese occupation of Singapore and Java, the Allies' access to about 90 percent of natural rubber sources was blocked. Synthetic rubber was developed—it was made from oil products residues.

As the leaders of the victorious countries, Churchill, Stalin, and Roosevelt appear in the famous pictures of the Yalta Conference in February of 1945, where they discussed the post–Nazi Germany world; however, victory on the Pacific front was still quite far off.

Nuclear Dawn

The war ended with the defeat of the dictatorships upon the complete surrender of the Axis's regimes and armies. Having endured the Allies' victory in Europe, Japan was the venue for the final stage of the war, which only ended after two nuclear bombs devastated the cities of Hiroshima and Nagasaki.

Raising the American flag on Iwo Jima.

Arguably, the end of that brutal war should—and indeed could—have been the catalyst for the realization of the illusive dream of world peace, ushering in a new era in energy as well. The idea of harnessing destructive nuclear power as a peaceful energy source seemed to dissipate as it became a doomsday weapon during the Cold War balance of power, and powers were deterred from massively incorporating it as a cheap, reliable, and safe energy source.

It is impressive that Japan successfully harnessed nuclear power to supplement its dependence on oil, though this achievement was shadowed by technical and human limitations during the 2011 Fukushima disaster.

During the energy price crisis of 2008, it was encouraging to see an increase in demand for nuclear energy for peaceful purposes.

Today, just like seventy-five years ago, as tyranny and dictatorship, terrorism, and fundamentalism threaten democracy and freedom across the globe, the dark shadow of a mediaeval war looms on the horizon and must be met with a firm determination to lead the world into a new era of sound, solid, and strong politics and energy security of supply.

Victory is needed today just as it was needed back in the Second World War.

4. THE COLD WAR TO WARS IN THE MIDDLE EAST, 1945–1973

———◆———

A. From the Marshall Plan to the Berlin Wall

From the Ruins

The vast destruction caused by World War II had visible effects, leaving Europe in a crisis long after the last bullet was fired. European countries' infrastructures were completely destroyed, leaving their economies in shambles.

One prominent restoration and reconciliation program was the Marshall Plan. The plan rehabilitated Germany and war-torn Western Europe; however, it also perpetuated the differences between the democratic capitalist world of the West and the communism that fortified Eastern Europe.

Not long before, two highly contrasting parties had come together to fight a common enemy. However, soon after, these one-time allies evolved into the two conflicting poles in the world of the Cold War: the Eastern versus Western blocs that formed the balance of terror over nuclear deterrence, as the sword of mutual assured destruction hung over the world. A series of proxy wars and conflicts across continents marked the inter-bloc bipolar frontline. During these wars, the use of oil increased greatly, and with this growth came the rising need for control over energy sources and security of their supply.

———

The Marshall Plan was a conciliatory initiative, mandated by a post–World War mindset, yet it emphasized the newly formed European Iron Curtain that was lowered between the two blocs. The plan was also conceived in order to prevent a replay of the degrading peace agreements signed after World War I that were seen as having sown the seeds of World War II. Yet an argument ensued between the victors over the spheres of influence over liberated countries and territories. Herein lays the root of the inter-bloc Cold War.

The Marshall Plan was aimed to bridge an economic and political abyss that resulted from World War II. The war had seen long-term economic ties collapse and be destroyed: private businesses, financial and insurance institutions, shipping companies, and countless other entities that were drafted to the war effort and nationalized were left financially drained and in complete ruins. In addition, new governments grappled with infrastructures that were gutted by years of war, as national currencies also lost their value and trust. As millions were displaced and their homes destroyed, soldiers returned from the frontlines only to face unemployment and poverty; entire populations suffered the crippling effects of war.

On June 5, 1972, German Chancellor Willy Brandt spoke at Harvard University during a conference commemorating the twenty-fifth anniversary of the Marshall Plan. Brandt recounted how the plan had been considered a beacon of light during its conception and implementation at the end of the war. Nevertheless, it was clear that victory did not exempt Germany or the victorious Allies from responsibility.

The plan was also drafted in light of concern over the rise of communism in an impoverished Europe, threatening the rest of the world, as defined by the Truman Doctrine during a presidential speech to the American Congress in March of 1947. Secretary of State George Marshall outlined the principles of the plan as a baseline for recovery of the European nations from the destruction caused by war. He also laid an important cornerstone in setting the United States as a global leader in what would become the Eastern nation's bloc and the NATO alliance.

Cold Front

With victory in 1945, the spoils of war were to be divided between the four main Allies at the time: the USSR, the United States, Britain, and France. Eastern Germany was now under Soviet order and rule; the remainder was divided between the three western democratic nations, with a firm, carefully planned border separating east from west. An island, within Soviet influence of East Germany, was Berlin itself, divided into four territories: American, Russian, French, and British. It soon grew into the microcosm of the Cold War, with ever more fortified borders and the complete separation of the capital by the Berlin Wall. The Soviet Iron Curtain was quickly unfurling, and would soon cast a grave shadow over all of Europe.

In June of 1947, all twenty-two European countries were invited to a special convention in Paris, in which the plan's details would be discussed. Russia refrained from participating and even succeeded in preventing Czechoslovakia, Poland, and Hungary from taking part. Under the supervision of a special American commissioner, the required funds needed to execute the Marshall Plan in a four-year timeframe were agreed upon.

The plan extended for three and a half years until December of 1951, due to the escalation of the Korean War. With a budget of $13.3 billlon, its short-term achievements were the supply of raw materials and production facilities that contributed to the prevention of an economic crisis as well as the moderation of the recession in Europe. Beyond economic contributions, it also assisted in the political recovery of the European nations, including the defeated countries. This was the largest economic program ever implemented during peaceful times, and it was widely considered to be the most successful.

On the other side of the Berlin Wall was communist East Germany, a satellite of the Soviet Union, a country with an economy and standard of living that had changed very little since the end of the war. East Germany served mainly as a strategic front facing NATO in a foreseeable and seemingly inevitable conflict.

The Iron Curtain.

Under the Wall

While the Marshall Plan proved to be a great success, it also emphasized and underscored the new inter-bloc division. Berlin was divided; the symbolic, fortified border passed through the center of the city, with the famous Checkpoint Charlie that beyond being featured in many espionage movies, acted as the concrete gateway between East and West.

The Iron Curtain was drawn across the heart of Europe, separating east from west. Yet, regardless of powers and conflicts, energy flowed between the blocs to where it was needed. In 1978 a gas pipeline from Siberia to Europe was proposed to ease the pain of the 1973 oil embargo and soften the harsh reality of Europe's reliance on Middle Eastern oil. The pipeline provided the Soviet Union with valuable hard currency, while shifting their dependence on Soviet gas. Despite being among the most fortified borders in existence, under the wall and over the Iron Curtain energy flowed uninterrupted.

The fall of the communist regime of the Soviet Union with its satellite countries in 1989, together with the fall of the Berlin Wall, resulted in the reunification of Germany for the second time within a century.

B. The Middle East until 1956

Warm Front: Powers and Wars

The Middle East had long held strategic importance to the British Empire, as well as other European countries, as a spearhead to the Near and Far East. As India gained its independence, and as internal political strife arose in post-World War Britain, the country was willing to invest the resources required to maintain its influence. The contest within Europe between Britain and France, which once spanned the globe, was now concentrated in the Middle Eastern region, as nations under European influence struggled for independence. Yet the strategic, geographical relevance of the Middle East was now overshadowed by its importance as the source of cheap oil for Europe, thereby reinstating Europe's dependence on Middle Eastern oil.

Upon the formation of the bipolar world, it became apparent that the Middle East had turned into another front in the battle between the United States and the USSR. Europe had already been divided between the two blocs. American President Harry Truman realized that in the new balance of power, stability of the world would need to be maintained through a clear division of spheres of influence and the building of military and nuclear deterrence.

The first signs of the formation of a nexus in the East-West conflict in the Middle East can be found as early as 1946 over a territory occupied in Iran during World War II. The Soviets refused to withdraw from this territory within six months of the end of the war. Thanks to the rigid diplomacy of President Truman, the crisis resolved.

As World War I was coming to an end, the two great European powers, Britain and France, were drawing new borders and devising new states and nations in the formerly Ottoman-ruled Middle Eastern region. When World War I ended, the newly formed states found themselves under British and French mandate rule. Consisting of various nations and different tribes, these new countries stewed with internal strife, and claims for independence soon emerged. The seemingly natural process of granting independence to countries in the region was only made possible after many local struggles that further exhausted the war-tired Britain and France. Thus, in the second half of the 1940s, Egypt, Syria, Iraq, Israel, Jordan, and Lebanon all gained their independence. The Persian Gulf states followed only later; perhaps their European patrons delayed relinquishing power due to these territories' great abundance of oil resources. Thus, Kuwait received its independence from Britain only in 1961, and Qatar and Bahrain a decade later in 1971.

These countries gaining their independence did not lead the region into the desired political stability Europe had had in mind. Military coups became a common post-independence trend. Starting with Syria in 1949, other countries followed suit. The 1952 Free Officers coup in Egypt—which would greatly affect the entire Middle East for decades to come— saw a military officer by the name of Gamal Abdel Nasser rise to power. A wave of "Nasserism" swept the Arab world, accompanied by Arab nationalism and an increasing aversion to the West. This set the stage perfectly for the two new global powers, the United States and the Soviet Union, to set a "warm front" in their Cold War.

Breaking the Rules

In 1956, Egyptian leader Gamal Abdel Nasser nationalized the Suez Canal in response to Western withdrawal of support for the critical project to build the Aswan Dam, a result of Egyptian cooperation with the Soviets. England and France, together with Israel, invaded the Sinai Peninsula and the Suez Canal in an attempt to restore British control of the Suez Canal. In fact, it was a campaign against an Arab ruler who "broke the rules" set by global powers.

The Baghdad Pact of 1955 marks the beginning of the escalation in the Middle Eastern front. This 1955 pact between Middle Eastern countries, namely Iraq, Iran, Turkey, and Pakistan, joined by the United Kingdom, was meant to offer mutual protection and support against the Soviets. With the assurance of American military and financial support, the pact marked a formidable frontline to hold back the Soviet Union's possible expansion across its southwestern border.

The agreement was met with great opposition, mainly by the Soviet Union and Egypt, leading to the Egyptian-Czech arms deal in September of 1955 that allowed for the supply of Soviet arms to Egypt. Bypassing, ignoring, or challenging the American-led Baghdad Pact. The USSR gained their much-desired foothold in the heart of the Middle East. As a response to Egypt's recent slant toward the Soviets, the United States revoked its support to build the Aswan Dam; a monumental hydropower production project on the Nile river. This sleight was answered by Egypt nationalizing the Suez Canal, which mainly hurt Britain and France.

Lack of American support now emphasized the rift that had torn open between Western allies, perhaps for the first time since the end of World War II.

A Shady Victory

The planning and execution of the Suez Operation in October of 1956, in collaboration with Israel, was a result of mutual interests of all parties involved. Israel in the 1950s had been subject to an internal political crisis, and the country was also facing increasing terrorist attacks, which were especially prevalent along the Egyptian border. France believed that a powerful move against Nasser would convey a strong and effective message to the rebels in French-ruled Algeria and assist in ending the crisis there as well. Britain, seeking to regain control over its prized asset, set out to defeat Nasser, who the British prime minister at the time, Anthony Eden, considered to be a second Hitler.

Despite swift and successful military maneuvers, the Suez Operation had far from satisfying results in the political arena for both Britain and France. American objection to a military solution furthered the rift in its relations with the European countries. Egypt lost the Sinai Peninsula and suffered great casualties, yet Nasser's prestige was boosted for his boldness in coming out against Western powers and interests. Nasser staying in power made France's desired outcome in Algeria unlikely. In Britain, Prime Minister Eden's administration lost power upon the enforcement by American diplomacy to end military occupation of the Sinai and Suez Canal. Thus, the loss of prestige and resources for both European powers was significant, once again signaling the end of the old empires' eras.

For the Soviet Union, the Suez Operation created a golden opportunity to solidify its rising power in the region. This was soon materialized in Soviet rearmament and resupply of the defeated Egyptian army.

Israel reached a crisis point in its relationship with the United States, as the latter led the demand for Israel's withdrawal from the Sinai Peninsula. The withdrawal followed an American guarantee to secure Israel's freedom of navigation in the Red Sea. The radicalization of the Arab world escalated as a direct result of the Suez Operation, the results of which would be seen within a decade, in May 1967.

The Suez Operation of 1956, much like the future wars in the Middle East, brought about the second oil crisis since World War II. This crisis resulted from the temporary closure of the Suez Canal and from the regional tension that followed, reiterating the prominence of the Middle East as the main oil supplier for the West.

C. The Middle East, 1967: Closure of the Suez Canal

Cold War Politics

Within the course of a decade, the 1956 Suez Operation was followed by the Israel-Arab Six-Day War of 1967. In addition, the East versus West struggle for power, influence, and control over oil sources intensified, spreading to other arenas. Political and military instability of the Middle East grew stronger; international intervention was required in Jordan in 1957 and in Lebanon in 1958 by British and American forces respectively, supporting these countries' regimes in pacifying unrest and fending off armed opposition. In 1959 a military coup took place in Iraq, and in Syria, the 1969 revolution brought Alawi minority ruler Hafez al-Assad into power, taking control over Islamic Sunni Syria. Yemen, Algeria, and Libya also experienced this cycle of political and structural instability during the 1950s and 1960s. As the Middle East became evermore shrouded in turmoil, the importance of the region as an oil source to the western world and Southeast Asia increased.

In West Germany, a new foreign minister named Willy Brandt was appointed in 1966, and three years later he was elected chancellor. Brandt pioneered the *Ostpolitik* strategy of normalizing relations with Eastern Bloc countries, first and foremost with the Soviet Union itself. The United States, on the other hand, had been confronting the Soviets head-on. In the following decade, the United States escalated its involvement in Vietnam with a lack of decisive military success, emphasizing the internal differences within the Western bloc, which now began to show its first signs of weakness.

At the same time, this was a decade of European collaboration with Israel overshadowed by dependence on Arab oil. The pro-Israeli policy of France, Britain, and West Germany was adjusted as a direct result of these countries' increased dependence on oil. This process further escalated when Israel achieved victory in the 1967 Six-Day War.

A Proxy Conflict

The war that broke out on June 5, 1967, was preceded by a seemingly short chain of events starting on May 14, when Egyptian President Nasser ordered a general military mobilization, and two days later declared a state of emergency. On May 17, Egypt demanded UNEF (United Nations Emergency Force) to depart; the force has been deployed in the Sinai since December of 1956 when French, British, and Israeli troops had withdrawn.

In May 23, Nasser ordered the closure of the Straits of Tiran in the Red Sea, which led to Israel's southern sea port of Eilat. This step was met with British rage as the United Kingdom advocated the freedom of navigation and upheld the international treaties securing it. The United States and France also rushed to declare their commitment to Israel's security, as Israel's destruction was a proclaimed goal of the general military mobilization in Egypt.

In his book, *New Diplomacy*, Abba Even, the Israeli foreign minister at the time, accused the Soviets of inflaming the events leading to the war, including false Soviet intelligence information that claimed that Israel had mobilized its army along the frontlines.

In their quest to build up a naval force in the Mediterranean and a countermeasure to the American 6th fleet in the region, the Soviet Union was looking for locations to host its bases. Syria and Egypt were willing to offer locations in return for Soviet military support and supply. On May 2, 1966, a military treaty was signed between the USSR and Syria, followed by a high-level Soviet delegation visit to Egypt later that month, headed by Soviet Prime Minister Alexei Kosygin. On May 22, 1967, a day before Nasser declared the closure of the Tiran Straits to Israeli vessels, the Egyptian president consulted the Soviet ambassador about the steps to be taken.

The war caused major global turmoil. In the context of the Cold War, this was a blistering defeat for Arab countries, which relied on the Soviet Union's support. In the inter-European struggle, pro-Israeli and pro-Arab parties were both shocked by the Arab countries' defeat. As dependence on Middle Eastern oil increased, the Suez Canal became the main shipping route for oil tankers from the Persian Gulf to Europe and to the Americas. All of a sudden the Suez Canal was closed once again—but this time it would remain closed for over a decade.

Cutting Losses

The closure of the Canal, as well as the fourteen vessels that were trapped in it during a routine passage as war broke out, shocked global oil and shipping markets. Closing the Canal added some 2,500 nautical miles to the route from the Persian Gulf to the Mediterranean Sea and Northern Europe—about ten additional sailing days—and sent a shockwave through global economies, affecting every oil and shipping-related industry. Oil from the Middle East now had to make a long journey around the Cape of Good Hope.

Until June of 1967, the probability of ships being trapped in sea straits and international passage routes had never been contemplated. This now changed as well, and marine insurance had to undergo great transformations, costs that were once again reflected in increased oil prices for consumers.

When the Canal closed, Egypt's income from transit tolls came to a halt. As years passed, its once indisputable importance to the global shipping industry dissipated. Oil markets started to recover in the following years. Shipping companies had to adopt a different approach to the new situation, with modern, efficient, and much larger tankers—vessels that would no longer be able to pass through the Suez Canal anyway. New economy of scale was introduced, and the costs saved on transit tolls compensated for the losses that resulted from much longer routes.

Egypt was also seeking a way to recover, as various peace initiatives were brought up by different parties, some of which bluntly rejected by Israeli Prime Minister Golda Meir's administration. The Egyptians also sought ways to get closer to the West, since some blamed the Soviet equipment that Egypt and Syria used for their defeat. At the time, the United States further established its influence in Iran and Saudi Arabia, which were both of great importance to the region.

As is nearly always the case, oil, its trade, and its pricing were again at the top of the global agenda, as the 1967 war in the Middle East brought about the third oil crisis. This crisis provided the drive for oil exploration and discoveries in new locations as the world searched for alternatives to Middle Eastern oil. Soon, drilling began in Alaska, North and West Africa, and the North Sea.

Warm Front

In August of 1967, an Arab League summit convened in the Sudanese capital of Khartoum, where it was decided to enhance military preparations in order to restore Arab territories that had been captured by force during the war in June. The Khartoum summit closed with the infamous "three NOs" resolution, stating that there would be *no* peace, *no* recognition, and *no* negotiation with Israel by the Arab League. It was during this summit that calls were first made to use the ban of oil as a weapon. This option was abandoned, however, and it was decided instead to utilize oil as political leverage on Western consumers. It was also decided that oil revenues were to be used in financing and supporting Arab countries in a war against Israel.

Acts of animosity renewed and continued into the early 1970s, in what came to be known as the War of Attrition on the Israel-Egypt front.

As the 1967 war came to an end, the European Union demanded that Israel withdraw from territories captured during the war. To further enforce this point, the French imposed an arms embargo on the region in June of 1967, mainly affecting Israel. It appeared that the Europeans wished to practice an independent foreign policy in Middle Eastern affairs, one that would separate them from the interests and influences of the Cold War. This conflict would soon reach its next climax in October of 1973.

A Global Game of Chess

On the Cold War front, it seemed that the Nixon administration was going into retreat and entering détente as the war in Vietnam continued to entangle the United States. Despite its prominent member status in the NATO alliance, Germany upheld its *Ostpolitik* policy, even after the Soviet Union invaded Czechoslovakia in the spring of 1968. Britain was about to withdraw from the Persian Gulf in 1971, in accordance with its agreements with the Gulf states, and the void left behind would seem highly attractive for Western-armed Iran and Soviet-sponsored Iraq—both nations had great aspirations for assuming control over the Persian Gulf and sought dominance in the region.

Iraq was strongly supported by the Soviet Union, both politically and militarily. In Iran, massive arms procurements were made as the Persian shah called on neighboring countries to join him and establish a federation of Gulf states.

The Cold War was waged on a global scale as the quest for supremacy spread to local fronts around the world by means of proxy conflicts and arm races. These, however, seemed somewhat stemmed by Nixon's historic visit to China in 1972; for the first time in the course of the Cold War, a window for diplomacy opened. Nevertheless, it would take another major war in the Middle East to trigger a real change in the region as the main oil source of the world.

Following the 1967 war, the Soviet Union continued to arm the defeated Egyptian and Syrian armies in preparation for yet another round against Israel. The arms race reached a critical point in time due to the French arms embargo on the region. Israel now turned to the Americans for armament and support. In this inter-power global game of chess, it seemed that the Israeli-Arab front had become the playing field.

Despite the closure of the Suez Canal in 1967 and the events of the war that followed, the West's dependence on Middle Eastern oil only increased. During those years, 64 percent of Europe's oil consumption came from the Persian Gulf.

As the importance of their oil in Western economies grew and seemed irreplaceable, the oil-producing countries felt more secure in considering using the resource for political leverage. In 1971, the Arab media openly discussed the usage of Arab oil resources to influence the West to support Arab causes. During the summer of 1972, various oil supply disturbances occurred, resulting in local and regional shortages across the world. Some blamed the oil-producing countries and the major oil companies to have deliberately produced insufficient supplies to meet demand in order to raise oil prices.

At that time oil was quite an affordable commodity, priced at less than $2 per barrel during the late 1960s and early 1970s. As the world became ever more dependent on Middle Eastern oil, it was clear that another war in the region was imminent.

5. POWER AND CONFLICTS, 1973–1979

———————◆———————

A. The Middle East, 1973: The Oil Embargo

The 1967 War followed by political and diplomatic stagnation in the Middle East. Diplomacy was taken by an armament spree across the region. Russian military supply to the defeated Arab countries reached its climax with the introduction of Soviet surface to air missile and Russian pilots flying in Egypt and Syria.

Repercussions of War

On October 6, 1973, Jewish Atonement Day (Yom Kippur), Egyptian and Syrian armies opened a well-coordinated surprise attack on Israel in a joint campaign on both fronts. The declared objective was to bring negotiations, aimed at regaining the territories lost in 1967.

The shockwave that hit Israel, and the devastating results of its first days, definitely marked a change taking place in the Middle East. Yet the desired outcome was still far away, and surely it would take more than the eighteen days of war waged in that autumn.

The war led to direct involvement of the superpowers, starting with an aerial supply train of American military equipment to Israel, and Soviet weapons deliveries to Damascus and Cairo. Later on, the military alertness level was elevated in both powers, as explicit threats were made regarding involvement in the area, with the prevailing threat of American nuclear might.

———————

The internal political situation in some of the Western countries was poor: in the United States, there were dying ripples of the Nixon administration, following the Watergate scandal; in Europe, economic and political strife was occurring in Italy, France, and the United Kingdom; on the other hand, the *Ostpolitik* and détente policies—the compromise policy toward the Soviet Union—had not yet resulted in any concrete outcome.

Four days after the war broke out, on October 10, 1973, Turkey notified the United States that American bases in Turkey were to be used only for purposes concerning the NATO alliance, making clear their utter objection to any use relating to the Israeli-Arab conflict. Three days later, Greece, Spain, and France imposed an embargo on military supply to all parties involved in the war. Other European countries, such as Portugal, the Netherlands, and Germany, continued their support of Israel. However, American supply flights to Israel, taking off from Germany, were now routed over the Atlantic Ocean, Gibraltar, and the Mediterranean Sea to Israel.

The long-range, direct flights from the United States to Israel were reduced due to re-fueling issues, resulting from the European ban on these flights. It is important to note George Pompidou's correspondence with Henry Kissinger on October 10, in which the French president stated that France could not take any risk of aggravating the relationship with the Arab countries due to its dependency on Middle Eastern oil.

The Oil Weapon

Iraq was quick in calling for an Arab oil ban on the West. Perhaps the first Arab producing country to act, a day after the war began, Iraq nationalized the assets of some Western countries in local oil companies. 47.5% of the shares of "Basra's Oil Company," held by American companies *Exxon* and *Mobil*, and Dutch company *Shell*, were nationalized. On October 20, Iraq also nationalized the remaining foreign-held five percent shares of Portugal in protest of it allowing American supply flights use its airports on the way to Israel.

The oil ban imposed by October of 1973 on the United States, as well as several other countries who had "committed a sin" in the eyes of OPEC supporting Israel, was only lifted six months later. Along with a direct embargo on oil sales to those countries, the ban also incorporated a well-planned reduced oil production throughout the producing countries, causing an *oil shock* which spread across the globe as prices quadrupled within weeks.

The ban landed on fertile ground, as years-long negotiations on oil prices between producing and consuming countries left the producing countries discontent with their current revenues. Oil price at the time was around two dollars a barrel, with average royalties of 1 $/bbl.

Despite OPEC members' feuds with the United States and its protégé State of Israel, at the time overshadowing nearly all other issues, the ban also brought to light conflicts of interest and disagreements among OPEC members themselves: the non-Arab against the forum created an inner ring called *OAPEC*—the Organization of Arab Petroleum Exporting Countries—within OPEC. Iraq's aggressive position stood out, calling for complete cease of oil production, as well as nationalizing all assets of Western oil companies within OPEC countries.

OPEC's first common resolution, issued on October 17, 1973, was to use oil as a political weapon by first cutting-back production, without resorting yet to a full embargo. The following day, however, Kuwait and the United Arab Emirates already imposed an embargo on oil export to the United States. Saudi Arabia, having previously opposed this move, joined the oil embargo on the United States a day later, in reaction to President Nixon's disregard of its warnings against American support of Israel.

The immediate production cut was set at 5%, and, later on, Saudi Arabia cut 10% of its own production as a further expression of its utter discontent with the continuing Nixon administration's policy. Portugal and South Africa were also included in the countries subject to complete embargo for their support of Israel.

In November, the Arab countries' production cut reached a 25–30 percent level, and caused an even sharper spike in oil price, reaching its peak in early 1974.

By then, the Saudis had become increasingly concerned that such price levels might destabilize the global economy. On top of that was the Saudis' growing concern that steep price increase might lead to future technological developments that would render oil unnecessary.

Oil-Shocked

Rising oil prices were the immediate result of the oil embargo, followed by drastic price increase in many other commodities, and energy related products soon followed as inflation destabilized the global economy.

The United States, which had a significant dependency on OPEC's oil, was now forced to enter negotiations for lifting the embargo from a weak position. And so, for the first time, negotiations over oil supply and prices included also political arrangements. This was now OPEC's official demand—along with oil prices and supply.

As the war ended with a cease-fire on October 24, negotiations with OPEC countries were still underway. Post-war talks between Israel, Egypt, and Syria, mediated by the United States, revolved around mutual withdrawal from the territories captured during the war. On January 18, Henry Kissinger succeeded in presenting a viable agreement, according to which Israel committed to withdraw from the territories it took west of the Suez Canal, with a continuing discussion on withdrawal from the Golan Heights in the Syrian front in northern Israel.

Following this event, OPEC lifted the embargo on March 1974. The ban on the Netherlands extended beyond that, as despite the embargo, Holland continued to support Israel politically and economically. This particular ban was only officially lifted four months later. The sights that time, of empty roads in Holland—as the government restricted vehicle driving on the weekends—left their mark. The fears and concerns of this oil shock endured for years.

By the end of the war it was clear that the next step would be diplomatic. It became clear that any diplomatic initiative had to come from the United States. Starting in winter of 1974, Henry Kissinger made personal shuttle trips, as part of the "step by step" policy he implemented. His efforts were fruitful, leading to a permanent cease-fire agreement, separating military forces, and withdrawal from the territories taken during the war. It continued with Israel's withdrawal further east of the Suez Canal, in September of 1975, which would soon lead to the reopening of the Canal for transit for the first time since June 1967.

For the United States it represented a victory of its diplomatic policy, having succeeded in forming a firm front against the Soviets, now consisting of Egypt, Saudi Arabia, and Iran, as well as NATO member Turkey. This was an important block of Muslim countries in the region, which helped stabilize the balance between East and West by securing also energy sources and therefore stable oil prices.

The oil embargo of 1973 drove the United States to announce its decision to strive for energy independence. Other means were to consolidate consumers in an organized entity, allowing them a better influence and potential control of oil prices, preventing future oil embargos and crises. This entity would later become the IEA, the International Energy Agency, with its 28 OECD members.

Other step to ensure its energy security was the creation of the USA SPR: the Strategic Petroleum Reserve, storing some 500 700 million barrels of oil.

Petrodollars

In recounting the oil embargo of 1973, one cannot ignore the rapid evolution oil prices have undergone during those years. Oil became the most important factor in trade between the Middle East and the West. It was now very clear that just as Western countries rely on Middle Eastern oil, so too did Middle Eastern countries depend on their trade with the West.

Oil prices climbed from below $2 a barrel in 1970, to $2.50 dollars in 1973, and peaked during the October War to $18 per barrel. The average price for 1973 was recorded at $2.83 per barrel, compared with an average $1.90 a year prior. Within a single year, 1974 ended with a staggering average price of $10.41.

The price range of $11 to $13 dollars per barrel held steady until the eve of the Islamic revolution in Iran by late 1978.

This dramatic price increases—quadrupling within only one year—more than anything else reflected the fragileness of oil price stability and how greatly the world depended on OPEC.

It should be mentioned, however, that even before the 1973 war, some OPEC members had already pressed for price increase. Libya led this line demanding a price of $5 for their higher quality oil. Algeria joined the demand for raising prices in September 1973, but it was denied by an OPEC resolution.

By October 16, an agreed price increase to $3.65 a barrel left the producing countries with about $3 gross income a barrel, to jump shortly after to $10 a barrel. Production costs remained nearly the same at about 50 cents a barrel.

The high revenues also increased the economic importance of the producing countries for the global trade. For example, the Arab League countries: in 1970, their share of global export was 4%, and increased to 8.5% between the years 1974–1978. In monetary terms, their export reached close to a hundred billion US dollars annually as of the mid-seventies, compared with approximately 25 billion dollars before 1973. Oil's share was 90% of that export.

On the other hand, a major part of the producing countries' revenues started to be used for import of Western commodities and goods. The total import to the Arab League countries, which was about 15 billion dollars in 1973, grew close to 80 billion dollars in the second half of the seventies. This import was mostly to the Persian Gulf States, Libya, and Nigeria.

In 1978, Europe imported 57.7% of its oil needs from the Arab League countries, which, along with other commodities purchased in these countries, amounted to 16.6% of the entire import value to Europe.

As revenues soared, a new term was coined: "petrodollars." Some of these huge revenues were deposited in Western banks, thus having the ability to affect currency rates and local economies.

While some capital was used for development of infrastructure and social wealth in the exporting countries themselves, a substantial share of it, like in Iran and Saudi Arabia, was redirected to armament and securing their regimes. In many other countries, however, petrodollars would only benefit the rulers and their very rich families and relatives in maintaining their reigns and basking in the fragrances of oil.

B. The Middle East, 1977–1979

Sadat in Jerusalem, Khomeini in Tehran

While the Six-Day War of 1967 resulted in a diplomatic and political standstill, the Yom Kippur War in October of 1973 opened the door for a long awaited and much needed peace process in the region. What started as meetings between Egyptian and Israeli military officers to set the cease-fire, soon led to the first separation agreements, and later on enabled the reopening of the Suez Canal. This process reached its peak in November of 1977, when Egyptian President Anwar Sadat arrived in Jerusalem, becoming the first ever Arab leader to visit the state of Israel.

On November 19, 1977, Sadat landed in Tel-Aviv, where he was formally greeted, before the astounding eyes of many Israelis who came to pay their respect to the Egyptian leader. In his speech before the Israeli parliament, the Knesset, in Jerusalem, with the Israeli Prime Minister Menahem Begin at his side, Sadat called for an end to the war between the two states, saying "No more war, no more bloodshed." Over three decades of war finally came to an end on March 26, 1979, with the Camp David agreement signed.

The Egypt-Israel agreement brought some hope and optimism to the region. Upon the tightening ties between the United States and Saudi Arabia and Egypt, Iraq blamed Saudi Arabia of taking part in an imperialistic plan to take over the Persian Gulf and the Middle East.

Yet, during the course of 1975, the Iraqi-Saudi relationship improved, and by April of that year matured to an agreement on a border dispute between the two countries. At the same time, talks between Iraq and Iran took place, which led to the signing of a border division agreement regarding the "Shat El-Arab" river.

The agreement was signed only to be breached by Iraq in September of 1980. Some hoped that the Israel-Egypt peace treaty would lead to an extensive reconciliation process between Israel and its other Arab neighbors. Such a process was hoped to initiate a pan-Arabic reconciliation, but the events taking shape in Iran cut these hopes, raising from the abyss the fundamentalist radical Islam.

On January 16, 1979, the Shah was forced to exile from his country. Two weeks later, Khomeini landed in Tehran.

On April 1, Khomeini declared the establishment of the Islamic Republic of Iran. In December 1979, the Soviets invaded Afghanistan, while riots broke out in Saudi Arabia. As a result, oil prices started climbing, and a real concern was raised in the markets for the security of supply, fearing a second *oil-shock* within less than a decade.

This crisis was also accompanied by speculations and apocalyptic forecasts on the complete shutdown of oil export from the Persian Gulf.

The world was about to face its *fifth oil crisis* since the Second World War.

II. GEOPOLITICS

6. CHECKMATE – THE ISLAMIC REVOLUTION, 1979

———————◆———————

Introduction

The Revolution in Iran, which brought Khomeini to power in 1979, in what appeared to be the beginning of a fundamentalist wave of Islam, would hit in full force 22 years later with the September 11 attack against the United States leading to the never-ending related Operation Desert Storm.

The descriptions of the revolution is rather long, since I found it very relevant to the ongoing Middle and Near East countries—from Syria to Saudi Arabia and its neighbor Yemen, from Morocco to Iraq; as well as to other countries all over the world, as the July 2016 events in Turkey proved.

It came crashing as a fierce and surprising freak wave; the type of wave that has been the fear of any seaman since the dawn of shipping. Ask any seasoned sailor and you'll hear the terrifying recounts of meeting such a creeping rogue wave—a sudden huge wall of water appears, rising higher and higher, threatening to crash down on anything in its path. Those left to tell the stories are only the ones who survive.

In 1996, a cargo ship sailed from Durban Port in South Africa toward the Mediterranean. The ship was loaded with general cargo of steel, granite, and paper rolls. Somewhere around the Cape of Good Hope, the ship was lost with its entire crew of 25 men. The Ministry of Transportation of South Africa, which investigated the accident, concluded that the cause was most probably a **freak wave.**

———————

The revolution in Iran followed a period of unrest, sending warning signs that were never seen or understood at the time. An entire nation turned its back on its leader and regime, and to the modernized way of life, and fought to return to religious fundamentalism. This is the scenario witnessed in Iran of the late 1970s.

It is important to understand this process in light of extreme yet possible scenarios for a replay of such a revolution in other Muslim countries. It may hit a Middle Eastern oil producing country, or another country essential to regional order and stability. Such a revolution in Egypt, Algeria, Saudi Arabia, or Malaysia may shake the global economic and political order just as happened during the Arab Spring of 2011 (though mainly due to civil unrest and not religious background). Later in 2014, when ISIS – "Islamic State of Iraq and Syria" introduce by its founder in northern Iraq, the fundamentalist jihadist militant aspect was clearly added to the religious aspect.

Another example can be seen in the military coup attempt in Turkey in July 2016. It surprised the world. Some voices describe the government acts against opponents after it as a different method of Islamic revolution.

The Revolution

The Islamic revolution in Iran removed the Persian Shah Reza Pahlavi from power. His regime seemed stable and solid to all those countries which invested billions in building up a modernized Iran. Iran enjoyed a fairly convenient status as a non-Arab Islamic country, yet behind the scenes, in back yards and mosques across the country, the people's unrest started to bubble.

The unrest leading to the revolution had a sound basis, such as the rule of the 1,000 families or the poverty and illiteracy that remained common within the masses. This fertile bed of civil restlessness produced an extremist leader, Ayatollah Ruhollah Khomeini, who enjoyed broad popular support, even during his exile in Iraq, mostly perusing outward to the streets of Iranian cities by the Imams and preachers in the mosques.

It only took a year from the moment the uprising began with relatively peaceful demonstrations in the squares of Tehran until Ayatollah Khomeini landed in the Iranian capital in January 1979 to inaugurate the Islamic Republic of Iran.

However, the story of the revolution is much more complex, and this was but the climax of a long progression, during which the Shah's power diminished following a series of social, economic and political processes, which had left too many dissatisfied or losing parties. A fighting opposition developed, despite the existence of a centralist regime with tough and ruthless security services.

In the background stood out a large religious establishment, such that did not hesitate to use all the measures at its disposal, faith and religion, to its needs. Thus, for example, the Shah was outcast as a "Yezid," or a traitor.

"Islamic Revolution" they named it.

Background

The long struggle to maintain the Shah regime in Iran was mainly focused between the Shah and the middle class. Apparently the conflict existed during decades in number of rounds.

The outbreak of each round of the struggle required pre-requisite conditions, the most obvious of them being: social-economic pressure, absolute regime, increased foreign involvement, and the spreading of modernization. In each round, religious leaders, intellectuals, and bazaar leaders could usually be found, succeeding in recruiting the support of the city masses.

But only a combination including a religious core led by a charismatic leader, who enjoyed freedom of action in exile, could have succeeded to such a degree.

Mossadeigh

A crisis with similar background was the one that took place during 1951–1954; yet relevant to our days. An opposition leader—Muhammad Mossadegh, one of the bluntest opposers of the Pahlavi dynasty—succeeded to harness some of the traditional power sources, like the estate owners, the intellectuals, and the bazaar leaders, to a significant political opposition.

This power stood against another opposition entity, the Marxist left, concentrating around the communist "Tudeh" party.

The Shi'ite religious priesthood during those years was moderate, and refrained from political involvement.

The crisis revolved around the attempt to nationalize the oil industry, and led to the deterioration of economic status and shook the relationship with the Super Powers. Thus, oil began playing an important economic and political role.

The royalties paid to the producing countries by the foreign oil companies were defined during the first years of oil production, and various agreements were inked in during the 1930s and 1940s. The common royalties amounted to several percent of the oil revenues, ranging between 5–12%. During the 1950s, the producing countries began demanding higher royalties, and later on, even full partnership with the production companies.

Iran's situation was not better off. During the 1940s, the Anglo-Iranian oil company paid 16.5 cents per barrel as royalties, but in later years of that decade, new agreements were signed, granting higher royalties to other producers: Aramco paid 33 cents to the Saudis; in 1948–1949, royalty agreements on 35 and 55-cent level were signed.

The highlight during that period was the "half & half" agreement, signed in December 1950 between Aramco and Saudi Arabia. This compliance was strongly influenced by a similar agreement that was formulated in Venezuela during the 1940s, which was described as a revolution and an important political and economic crossroads for the oil industry.

The Anglo-Iranian Oil Company (AIOC) was an Iranian-British partnership, in which the Iranian government owned 49% and the British government owned 51%. So when it became apparent that during the last five years the AIOC's profits were 250 million pounds sterling, compared with the 90 million it paid as royalties to Iran—it serve as the perfect background for the Iranian government to demand the increase in royalties.

Mohammad Mossadegh, who headed Iran's parliamentary oil committee, called for full nationalization of the AIOC, but he faced the objection of the Prime Minister, Ali Razmara, who was murdered in a "holy jihad" by Muslim terrorists in March 1951.

The seed of calamity was planted. Few days later, the Minister of Education was also murdered, and the Shah's position weakened. On April 28, the Parliament (Majlis) elected Mossadegh as Prime Minister, naming his first mission to nationalize the AIOC; the Shah, who was merely a figurehead, gave his stamp of approval, and the company was nationalized on May 1.

As a result of the conflicts and the foreigners' departure, the Iranian oil production decreased, and the world faced its *first oil crisis* after the World War II. A crisis signifying the future, a crisis that originated in the Middle East. However, different from the three to follow, this crisis was not derived from the Israel-Arab conflict, but from an internal conflict in a developing Muslim country.

The crisis had two aspects which remained relevant to later crises: the first is the West's preparation of reciprocal oil supply, mainly by British and American companies, just as they did in the Second World War with the "oil committee" to increase production of the other producers in order to compensate for the loss of the Iranian production.

Another important aspect was the total British embargo on Iran. It led to the deterioration of Iran's internal economy, yet some preferred that as a price of their blossoming national pride. In early 1952, the situation deteriorated, which compelled Mossadegh to take harsher and less popular steps to maintain his regime. The Shah still remained helpless.

The Powers were left only with the military option. However, in an initiative coordinated with the Shah, they pre-empted a counter-revolution, which brought the Shah back to power in August 1953. Now the task was to restore Iran's oil supply to global markets. In October 1954, three years after the deportation of the British from the giant refinery in Abadan, the Iranian oil export to the world resumed. In order to enable Iran's return to the market, the other producers in the Gulf were forced to give up a relative part of the production.

This was a price they all agreed to pay in order to regain stability in the area.

The White Revolution

The "White Revolution" is based on the Shah's efforts to improve the peoples' welfare. It included better allocations of the oil revenues, aiming at turning Iran, by the end of the 20th century, into a modern industrialized country. The revolution included also some social reforms, from women's status to modernization of the army, aiming at turning Iran into the strongest power in the Gulf—the one to safeguard the free export of oil.

Another objective was the national-cultural roots with the pre-Islamic glorious Persian history, which the Shah wished to renew, as he believed the current culture blocked the country's development.

The White Revolution promoted economic progress. The substantial investments in infrastructures and development were enabled by the increased oil revenues from 0.55 billion dollars in 1963 to 1.2 billion dollars in 1970, and a giant leap, following the 1973 revenue, of 20 billion dollars in 1975.

The first 5-year plans for the 1960s focused on the development of agriculture, transportation and infrastructures. Later plans were focused in the development of industry, electricity, communication, and society, with investments in health and education.

In 1976, there were already 2,800 clinics, compared to only 700 a decade earlier. The number of hospital beds doubled and reached 48,000. The life expectancy and birth rate increased, and in 1976 the population grew to over 33 million.

Yet no political change was offered.

Social Classes in Pre-Revolution Iran

In the mid-1970s, the urban population was divided into four main groups: (**A**) the upper class was referred to as "The Thousand Ruling Families," which included the royal house, the aristocratic families, and about two hundred families of veteran politicians and high-ranking military officers, who retired and were busy with the government huge procurement contracts. These well-established families held about 85% of the large private business in banking, industry, foreign trade, insurance, and construction. The majority were Muslims, with few minorities Christians, Jews, and Baha'is. (**B**) The upper-middle class: the echelon of high-bourgeois, which included about a million families. This group was divided into three main subgroups: The Bazaar community, which formed about a half of the entire group; investors in stores, workshops, farms, and small to medium factories; and a third group of religious people. They had 5,600 city mosques, large seminaries, and additional Waqf (Muslim mortmain property) assets. They enjoyed the financial support of the Bazaar people. (**C**) The working middle class: the lower bourgeois class; a class that grew together with the economic growth and the development wave of the 1970s. The kernel of this class was the white-collar people, including teachers, engineers, managers, and civil servants. (**D**) The working class: a class that multiplied by five during the 1970s. The kernel of this class was approximately 880,000 workers of the oil and heavy industry, and railways. This totaled about 3.5 million employees.

At the same time, in the agriculture sector three main classes formed: (**A**) "Absent" farmers, included the royal family, religious leaders, and veteran landowners that did not live on their lands. (**B**) Independent farmers, including over 1.5 million families, which reached land ownerships thanks to the reform. This echelon expanded significantly from 5% to 75% of the rural population. (**C**) The common villagers, who did not enjoy the reform, and were the working hands. This echelon included about 1.1 million families.

Opposition and Enemies

As part of these reforms, the Shah tried to change laws that were set in the Shariah, the traditional Muslim laws. Like the ban to wear the Burka, a religious scarf, in campuses. The religious priesthood opposition grew, as they were considered to be the keepers of Islamic principles.

During 1974–1975, the detrimental influences of the increase in oil revenues started to manifest themselves: bottlenecks in import, delays in arrival, and delivery of goods, and an increase in housing and product prices, resulting in inflation. The expectations for rapid improvement of their condition did not materialize, and an intense frustration was directed to the Shah.

Yet, the White Revolution contributed to the expansion of the working educated class in the cities. The middle class bourgeois no longer settled for only financial improvement, but started to demand political change as well.

The traditional opposition that the Shah used to call "Red and Black," named after the communists and the religious leaders, began expanding right under his nose. The Shah also added the Western media and the oil companies, which he blamed for the intervention in Iran's internal affairs.

Thus, despite the tight supervision of the security forces, an extensive opposition activity developed, originated from three main directions: political parties from the liberal and the Marxist block, religious opposition, and guerilla organizations that were divided into the Marxist Fedayeen and the Islamic Mujahidin.

The Religious Opposition

The religious opposition was divided into three main groups:

(**A**) The large group of religious men, the "ulama," politically conscientious men who refrained from politics and believed that their role is to focus on the spiritual aspect of Allah's work and to train new generations of theologians. Between the years 1975–1977, the "ulama" were driven to political involvement as a result of the government activity against their religious opinion.

(**B**) Moderate opposition from religious men, led by the Ayatollah Mohammed Riza Golfairani and the Ayatollah Kazim Shriatmadari, who were the chief theologians in Qom. Their objection to the government was directly derived from the change in women's status and the agrarian reform. The group maintained its ties with the government, in order to moderate and influence steps to which they objected. They did not call for the removal of the Shah, but rather for the establishment of a constitutional monarchy.

(**C**) The third group can be described as a militant religious opposition headed by Ayatollah Khomeini, who had been exiled in Najaf, Iraq. The group was supported by religious leaders in Iran, and its activity was aimed directly against the Shah. A rivalry and deep personal animosity developed between Khomeini and the Shah. In 1962, as part of the Shah's agrarian reform, Muslim Waqif's lands were given to farmers, and women were allowed to be elected to local councils. This led to an open war by Khomeini, which ended in his exile. In 1964, a law that passed, granting ex-territorial rights to American oil companies, led to the renewal of propaganda by Khomeini, who described it as "cultural imperialism," fearing the Iranian society would turn into a Western one. Khomeini wanted an equal Muslim society, without large social gaps.

His exile allowed him to express himself freely, and from there Khomeini clearly called for the overthrow of the monarchy and the creation of an Islamic religious state led by religious leadership.

Supporting Powers

The main elements that supported the Shah by the eve of the revolution were the army, the police, and the secret service (Savak). The army with about half a million soldiers, in a well-organized and developed organization, also enjoyed the collaboration with the American and British armies. The military budget soared from $293 million in 1963, to $1.8 billion in 1973 and $7.3 billion in 1977, and military equipment orders were placed in the scope of $20 billion for 1978–1980.

The Shah built a modern army, with expensive and sophisticated equipment which have not been purchased yet even by NATO members. The modernization was mainly focused on the air force and the navy, which grew to become the largest navy in the Persian Gulf. The air force included Phantom airplanes, and, in 1976, it became one of the first foreign air forces to acquire the advanced F-15s.

The land forces were equipped with hundreds of modern tanks, placing the Iranian army as the fifth military force globally. The grandiose purchasing plans invoked wonder and criticism both in Moscow and Washington. The criticism by Moscow, due to the Cold War, was understandable. In the United States, however, an argument ensued between the supporters and opponents.

Supporters were mainly in the Pentagon, who perceived as important having an advanced military equipment reserve, held by an ally, in the Middle East. These arms sales also lowered the unit costs of expensive equipment for the U.S. Army. Yet, criticism developed within the U.S. State Department. Their argument against the purchasing plans was rooted in the fact that the Shah was considered to be a dictator. Other mentioned that a huge modern army must have proper technology support and manpower, which Iran lacked.

An additional $20 billion were allocated to the development of a nuclear power plant which the Shah considered a necessity. Was it due to the military characteristics of such a program, or the Shah's broad view on alternative energy?

Beside the police and the gendarmerie responsible for public order, there was also the secret police, the "Savak," with about 5,000 full time agents and another large number of collaborators and part-time agents—according to some estimations, up to half a million people. During the 1970s, the Savak became the symbol of the Shah's tyrant regime, the secret police had unlimited supervision and censoring authority, and its measures included arrests and torture of regime opposition activist

Liberalization – Too Little Too Late?

During 1976 and 1977, certain liberalization steps were taken by the Shah, but the opposition became stronger. The opposition had already listed local and foreign students, intellectuals and left wing activists. The Shah remained with a relatively small support circle. Protest letters and pamphlets were openly published and distributed, almost without any prevention steps by the Savak, as commonly practiced in the past.

The liberalization and relative sense of freedom were interpreted as a weakness of the regime, and spread through the mosques where political activity began to develop. The speeches of Khomeini were smuggled from Iraq in cassette tapes and openly sold in Tehran and Qom.

The process soon led to a series of determined and even more extreme demands by the Islamic opposition, which included: (1) Return to a democratic constitutional regime, and operating the Five Mujahidin Committee. (2) Allowing Khomeini's return. (3) Cancelling the reforms contradicting the Sharia; mainly changing women's status and eliminating the Persian calendar (that replaced the traditional Muslim calendar). (4) Eliminating corruption and the Western entertainment institutions. (5) Casting out the foreign workers; mainly the American specialists. (6) Revoking the large investments in the military (due to the concern of the military as a support base for the Shah). (7) Cancelling the agrarian reform.

The Freak Wave Turns into a Tsunami

In November 1977, the opposition's activity spread to the streets and campuses. At the same time, during a royal visit of the Shah to Washington D.C., demonstrations against him took place and were reported in the American press.

November 19, 1977 listed the first death during a demonstration. The demonstrations and riots that took place on the 40th day of the mourning period accelerated the deterioration. However, that yielded a relatively weak response by the regime.

The last stage of the revolution was underway, and since January 1978, the riots reached new scale of violence. The cycle of the recurring demonstrations of the 40th day anniversary was enhanced with additional violence and casualties.

During the revolution, the military maintained its loyalty to the regime, but was almost not required to act since the Shah believed in non-use of military force to repress civilians. The military was a reflection of the population, including those that were mentally and ideologically connected with opposition powers. The military command was concerned that a struggle between the opposition forces and the government would cast the country into chaos, destruction of the reforms' accomplishments. They knew that the main looser might be the army.

It is possible that part of the military command was influenced by religious leaders, or simply concerned for their own skin when they concluded that the revolution was about to succeed.

It seemed that nothing would stand against this revolution and change the course of history. Despite this, during May–June 1978, it appeared that the government was back in power. The Shah understood the severity of the situation, and changes in certain development plans were announced in order to mitigate the resistance of the religious and the Bazaar leaders.

These steps brought several moderate religious leaders to call for order, and the Prime Minister even declared that the crisis had passed. But Khomeini did not let go, and from his exile in Najaf he continued to instigate. By the summer of 1978 the renewal of the riots was now turning into a huge wave. The demonstrator's number grew by many workers, forcefully unemployed due to the strikes. On August 5 the Ramadan month started, further escalating the events.

The Shah replaced the Prime Minister once again, nominating Sharif Imami, who was awarded extensive authorities and strived to restore order in the streets. Among the steps taken by Imami was the deportation of Khomeini from Iraq to France. This step turned later to be a fatal mistake, since it gave Khomeini utter freedom, and a global stage for his preaching against the Shah.

The end of the Ramadan and the Eid al-Fiter celebrations led to larger and more organized demonstrations. The voice calling for the return of Khomeini to Iran began to be heard; as well as calls to soldiers and policemen not to hurt the protesters who could be their brothers.

On September 7, the largest demonstration ever seen in Iran took place, with about half a million demonstrators (less according to other estimations). This development drove the Shah to declare a military regime that evening. The public response soon followed, with another large demonstration, where the army had to open fire in order to disperse the crowd.

It was the "Black Friday" of September 8; many were killed (estimated from few dozens to several hundreds). It brought the Egyptian President Sadat to offer the Shah immediate asylum in his country.

The following day, a more substantial strike wave began, deteriorating even further the damaged economy, as the 700 workers of the Tehran refineries began a strike. Two days later workers in other refineries joined the strike. In October, most of the country was on strike—including oil facilities, bazaars, universities, high schools, banks, transportation, ports, newspapers, government ministries, and hospitals.

Khomeini in Tehran

On October 6, 1978, Khomeini landed in Paris, where he was met by an anticipating global media. The riots in Tehran and the public protests went out of control, and forced the Shah to leave Iran. On January 16, 1979, the Shah departed to exile in Egypt.

On February 1, Khomeini landed in Tehran.

Oil Shock

The world recorded its *fifth oil crisis*, just as the market recovered from the 1973 oil crisis, but yet remained vulnerable. The potential improvement in the Middle East, as Israel and Egypt were about to sign the peace agreement and the Suez Canal was about to be opened, dissipated.

The "Oil Shock" hit the markets with the same force as the oil embargo six years earlier in 1973, and was severe enough to spike the oil prices to new records.

Rising from $13 a barrel to $34. Upon the break out of the Iraq-Iran War in September 1980, prices went up to $40 per barrel.

Much like most crises before, there was no shortage of oil in the markets. Moreover, during the late 1970s, the European dependency on Middle East oil reduced, as oil started to come from the North Sea, Mexico, and West Africa.

*It is possible that this energy crisis could have been prevented or solved in a practical and realistic manner if it would have been managed properly. **Crisis management** is what the industry lack.*

*This is what our newly introduced **'Independent Energy Security Agency'** will cover.*

From Revolution to War

The crisis continued to aggravate, as some time was needed to stabilize Iran's economy after more than a year of unrest. Apparently, the street mobs continued to celebrate. On September 4, 1979, the siege of the American hostages in the American Embassy of Teheran took place and continued for 444 days, until January 1981.

In September 1980, Iraq attacked Iran, starting the 8-Year War in the Persian Gulf. Was it the Sword of Islam, or the national heritage of old Persia driving the killing fields there? However, there should be no doubt that the revolution and the war continued to reflect in the world since then.

The fundamental Islam rising from Qom and Tehran, and the so-called holy war between the two Islamic countries, continued since then between the different parties and rivals in that region, spreading out like a huge bomb blast in the Western world.

Since then, the world has entered tough bloody period that looks more like a mediaeval war. Wars we thought have left the world hundreds of years ago, and definitely should not be part of the 21st century.

7. THE SWORD OF ISLAM:
1980 TO A THIRD WORLD WAR

———————◆———————

A. Geographic Holy War, 1980–1988: The Iraq-Iran War to the First Gulf War

Terror State

Contrary to jihadi terrorists, who act in the dark in fear of the long arm of the regimes, Saddam Hussein's terror was rooted within his state of Iraq. A tyrant in his country and over his people, Hussein terrorized members of his government, various minorities such as Iraqi Kurds and the Shiite population in Iraq, and his other various opponents—even his own family: his sons-in-law were assassinated in cold blood when they returned home from Jordan at the end of the first Gulf War. In doing so, Hussein was never hesitant in utilizing any and every weapon in his arsenal, including chemical weapons against Kurdish civilians and surface missiles against civilians cities in Iran during the Iran-Iraq War in the 1980s.

One may suggest, however, that it was the Iraqi people who have been the main target of the insanities of terrorist regimes in their country; a country with immense oil and gas resources that was once a well-founded energy and agriculture economy. This fertile land, at the heart of Mesopotamia, once the cradle of human civilization, with its abundance of water from the Euphrates and the Tigris rivers, has since been left in ruins, torn by decades of mad dictatorship and devastated in an endless series of oil and religious wars.

The local terrorism expanded across the Iraqi borders into Iran in a September 1980 attack that began eight years of war between the two countries. When the war ended, both countries were left with shrinking economies, damaged oil industries, and an unresolved territorial dispute. A war between two Muslim countries, Arab and non-Arab, was perhaps the first major clash between Islamic Sunni and Shia in modern history. Throughout the eight years of war, an ongoing threat hung like a cloud over ships conducting international trade. Freedom of navigation was threatened by what was called the Tanker War.

Double-Edged Sword

Historians of the Middle East tend to classify the Muslim world with a comprehensive division between Arab Muslim countries and non-Arab Muslim countries. In the Middle East, the non-Arab countries are Iran and Turkey, both of which have been highly influential and very prominent in shaping Middle Eastern and world politics for centuries. There is also a secondary religious separation between Shiite and Sunni Islam.

In this sense, the war between Iran and Iraq, which originated from a territorial dispute as well as a struggle for control over more oil resources, soon translated, according to the Middle East tradition, into an all-out war in which the strong prey on the weak. Naturally, Saddam Hussein's Ba'ath Party, a secular-Sunni regime, had a lot to say about Khomeini's Shiite revolution, due to the animosity Khomeini held for his Sunni neighboring country. The fact that Khomeini was granted political asylum in Iraq until 1978 did not contribute to mitigating the gaps between the adversaries; each side feared its neighbor's sect of Islam and was ready to draw the sword in a moment's notice to defend itself.

The thought of the large bounty represented by ruling over not just both sides of the Shatt al-Arab river, which bordered the two countries flowing into the Persian Gulf—but also the abundance of oil resources along its path—was most likely what motivated Hussein in the autumn of 1980.

It seemed more like an attempt by Iraqi rulers to exploit a potential weakness of the post–Iranian Revolution regime. The climax of the conflict was symbolized by the Tanker War, with air and naval forces on both sides attacking foreign tankers carrying the other country's oil in the Persian Gulf to be exported to global markets.

The Persian Gulf, also called the Arabian Gulf, stretches five hundred miles from the Shatt al-Arab northern delta to the gulf and through the Strait of Hormuz. It is subject to complete Iranian dominance from the north and Saudi Arabia from the south. Iraq has a narrow exit to the gulf with long borders with Iran in the east and Saudi Arabia in the south.

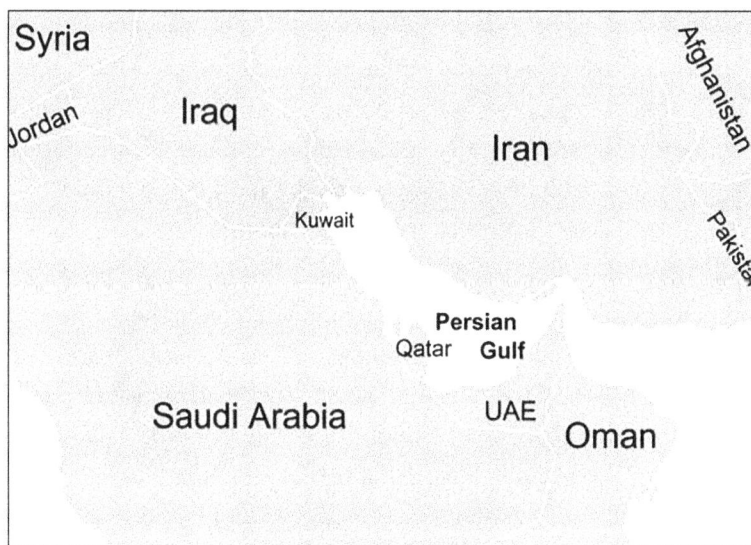

The Persian Gulf

The sword of Islam hit both the attacked and the attackers with heavy losses of life and property. The scene of children being led to the frontlines as a mine-clearing workforce remains a vivid memory. The common ground shared by both parties was their faith and the call to fight and die "for Allah," something that seems to have been taken from other eras in history. The sanctity of death became the highest value and a tool in the hands of the regimes, seeking the grace and protection of the same god, under the same religion, and waving the same sword—the sword of Islam.

To finance the war, Iraq took out billions of dollars in loans, mainly from Saudi Arabia, Qatar, the United Arab Emirates, and Kuwait. The Gulf War between the two Islamic rivals initially drove oil prices to new peaks, but prices dropped dramatically as the war continued.

The war ended in August of 1988 with UN Security Council Resolution 598, which ultimately determined that Iraq was the aggressor. Iraq was also accused of disrupting international peace and security. It was the longest war in the twentieth century. Some tried to analyze why the war lasted as long as it did despite several good opportunities for both sides to end it; the crash of oil prices in 1986 was among them.

The price crash completely stifled the oil revenues funding the war and had an equal impact on both countries, much like the losses of lives, both strategically and morally. But in dictatorships with such fanatic rulers, the war was seen to have served the nationalist nature of both rulers well, and they harnessed it to fortify their regime.

Once the fog of war cleared, it was obvious that no side had obtained its goals. Saddam Hussein also failed to stop the Shiite Islamic Revolution in his neighboring country, and at the end of the war he remained without any territorial achievements justifying even a single day of battle. Iran also failed, waving the flag of Shiite Islam in hope of eradicating the secular Iraqi Ba'ath rule by expanding the Islamic Revolution into Iraq, where half of the population is Shiite, and where some historical and sacred shrines and landmarks for the Shia have stood for centuries.

The Seeds Were Sown

Another important detail to note in the Iran-Iraq War is the limited involvement of the great powers in this seemingly isolated religious war between two fanatic Middle Eastern regimes. In the bipolar Cold War, the powers usually held contradicting interests, supporting opposite sides in various proxy wars and conflicts, but it didn't seem that the bloodshed at the heart of the oil fields of the Persian Gulf caused these leaders to lose any sleep. Indeed there was no shortage of oil in the markets, and oil prices reached an unpreceded low during the war.

When the war broke out, oil prices were still at the high range that had resulted from the Iranian Revolution of 1979. The average price during the first three years of the war, 1980–1982, was at the $33 per barrel level. During the years 1983–1985, the average dropped to $27 per barrel. During 1986–1989, there was a significant decrease to an average of less than $16 per barrel. Despite the war and the daily coverage in world media of losses on both sides and grave damages to international navigation and free trade, tankers, and oil facilities, not a single barrel of oil was missing.

Could it be that the oil industry and global markets had finally learned to ignore such local and isolated occurrences in various parts of the world? Had the Persian Gulf and the entire Middle East truly lost their traditional role in raising concerns of shortages and striking fears of yet another oil shock or crisis? Indeed, during the early stages of the war, the market could have found confidence that it was but an internal, regional dispute—consumers around the world and the oil industry were revealed to be much stronger than any local conflict. Prices soon spiked and crashed again throughout both of the Gulf Wars that followed in 1990 and later in 2003. The world had come to a crucial realization that it could in fact do without Middle Eastern oil.

This is the precedent we need to strive toward when confronted with a possible conflict with any major oil supplier or when encountering interruptions to oil flow to the markets. The oil market has already experienced real crisis on a large scale, so it needn't fall prey to any speculative crisis that may occur.

In contrast to the panic that swept over OPEC, crisis management by oil-consuming countries helped mitigate the effect of the war on the markets, leading to the low prices of the mid-1980s. Low oil prices, even at the peak of the war, acted as resonating proof that during that time the world had learned to manage without Iraq or Iran.

As for the great powers' involvement in this long and brutal war, both the Americans and the Soviets benefitted by selling weapons to the rival countries, as well as spare parts and aging weapon systems. During the war, it was a common occurrence to see in the cargo terminal of the Orly Airport in Paris, just like in many others, an Iranian cargo plane loaded with military equipment, followed immediately by an Iraqi airplane loaded with similar cargo—an intensive aerial train from around the globe to feed the killing fields.

Whereas the Iraqi army relied mostly on Soviet supplies without interruption throughout the war, the Iranian army were supplied with the best of American weapons at the start of the war but soon faced recurrent shortages due to wear and tear and no spare parts. Another major problem was the shortage of skilled, trained officers and soldiers after the severe hit they took during the revolution. The United States' strict embargo on all arms shipments to Iran, effective immediately due to the hostage crisis in the American embassy in Tehran, was fatal to the Iranian army. In November of 1979, the 444 days' US Embassy fiasco severed whatever ties still remained between Iran and the United States after the revolution. The United States became "the Big Devil," as it was called after Khomeini came into power.

Even a seemingly clear-cut weapons embargo can become selective at times of need, and can be overcome with the right political, diplomatic, and economic maneuvers. Above all, embargos can be overcome by engaging in intricate relationships between politicians, intelligence entities, and arms dealers.

These various impeachment acts of the embargo climaxed with the infamous Irangate—the Iran-Contra affair—which made huge waves when it was exposed in all its intricacy and global scale. And so spare parts for American military equipment, from armored vehicles to Phantom airplanes and helicopters, found their way to Iran along winding paths, and the Iranian army was able to overcome the intense wear of the long war.

Tanker War

At the height of the war, both sides proceeded to attack civilian tankers loaded with oil. As soon as these tankers left and sailed southward through the Persian Gulf toward the Strait of Hormuz, they became highly vulnerable and desired targets. Every tanker sunk or disabled marked another blow to the other side's struggling wartime economy and ability to fund the war. Since oil was abundant, even though many oil tankers were hit, no panic was registered in the markets; no trader or analyst expressed concerns and fears regarding the security of the global energy supply.

Yet the use of advanced air-to-surface missiles by both parties during the last stages of the war did raise concerns mainly in the shipping industry capital of London, where top maritime insurance companies and major shipping brokers and owners began to worry about the possibility of oil transport stoppage in the Persian Gulf and its effect on world trade and prices. With the increasing aerial attacks on civilian oil tankers in the Gulf, insurance companies refused to insure tankers in the Persian Gulf. Contrary to other conflict zones in the world, where insurance is immediately cancelled upon the outbreak of battle or dangerous events, at the peak of the Iran-Iraq War, insurance was only restricted to areas of the Gulf where vessels were not under threat of aerial attack.

Maritime insurance was following the geographical latitude of the attacks, as they advanced farther south through the Gulf. Tankers sailing in the southern part of the Gulf remained covered by insurance, while any northbound deviation beyond a specific latitude where the last marine casualty was recorded resulted in the immediate cancellation of insurance coverage in that area.

The Tanker War peaked in 1986 with a loss of 102 ships, including 80 tankers out of about 6,500 vessels that passed through the Strait of Hormuz that year

In traditional marine insurance, the idea of an uninsured vessel sailing the seas was nothing less than a fundamental breach of experience and conduct. Nevertheless, although some 150 oil tankers were lost, oil trade in the Persian Gulf endured.

Despite not being the main focus of the Cold War, local disputes and conflicts almost always played to the interests of the two world powers one way or another. This was hardly the case with the long war in the Persian Gulf; the interests were both contradicting and similar, to the extent that they seemed to cancel each other out.

The war could have continued for many years, uninterrupted by world intervention and constantly fed by American and Soviet arms, with mass bloodshed and losses on both sides. This was what Ayatollah Khomeini and Saddam Hussein used to strengthen their rule.

With the July 1988 UN Security Council Resolution 598 that resulted in a cease-fire, both sides celebrated their triumph.

B. Geographic Oil War, 1990–2003

Hussein's triumphant parade was held in Kuwait City. By the swing of Hussein's sword, the oil market was hit with the **sixth oil crisis**. Helicopters carrying Iraqi commando forces landed in the center of Kuwait City, in August of 1990, to begin a six-month spree of robbing and looting the treasures of a sovereign neighboring Arab country.

The effect on oil prices was immediate. The world, having learned to manage during the long war between Iran and Iraq, was now horrified as Iraqi aggression smashed Kuwait. Oil prices began to climb after some years of relatively low prices, reaching levels only before seen in the late 1970s.

This very drive to gain increased control over oil sources probably motivated Hussein to invade oil-rich Kuwait. Although declared by

Hussein an inseparable part of Iraq, Kuwait was nonetheless a sovereign Arab country and a prominent oil producer in the Persian Gulf.

The same triumph intoxicated Iran. It also continued its strive to power, including nuclear capabilities, which furthered its threat to neighbors in the region and world order.

International Coalition War

The first Gulf War began with the United Nations–American led coalition forces landing in Kuwait in the winter of 1991. Hussein's response was to shoot long-range ballistic missiles at Iraq's neighbors and Israel some five hundred miles from Baghdad. It took the coalition less than two months to force Hussein back to Iraq and Kuwait to regain control.

The market regained its balance and oil prices returned to prewar levels. Hussein's sword of Islam had been returned to its sheath. However, this time it would be subject to international supervision, which was also meant to reinforce the sovereignty of Western-influenced Gulf countries with the intent of diminishing the constant threat of aggressive regimes in the region.

As the world entered the twenty-first century, the sword of bitter rivalry and animosity between neighboring oil and gas producers in the Middle East would continue to cast a shadow over the security of the world's oil supply.

C. Religious Global War, 2001–present

Third World War

The sword of Islam was once again pulled from its sheath, rocketing in the clear sky of New York airspace and crashing low in the world's worst terrorist attack ever, sending world order and economies into recession and chaos. The long war that continues to this day in the

Middle and Near East had begun. The American invasion of Afghanistan, where Bin Laden found refuge with the Taliban, followed by the limited coalition sent to Iraq after Saddam Hussein's regime. Hussein's regime collapsed, sending the region into a complete, devastated chaos that continues to this day.

Iraq became killing fields in endless attempts to restore order and establish regimes between too many conflicting powers, sects, and religiously torn people. The situation was reminiscent in a way of the civil war in Lebanon with numerous attempts to gain power by different factions—attempts that would never end in peace.

On September 11, it was brutally clear that the world had changed. The first headline published by the well-known British weekly magazine *Flight International* after the terrorist attack was "The Day Civil Aviation Changed Forever." And it was not only civil aviation that changed. Past terrorist attacks around the world had not been handled the way they should have been, nor were they seen as warning signs of what the future held. Fifteen years earlier, in April of 1986, an attempt by Syrian intelligence to blow up an EL AL Airline 747 about to depart London with more than two hundred passengers aboard was prevented just before the human bomb boarded the plane. British airport security was upgraded as a result, together with some minor changes in American civil aviation defense.

The first attempt by Muslim terrorists to blow the World Trade Center in New York happened in 1993, which somehow did not result in major changes to homeland security.

Other signs were minimized and excused as being related to local minor rivalries, disputes, and wars; and not to the Sunni Wahhabi Salafi interpretation of Islam. The world had forgotten that this mega-terror tactic, and terror against innocent civilians, had been the trademark of Palestinian leader Yasser Arafat since the late 1960s, with one of the first mega-terrorist attacks in which four jetliners were simultaneously hijacked in 1970—Pan Am, TWA, Swiss, and BOAC—flown to Jordan, and blown up. Other aviation attacks followed, among them the TWA flight in Beirut in June of 1985. At the time, this terror had political roots and not the religious fanatic jihadist agenda of death the world faces these days.

"Turning Point, How 11 Sept 2001 will change civil aviation forever"
Flight International 18-24 September 2001

Terror that turned to jihadi holy war against Crusaders and Jews, against neighbors and worshipers of different sects in other mosques. Shootings and bombings of innocent civilians became a "legitimate" practice for radical Islamists of different sects. A mosque in Pakistan, just like one in Iraq, or a marketplace in Damascus—the road that led to the rise of ISIS in the Levant and the rest of the world was much shorter than anyone could imagine.

Then there was the 2002 Bali terror attack with 202 victims, most of them Australian tourists. Europe became a target with the 2004 Madrid train bombing that killed nearly two hundred, followed by the July 2005 attack in central London that killed fifty-six people. In Russia, the Moscow theater hostage crisis of 2002 ended with hundreds of deaths, as did the Beslan School siege in September 2004, where brutal terror against young pupils ended in a massacre of nearly four hundred deaths.

The January 2015 attack on the satirical weekly magazine *Charlie Hebdo* marked another fundamental approach of radical Islam: brutal, violent silence to any opponent, even the freedom of expression that is so highly valued in Western society.

In 2015 through 2017, Europe became a killing field for more terrorist attacks, from Paris to Nice, from Istanbul to Munich and London. What was first demonstrated in London with second-generation Muslims becoming terrorists acting against their European homeland became prominent in France and Belgium. The above is just a partial list.

Attempts to reduce the impact, effects, and causes of this terror, by connecting them to certain social aspects, unemployment, and other causes, were met with the bitter truth. The wild, brutal approach of Al Qaida turned to ISIS ideology. ISIS, which stands for Islamic State of Iraq and Syria, nonetheless sends its jihadi troops across the world. It builds the infrastructure of an organized state with an economy based on looting anything of value. Trading oil on the black market became a symbol of the collaboration of some regional players.

ISIS eliminates any evidence of a history other than the one they promote. The destruction of fascinating archeological sites is just part of it. In this case, what was said of the Nazis in the 1930s, "Where they have burned books, they will end in burning human beings," need not be explained, as ISIS has already done this and done it well.

With these radical terrorists announcing that their goal is to establish a world Islamic caliphate, a kingdom that adheres to strict Sharia law, a devastating world war is looming, only this time with the participation of Muslim countries and communities. It is possible to eliminate this fanatic ideology and prevent the expansion of its brutal, mediaeval death passage.

The different world powers that unite in one way or another to fight ISIS can win this war, but only massive cooperation will lead to victory.

The twenty-first century brings a different challenge and with it a different world war to win.

8. PETRODOLLARS

---◆---

Oil Revenues Distribution: The Kingdom of Saudi Arabia as a Model

The dualism of the Kingdom of Saudi Arabia's advanced oil producing capacities and its stunted human rights development is often seen as an enigma. The Kingdom was the largest oil producer in the world until 2014 and is to this day among the top three. Until this past decade, the Kingdom also had the largest share of proven oil reserves, a position that was overtaken by Venezuela, though Saudi Arabia still has the second largest share at 15.7 percent, lagging 2 percent behind Venezuela. This remains a very impressive position, since the next is Canada with just 10 percent and Russia with 6 percent. Despite being so rich in resources, Saudi Arabia is also an Islamic religious kingdom where women are forbidden to drive and the law states that the punishment for theft is amputation.

Since Saudi Arabia is crucial to the stability of the world oil market—as so many claim—the country enjoys a very special, warm relationship with the United States, the world's number-one oil consumer. King Fahd received a royal welcome when he visited President George W. Bush's farm time after time, and the king had a close bond with President Obama as well. It became even closer with the Trump administration, as was proven during President Trump's visit to Riyadh in June 2017. This warm relationship between Saudi Arabia and the United States exists despite the fact that fifteen out of the nineteen terrorists involved in the September 11 attack were Saudi Arabians and followers of Bin Laden.

Saudi Arabia was founded in 1932 by Abdulaziz, also known as Ibn Saud, after a long struggle with mainly nomadic tribes, all of whom wanted to be in charge of the regional birthplace of Islam in the Arabian Peninsula. It was crucial to the Turks of the Ottoman Empire to secure a free and safe passage to places that were necessary to holy pilgrimages—Mecca and Medina—and to monitor and control the Red Sea and Persian Gulf coastlines.

For the British, those territories were important because of Saudi Arabia's geographical location close to the Red Sea and the Persian Gulf, and later as a transit and mobilization point for the British Army during the British occupation of Palestine and Transjordan, territory that was taken from the Turks toward the end of World War I.

"The Sick Man on the Bosporus"

The famous romantic story about Lawrence of Arabia has historic roots that can be traced to British officer T.E. Lawrence, who trained, commanded, and led Arab tribes as part of a British offensive from the desert of Arabia into the heart of Middle Eastern territories. This offensive was successful in taking over important sections along the Mediterranean coast, Jerusalem, and Transjordan, and achieving victory over the Turkish Ottoman Empire. The Kingdom of Saudi Arabia was born from the storm that hit the whole world at the end of World War I and the death throes of the Ottoman Empire—"the sick man on the Bosporus," as it was dubbed by enemies and neighbors—an empire that had ruled the region for centuries and was responsible for mass conversion to Islam. The victors of World War I competed with local tribes for power over former Ottoman territory.

Throughout history, the desert and the holy cities of the Arabian Peninsula have maintained their traditional importance to Islam. Religious influence was very prominent and since the late eighteenth century the region has been under the influence of the Wahhabi movement, which was the most conservative religious sect at that time and was based on traditionalist Islam.

The Saud family, located in the Najd region, accepted the principles of the Wahhabism movement from its founder, Muhammad ibn Abd al-Wahhab, and began enforcing them among its associates and neighbors.

The movement succeeded in taking over the holy cities of Mecca and Medina. The journey to occupation was extremely violent and destructive. Most existing structures, including places of holy importance to Islam, were destroyed.

As long as the Wahhabis remained isolated in their desert areas, their existence didn't bother the Ottoman Empire, but with that brutal, destructive passage, the Wahhabis awakened the rage of the Turkish sultan in charge of that area. In response, the sultan sent the ruler of Egypt, Mohammed Ali, to regain control of the holy cities. In 1818, Mohammed Ali reoccupied Najd for the sultan, and Abdulla bin Saud was taken prisoner and executed in Istanbul. Yet the Saud family house survived, and with the weakening of Egypt in the late nineteenth century, the family returned to the area, fighting other tribes for dominance, losing again temporarily to the Rashid tribe, only to regain control in the early twentieth century and reestablish Wahhabism and its rein over the region.

As early as the seventeenth and eighteenth centuries, the British had been looking for a foothold in the Persian Gulf region. They fought the French, Portuguese, Dutch, and Italians in the region, all of whom sought to gain control over the geographically important region. Oil was not on the agenda yet, but trade and territories determined this overseas activity.

Many had hopes to control the Persian Gulf and its shores. During the nineteenth century, Britain managed to establish itself as a power in the Persian Gulf region, mainly by fighting pirates that disturbed their shipping routes to India and by struggling to end slavery in the region.

The British managed to achieve a dialogue with the Turks in order to work on some understanding of their activity in the Persian Gulf. However, with the beginning of World War I, it all collapsed.

It is important to note that the Turkish efforts were made to strengthen their control and to prove their importance as the guards of Islam's holy places. In the early years of the twentieth century, they built a railroad from Haifa through Transjordan to the Hejaz region and the city of Medina. It was dubbed the Hejaz Railway and it had been built to allow pilgrimage to the holy cities.

The war that broke out in Europe in August of 1914 quickly made its way to the Middle East. The British already controlled Egypt, the Suez Canal, and they had a massive presence in the Persian Gulf where oil had been discovered back in May of 1908. Persian oil was crucial to Britain's war efforts; it was needed to fuel the British Royal Navy.

In the Arabian Peninsula, the British acknowledged the Ibn Saud regime in an agreement that allowed them to focus on their war with the Turks over the control of Palestine and Transjordan.

But in the Hejaz region, Hussein Bin-Ali Hashem, the Sharif of Mecca, remained of great importance. In June 1916, local tribes began the famous Arab Revolt that was meant to help the British conquer Palestine and the surrounding areas to take control from the Turks.

In November of 1917, the British arrived in Jerusalem, and in October of 1918 they advanced into Lebanon and Syria. Arab rebel forces were given the honor of being the first to enter Damascus.

The progress of the rebels' army campaign in the eastern arm of the British attack of Palestine helped the British a lot, and was in fact crucial for their victory over the Ottoman Empire.

The British remembered clearly and acknowledged their obligations to Saud; however, the British were left with their commitment and responsibility to Hashem on one hand, and to the Saud family on the other.

Saud Family Dominance

The solution was to make a geographical separation and division of the huge territories of the Arabian Peninsula, Transjordan, and Mesopotamia between the different princes and families. And so Ibn Saud was made king in Saudi Arabia; Hashem was given the territory of Transjordan; and Iraq was the fee paid to King Faisal, who was crowned in August of 1921. The straight line of a border that had been drawn and the prize or bribery given to these different rulers and families would later rise as spoiled seeds, leading to miserable and bitter chaos in most of the Middle East.

In Saudi Arabia, the struggle between the Hashem family and the Saud family continued during the 1920s and 1930s as the Saud kingdom was established under the hegemony of the Saud family.

Most of the development in Saudi Arabia was done after World War II, since oil wasn't discovered in the Persian Gulf until 1938. This is how and why during the 1930s and 1940s Iran and Iraq were more important economically and logistically to Britain than Saudi Arabia.

Oil from Iraq had been piped to a Haifa refinery since the 1930s, and Iran already supplied oil to the United Kingdom. However, the huge oil fields discovered in Saudi Arabia, along with the ease of producing oil from these fields, allowed Saudi Arabia to quickly become the most important oil producer in the world.

Pipelines were laid to allow the Saudis to export oil out of the Red Sea, and another pipeline was laid in the second half of the 1940s to pipe oil to the Haifa refinery on the Mediterranean Sea. The Tapline (Trans-Arabian Pipeline) could not be completed as originally planned, once Israel gained its independent in 1948; the pipeline was diverted to the Sidon refinery in Lebanon instead.

Since 1973, oil revenues have grown dramatically, increasing the Kingdom of Saudi Arabia's GDP and its potential regional and international influence.

Saudi Arabia is an absolute monarchy whose kings have been children of its founder Abd Al Aziz ibn Said Al Saud. The king is assisted by a crown prince, who is usually appointed by the king. The Saudi royal family, the largest in the world, numbers over 5,000 males, out of a total population of nearly 32 million. Over 30% of the total population in 2015 were immigrants or foreign nationals. The estimated 2015 rate of population growth is under 1.5%. However, according to *The CIA World Factbook 2017*, the estimated 2016 GDP per capita was $54,100, with only a slight increase over the previous year. In the year 2008 it was $19,505. The unemployment rate in the 15-24 age group is approximately 30%. Birth rate and population growth is high, as evident by the fact that the population was just 15 million in 1989.

A UNESCO report from 2006 states that in the years 2000–2004, the illiteracy rate was 20.6 percent, better than the average of 37.3 percent in Arab countries. The Palestinian Authority leads the Arab world with an illiteracy rate of 8.1% percent, followed by Qatar and Jordan with slightly more than 10 percent. In Nigeria, the largest oil producer in West Africa and an OPEC member, the illiteracy rate stands at 40.3 percent.

According to the International Energy Agency, in the years 2006–2007, Asian countries, including Japan, China, India, and South Korea consumed about 50 percent of Saudi Arabian oil exports, while the United States consumed about 16 percent. For China, Saudi Arabia was the largest oil supplier with about half a million bbl/d (barrels per day). In 2010, China signed an agreement to purchase a million bbl/d from Saudi Arabia. In the United States during this period, Saudi Arabian oil accounted for 12 percent of the total crude oil imports to the country.

During the years 2008–2011, Russia and Saudi Arabia competed for the position of the world's top oil producer. In 2009, Russia produced 10 million bbl/d and Saudi Arabia produced 9.7 million bbl/d (a 10 percent decrease from 2008); in 2010, Russia produced 10.15 million bbl/d and Saudi Arabia produced 9.95 million bbl/d; in 2011, Russia produced 10.28 million bbl/d and Saudi Arabia produced 11.16 million bbl/d, which accounted for 13 percent of the world oil production, which was 83.6 million bbl/d that year.

In 2015 the United States became the top oil producer, with 12.7 million bbl/d. Saudi Arabia was second, with 12.0 million bbl/d, and Russia third, with 10.98 million bbl/d. Total world oil production was 91.67 million bbl/d. In 2016, Saudi Arabia maintained its second position after the United States, with only a 6,000 bbl/d gap.

The process in which a desert country turned into an oil superpower came with problems in Saudi Arabia as well as in other oil-producing countries; some of these problems were solved and some continue to place enormous stress on the different regimes. These problems include rising inflation; immigration of people seeking wealth; foreign labor forces brought in, from engineers to housekeepers to drivers; rapid urbanization; an increase in importation of consumer goods; and an increased standard of living that has not been supported with necessary infrastructure.

Saudi Arabia always flies under the radar of the rest of the Arab world due to its important role as the guard of the holiest places in Islam. Millions of Muslims make the pilgrimage every year for the holy Hajj. This allowed the regime to become even stronger. But in recent years, the dangerous combination of a very conservative and extremely wealthy monarchy has led to an increase in jihadist activity in the country.

On the other hand, there are also Saudis who support initiatives to invest their wealth to create a better future for the country. One example of this is the nation's attempt to develop an agricultural industry and a general industry to achieve a self-sustainable food supply with the goal of growing wheat in sufficient volume to meet local needs, and even allowing for some profit through exportation. This unique program was promoted by the government in the early 1980s and has been successfully implemented. However, it has suffered in recent years due to lack of water for irrigation. During the mid-2000s, wheat growth totaled 2.5 million tons, a dramatic decrease from 2008, which forced the country to begin importing wheat again.

Saudi Arabia also makes efforts to decrease its dependency on oil by investing in petrochemical and other heavy industry, though these industries are still dependent on oil, but this diversification allows the country to export some products instead of just a raw commodity.

The Future of an Oil-Based Economy

The Saudis' decision in May of 2016 to pursue a different economic reality than the one based on oil export was impressive. This decision was aimed at sophisticated industries, including the defense industry. The official plan targets the year 2030 to achieve its goal, likely as a response to the world's decarbonization program and some of the country's main oil customers becoming self-sufficient for their energy needs.

The enormous funds streaming into Saudi Arabia and other oil-producing countries could have been used to solve many of the world's biggest problems, including poverty, illiteracy, and the most recent refugee crisis in the region.

In a report taken from the Strategic Arab Club, an institution established by the ruler of the United Arab Emirates, Mohammed Bin Rashid, examines the conditions of society, politics, and economics in the Arab world and how to adapt to modern times. The author mentions that the richest oil-producing countries have a golden opportunity to make a real change and improve the human condition throughout the world. However, this opportunity has thus far been poorly used, if at all.

Instead, many of these rich countries have used the money for massive investments in unnecessarily large armed forces. Saudi Arabia owns modern military equipment worth billions of dollars, which, some argue, will not be useful as there are not enough skilled personnel to maintain and operate it.

Other unsolved issues and persistent problems were exposed during the Arab Spring that quickly became the gloomy Arab Winter of 2011 and 2012. However, it is very important to global and regional stability that Saudi Arabia's powerful regime remained stable during the storming events across and around the surrounding Arab world.

Is Saudi Arabian oil the solution for the world's energy problems, or a solution for the problems of it civilians and the region? It seems like the nation has found a perfectly balanced approach between tough, conservative religion and state law, while still able to maximize oil revenue. However, there is danger from radical Islamic terrorists and sects that find fault with their Muslim brothers, just as they find fault with Christians and Jews, giving these terrorists good reason to continue their jihad, or holy war.

The Kingdom's alliance with the West, mainly with the United States, also stems from domestic Saudi needs; however, it does not seem like this collaboration will be everlasting. Oil production and reserves gave Saudi Arabia a secure and stable status in the eyes of oil-consuming countries west and east of the Strait of Hormuz. New oil and gas discoveries will challenge that status, as will decreased dependency of the United States on Saudi oil.

In light of the Arab Spring of early 2011, the struggle within the Kingdom of Saudi Arabia, and a growing conflict with Yemeni rebels, the region still poses a threat to the security of the world's oil supply. However, with the Gas Revolution and other energy alternatives, it seems that the world has learned its lesson and is better prepared to handle any threat to the security of its energy supply.

Doctrine and Leadership

The 2016 Saudi plan and vision to shift from being an economy based solely on oil revenues to a more developed industrial state by 2030, needs to be further developed and implemented. A big challenge to its leadership is eliminating radical ideology. But before reaching a more sustainable society, other challenges must be addressed, such as its hegemony in the Arab world and its relationships with Iran. Iran and Saudi Arabia in general adhere to different sects of Islam and often criticize the other's beliefs. The Obama administration's policy of noninterference in Saudi-Iranian rivalries was clear, which raised concerns in Saudi Arabia, as evidenced by King Salman's strategy to take responsibility and leadership in the region with the United States at his side.

Two drastic events during the month of June 2017 flashed and attracted the world to the kingdom again.[1] The June 5 vengeful encirclement of the tiny rich emirate of Qatar and its ruler Tamim bin Hamad Al Thani. A certain "game of thrones," driven by faulty assumptions, with huge risk of backfired serious unintended consequences. Riyadh's claim that Doha is a key supporter of terrorism is both disingenuous and hypocritical. It also distorts reality and ignores the recent history of the Saudi role in the past three decades in supporting and financing terrorist groups. Compared to Saudi Arabia in this bloody game, Qatar is a junior partner at best. This is an ongoing event and the war against the Houthi government in Sanaa, recognition of the kingdom as the hegemon of the Sunni Islamic world, and cowing Iran into submission.

The other event being the 81 year-old King Salman naming his 31 year-old son from his third spouse, Prince Mohammed bin Salman, as the crown prince and heir, bypassing his 56 year-old nephew, Prince Mohammed bin Nayef.

As all parties in the Gulf will do utmost to avoid the threatening big blast of the Saudi Arabia–Iran war which would be a total destruction to the region and the world, a hegemony struggle between the two reflects daily with the war in Yemen and elsewhere in the Levant against Shia Iran and its supporters, its influence.

We should not rule out the possibility of another scenario like the 1979 Islamic Revolution in Iran happening also in Saudi Arabia. We should ask ourselves if we can survive a certain degree of disruption in the supply of Saudi Arabian oil. We should always be ready and prepare for the worst case scenario.

---

1   Emile A Nakhleh, Ph.D., Research Professor and Director, Global and
    National Security Policy Institute, University of New Mexico.
    http://lobelog.com/saudi-bullying-of-qatar-a-spurious-game-of-thrones-crumbling/
    http://lobelog.com/saudi-arabia-and-qatar-tribal-feud-with-regional-and-global-
    implications/

9. OTHER OIL PRODUCERS:
QATAR, NIGERIA, VENEZUELA, AND BOLIVIA

———————◆———————

Qatar

An expert on the Arabian Gulf describes the Gulf countries' "sustainable energy policy" as a "paradox or complex" issue. In a presentation back in 2014, the professor focused mainly on Qatar, but it is important to broaden the case to three other oil producers: Nigeria, Venezuela, and Bolivia. They are strongly dependent on their natural gift of fossil fuel, but only Qatar has transformed the fossil fuel resources into becoming a world leader in LNG production, leaving the other countries lagging behind.

Qatar has the advantage of being a member in the Gulf Cooperation Council, founded in 1981, to which only six of the oil-rich Arab countries—Qatar, United Arab Emirates, Saudi Arabia, Bahrain, Oman, and Kuwait—belong. Together they boast a GDP of $1.7 trillion and are home to 50 million people, which amounts to $32,000 per capita. Qatar's 2016 GDP per capita was $152,509 compared with $53,600 in neighboring Saudi Arabia, although the Saudis do have a population twelve times larger than Qatar. Nigeria, with a population of 186 million, has a GDP per capita of $5,900; Venezuela, home to 31 million people, has a GDP per capita of $15,100; and Bolivia, home to 11 million people, has a GDP per capita of $7,200.

In the GCC charter, the organization does not refer directly to the day when fossil fuels will no longer be in use, but it states that its goal is ". . . to stimulate scientific and technological progress in the fields of industry, mining, agriculture, water, and animal resources; to establish scientific research, joint ventures, and encourage cooperation by the private sector for the good of their peoples."

When describing its goals, the GCC mentions mostly how to achieve more from its oil and gas in order to develop a long-term petroleum strategy for the Member States. . . . Reducing the dependence on oil as the main source of national income. . . . This strategy is also based on the political and economic importance of the GCC Member States at the international level and their leading role in the oil industry and their oil weight, as the Member States possess the biggest confirmed oil reserve and form the largest area of oil production and exportation. This confirms the importance of enhancing the political and economic position of the GCC Member States and their worldwide role through enhancing their role and oil weight.

The above resolutions were approved in early 2012.

In recent years there has been more activity to promote energy preservation and the usage of renewables of all kinds. Saudi Arabia, as a leading member in the GCC, set a target of 33 percent renewables by 2032. For Qatar, where hydrocarbons account for 95 percent of government revenue and 99 percent of Qatar's population works for the government, oil and gas price drops can pose a significant problem. The Qatari government is now investing more and more in heavy industry, petrochemical, and gas-to-liquid technology (GTL), which is related to oil and gas. Yet Qatar's major problem is a critical shortage of professional workforce, from engineers to project managers.

It is important to remember that 100 percent of its water is desalinated through gas-to-water projects. Both the lack of skilled workers able to overcome difficulties and challenges related to the nation's dependence on gas and its ambitions related to agriculture depend on proper irrigation.

With gas reserves declining slowly in Qatar and dramatically in Yemen, Oman, and Bahrain, it is important to note how little attention is given to the issue of energy conservation. The paradox of free energy that allows people to consume as much as they like complicates the efforts to move away from dependence on this resource.

From the BP statistical review of 2015, it is notable that Qatar's population of 2.2 million consumes 17 percent of its 1.9 million bbl/d production and 11 percent of its 181 Bcm (billion cubic meters) yearly gas production. In addition, Kuwait's population of 2.8 million consumes 17 percent of its 3.1 million bbl/d production and 20 Bcm of its gas, although it produces only 16 billion cubic meters of gas making it a net Arabian Gulf gas importer. Lastly, Saudi Arabia's population of 28 million consumes 32 percent of its 12 million bbl/d production, and all of its enormous 106 Bcm gas production.

These statistics raise a major concern for the region, despite Qatar's position as the world's third largest gas reserve, which ensures it will have enough gas for decades to come for both local consumption and for export.

Qatar, the world's largest exporter of liquefied natural gas, must prepare itself for a looming glut of LNG. It is already the most efficient country in terms of LNG production and also one of the most profitable LNG sellers, having taking advantage of its industry's lowest production costs while maintaining control over supply routes with its huge LNG tanker fleet that allows it to redirect LNG between markets to exploit opportunities.

Global LNG output is expected to rise by a third to about 330 million metric tons annually by 2018. Most of the new production will come from the United States and Australia, with Australia poised to topple Qatar as the biggest supplier. Unlike Saudi Arabia, the largest oil supplier, Qatar won't be fighting for market share at the expense of earnings.

"A lot of people have gas, but we have an integrated project, we are aware of the market change," RasGas's vice chairman Ibrahim said recently. "We are in a good position. Nobody can compete with us…. We are not trying to maintain a leadership role."

The Persian Gulf nation faces a challenge similar to the one Saudi Arabia has grappled with in oil markets. Competitors have taken part of the market share and driven down prices by more than 60 percent since 2014.

Even with the latest LNG market changes, Qatar has been able to maintain its astounding 77-million tons a year export target. In 2014, Qatar shipped 76.4 million tons of LNG, 32 percent of the global supply. This 77 MT target, reached back in 2006, took the two Qatar LNG companies (RasGas and Qatargas) ten years to achieve by building and operating fourteen liquefaction plants.

Thus, Qatar will not invest billions more to increase capacity, and instead of fighting the expanding American producers head on, Qatar has joined them. It has a 70 percent stake in Golden Pass Products LLC, a venture with ExxonMobil, and other similar international ventures already in the works. Another important factor behind their strength is the joint ventures between state-owned Qatar Petroleum and foreign partners, including ExxonMobil and Royal Dutch Shell, to develop GTL technology and other petrochemical projects.

Qatar is currently the lowest-cost and most profitable producer of LNG. Its break-even cost for RasGas to produce 1 million British thermal units (MMBtu) of LNG is $1.60, compared with $7.60 in the United States and as much as $13.50 for Australian companies, according to reports by Columbia University's Center on Global Energy Policy and the Oxford Institute for Energy Studies. However, American producers have recently lowered their estimated liquefaction costs to about $3.00 per MMBtu, on top of their feed gas price indexed to the Henry Hub price, and averaged $2.17 during the first half of 2016. In 2014, it was $4.35, and in 2015, $2.60.

With its control over production, liquefaction, transportation, and import terminals, Qatar was able to move cargo from Europe to Asia, where LNG rates surged in 2011 after Japan switched off its nuclear power production following the Fukushima disaster. Qatar continues to be flexible in a changing energy and geopolitics environment.

Will Ibrahim's statements prove to be true in the new energy era? It looks like Qatar will continue to contribute greatly to the world energy security.

However, having said all the above, as the events of June 2017 just started with a call to Qatar to stop its support of radical Islamists institutes and activity, it will be interesting to see the developments within the Gulf states; and between the surrounding powers—the United States, Russia, Turkey, and Saudi Arabia. Each fuelled by its own complex interests, threats, and ongoing manipulations in the region.

The intra-power struggles of the main Islam sects, the Sunna and the Shia, in parallel with the foreign powers involvement there, may threat the Gulf States contributions to global energy security. Though on the other hand it proves that the world can do without any of them, big or small, single or more. The world energy security is no longer in the sole hands of certain country or certain region.

Nigeria

Nigeria has emerged as Africa's largest economy, with its 2015 GDP estimated at $490 billion; this still leaves the country, with a population of 182 million, with a GDP per capita of a mere $6,100. However, there are some world energy majors involved in developing the country's rich fossil resources further. All efforts aim to get more oil and gas from Nigeria, which contributes back to Nigeria's overall wealth. It has allowed Nigeria LNG production, which started back in 1993 out of Bonny Island, to grow to nearly twenty million tons of export volume in recent years (about 8 percent of the world production in 2014).

Meanwhile, Nigeria, the most populous African country, lags behind all other oil producers, or any of its neighbors, when it comes to GDP. The LNG production could grow larger, but major delays in new development due to lack of security and stability will keep it from improving for a while.

Venezuela and Bolivia

In contrast to Qatar's strong position, Venezuela and Bolivia must be mentioned with great expectations of becoming potential major LNG producers in the future. This is because Venezuela and Bolivia, the two South American producers, have a tumultuous love-hate—and mostly hate—relationship with their powerful neighbor, the United States.

Venezuela and Bolivia are both rich in fossil fuel sources (crude oil in Venezuela and gas in Bolivia). Yet both are in internal turmoil as Venezuela is still recovering from the Chavez regime and Bolivia from Evo Morales's exploitation of gas resources. Venezuela, with 3 percent of the world's known gas reserves, has witnessed its island neighbor of Trinidad and Tobago, which has less than 10 percent of Venezuela's reserves, successfully become an LNG producer and exporter for years.

Bolivia has also been a resource-rich country with strong growth attributed to captive markets for its natural gas exports—Brazil and Argentina. Gas accounts for roughly 50 percent of Bolivia's total export and its 2015 budget. However, the country remains one of the least developed countries in South America because of state-oriented policies that deter investment and growth.

The global decline in oil prices of late 2014 exerted downward pressure on the price Bolivia received for exported gas. This also resulted in lower GDP growth rates and losses in government revenue in 2015 and 2016.

The new energy era encourages consumers to select their suppliers and to choose whom to respect, whom to suspect, and whom to trust.

10. RUSSIA, SUPERPOWER: FROM THE SOVIET UNION TO THE RUSSIAN FEDERATION

———————◆———————

Fall of the Iron Curtain

The dissolution of the Soviet Union following Gorbachev's *perestroika* may have resulted from the USSR leadership's realization that it could not compete with American economic and technological supremacy, as was manifested more than anything else by President Reagan's "Star Wars" vision of waging wars from space using advanced American technology. Another major contributing factor may have been the Soviet defeat in Afghanistan; it withdrew its forces in February 1989 after nearly a decade of wallowing in the deep Afghan swamp. Whatever the reasons may be, the 1989 dissolution led to dramatic changes. The former USSR countries, mainly the Warsaw Pact members, which now found themselves independent for the first time in decades, were suddenly faced with internal political, religious, and economic challenges. They would come to be known as the CIS, the Commonwealth of Independent States.

From an economic perspective, some see the fall of the Berlin Wall in November of 1989 as the onset of the globalization process of the late twentieth century, as realized in several key events: the bridging of the economic gaps between East and West, mainly between China and Western economies; the European Union expanding from sixteen to twenty-eight countries, of which nineteen use a common currency that prevailed despite many doubts; Russia shifting during the same period from a trade deficit of $4 billion in 1989 to a $170 billion trade surplus in 2009, mostly attributed to the oil and gas industry.

Newly independent oil-producing countries like Turkmenistan and Kazakhstan had gained new status and were wooed by the West. Despite trying hard to establish themselves as independent European nations, other former USSR countries, including Ukraine and Georgia, remained highly dependent on Russia in its newest form. The Russia-Ukraine crisis over the annexation of Crimea in March of 2014 proved once more the strength of Russia's influence on its former Soviet protégés.

Enormous efforts have been made in recent decades by Russian president, prime minister, and president again Vladimir Putin, to restore Russia to an energy superpower status by reclaiming control over independent Russian oil and gas players, returning it to government hands, and by expanding the production and supply of both oil and gas, mostly to European countries.

These steps to secure Russia's advantageous energy superpower status have been accompanied by Russian objection to any potentially competing projects. One example is Georgia; after seeking to maintain its independence from Russia, Georgia faced Russian objection that manifested as acts of aggression in 2008. Another example is the immense pressure Russia puts on parties and entities involved in the doomed international *Nabucco* project, a gas pipeline from Central Asia to Europe that bypasses Russia. Whether such aggressive moves against its competition will be fruitful remains to be seen.

"A Soviet Economical Attack"

Russia's affiliation with OPEC raised the possibility of its joining as a full member. However, this remains highly unlikely, because to do so would mean relinquishing its superpower status. The possibility of a "merger" is brought up from time to time to serve various interests; for example, necessary oil-price rises, or to support a rising political power.

In light of its relationship with OPEC, Russia signed a treaty forming a gas alliance with Iran and Qatar in 2008, the so-called *Gas Troika*. With this move, Russia succeeded in establishing its own OPEC-like organization, controlling almost half of all known conventional gas reserves worldwide.

The Russian Empire has held the status of prominent oil producer and exporter since the second half of the nineteenth century. This status was earned with the assistance of key figures in oil history, such as the Samuel brothers' Shell Company, and the world-renowned Nobel and Rothschild families. All these major players helped bring Russian oil to European and Southeast Asian markets. These exports came to a sudden halt at the start of the Russian Revolution of the early twentieth century and was only renewed many decades later by the USSR.

Oil export was a significant factor in establishing the Soviet Union's economy, thanks to the hard currency revenue it generated. Even during the Cold War, Russian oil and gas was highly important to the security of the European oil supply. The cheaper prices for which Russian oil was offered, mainly to European markets, forced the major Western oil companies to offer competitive prices. Since the 1950s, cheap Soviet oil has flowed uninterrupted into Europe, in what was referred to at the time by the Americans as "a Soviet economical attack."

Some see this price war as the foundation on which OPEC would later be established, since other oil-producing countries, having seen Russia's rise to energy grandeur, also wished to increase their overall revenues as well as their royalties from Western oil companies. During the 1960s, among the USSR's customers in Europe were Italy, Germany, Finland, Sweden, and France. As crude oil was being exported to these countries in great volumes through the Black Sea and Baltic Sea ports, Soviet ambitions to export natural gas to Western Europe suddenly became a reality.

Immense gas reserves were discovered during those years in the Siberian plains and the Soviet states of Central Asia. All these new gas resources now required new export markets. Moreover, in order to maintain the Soviets' own domestic consumption needs, substantial funds and foreign currency were required for investment in exploration and production. These would be obtained from massive export to the West.

A Line to Europe

During the 1970s, work began on the Soviet Trans-Siberian Pipeline. It would soon transport natural gas from the Siberian plains and Central Asia straight to Western and Central Europe. The massive pipeline, which required astounding engineering efforts, ran from the Tyumen region, in northern central Siberia, in two main lines—one running north of Moscow, through Belarus to Poland and Germany, and from there to the rest of Western Europe; and a southern pipeline laid through Ukraine and Czechoslovakia to Austria and Italy and from there to southwestern Europe.

The Soviet gas supply network became the heart of the gas supply system in Europe, and a crucial element of the USSR's economy, which allowed it to maintain its prominence in post-Soviet Russia to this day.

Soviet efforts to become a gas exporter to Europe drew the attention of the American CIA, which started surveilling this ambitious plan. A classified CIA document from 1970, declassified three decades later in 1999, stated that the USSR had made great efforts toward signing export contracts with Austria, West Germany, and Italy during 1968–1970; their efforts were fruitful, and led to gas supply agreements with these countries starting in 1975. Having signed the contracts, the Soviets began extensive and complex engineering works required to lay the pipelines. Despite an American objection to this Soviet project, special American-made earthworks and pipe-laying equipment was purchased for the project. In addition, during the negotiation of these contracts, Soviet oil and gas construction minister at that time, Alexey Kortunov, said that the USSR might even sell liquid gas to the United States itself sometime in the future.

Gas supply to Europe commenced in 1975 with an annual volume of 9 Bcm and reached 130 Bcm by the end of the 1990s. By the late 1980s, Russian gas supplied 31 percent of the gas consumption in France, 30 percent in West Germany, and about 40 percent of Italy's gas needs. In 2016, Russia supplied 191 Bcm by pipeline to Europe and the CIS. A decline from the 193 BCM supplied in 2015, reflecting the loss of the 7 BCM it sold to Ukraine but stopped,

American President Ronald Reagan strongly criticized European countries for their economic support of the Soviet Union after the 1979 Soviet invasion of Afghanistan. In a reminder of the espionage and intrigues during the Cold War, in 1982 the CIA made a failed sabotage attempt on the Trans-Siberian Pipeline. Yet to the great dismay of the United States, a year later the total natural gas production by the USSR exceeded that of America itself: 536 Bcm compared with 456 Bcm, respectively. A quarter of a century later, in 2008, gas production in the United States reached 571 Bcm, while Russia's production soared to 602 Bcm. A year later, this trend changed in favor of the United States, and in 2014 American gas production was 728 Bcm, while Russia's was only 579 Bcm.

In the course of few decades, the Soviet Union became a leading energy exporter to Western Europe. Achieving this longstanding goal did not come without a cost, since the USSR and then Russia has become highly dependent on these energy revenues, much like the dependence of Western Europe on the Soviet Union for its energy supply.

Russian supply to Western Europe has persisted over the years, or, to be more precise, has yet to be put to the test, as was the case with Ukraine, which faced a Russian supply cut in the winters of 2008 and 2009 as a result of a financial dispute over gas prices.

Russian dependence on its energy resources is evident when examining its income sources of recent decades. In 1971 only 25 percent of the Soviet GDP was based on energy export, while ten years later energy revenues exceeded 50 percent of the total GDP. An additional 25 percent came from arms sales and gold export in 1981 alone, when rising gold prices offered Russia a golden opportunity to sell some of its gold reserve at peak prices.

In 2015, American production rose 5.5 percent to 767.3 Bcm while Russian production declined by 1.5 percent to 573.3 Bcm. This was also accompanied by a 5 percent reduction in domestic Russian consumption, which further declined in 2016 by 3.2%. In 2016, the total US production declined by 2.5% to 749.2 Bcm, while Russia's output increased slightly by 0.5% to 579.4 Bcm.

New Markets for Russian Gas

During the two years following the fall of the Berlin Wall in November of 1989 and the declaration of the dissolution of the USSR in December of 1991, Russian revenues from oil and gas export dropped dramatically. This was due to two main reasons: a global decrease in oil prices, and a reduction in Russia's overall production. The latter was the result of the exhaustion of existing wells. Despite decreasing volumes from once-rich reservoirs being traditionally met by new investments in E&P (exploration and production of fossil fuels), these much-required funds were now diverted elsewhere, which resulted in a drop in production.

Reduction in energy production continued during the early 1990s and reached a 7 million bbl/d low in 1996. The Russian Federation took almost a decade to return to the production levels of the peak Soviet era. Some 10 million bbl/d were produced in 2007, similar to 1988 levels on the eve of the fall of the Berlin Wall.

During 1989–1990, global oil prices decreased along with the dissolution of the USSR. This trend reversed, however, as prices spiked with the Iraqi invasion of Kuwait in August of 1990, followed by the First Gulf War in 1991. This once again proved that a lack of price stability and security of supply affect oil producers and consumers alike.

In 1999, Russia started to export oil to the United States. This was an almost inconceivable scenario, considering the countries' bitter rivalry during the Cold War and the more distant history of tough competition over international markets during the early days of the industry in the nineteenth century. This export reached nearly half a million bbl/d in 2008. Although it comprised less than 4 percent of the total American oil import at that time, and some 5 percent of Russia's total oil export, Russian oil supply to the United States played an important symbolic role in establishing its international supplier status.

The symbolism of this first-ever Russian-American energy trade, which began in 1999, became quite apparent when the Russian oil company Lukoil opened gas stations across America. Having purchased the large American independent distribution company, Getty, in November of 2000, Russian Lukoil gas stations, with their famous Russian logo, could now be seen along American highways.

In the autumn of 2009, voices were already heard in Russia, warning against its growing dependence on the export of raw materials and energy products.

The OPEC Connection

A factor of great importance to Russia's energy superpower status is its relationship with OPEC and its members. Since the organization was established, the Soviet Union has maintained various relationships with OPEC members. Russia sustained better relationships with countries that were loyal customers of Soviet arms for years, while they were somewhat tense with nations more closely aligned with the West.

Of the latter, a relationship that stands out is the one between Saudi Arabia and the Soviet Union. Saudi Arabia has always maintained a dislike of this anti-religious communist country. Added to that was the natural rivalry between Saudi Arabia, the Soviet Union, and the United States, the three largest oil producers in the world. Over the years, the Kingdom of Saudi Arabia strived to weaken the USSR both politically and economically. The Saudis' weapon of choice was waging a constant price war against the Soviets, as well as maintaining a close relationship with the United States.

At times, the Saudis desire to disrupt the USSR's oil revenues was even reflected in the kingdom's price policy. Supporting its highly competitive prices was the fact that production costs in Saudi Arabia are some of the lowest in the world.

Upon the dissolution of the Soviet Union, diplomatic relations between the two oil powers were renewed, but tensions endured, rooted both in past animosity as well as in the close relationship Saudi Arabia had with the Unite States. During recent years, in light of Russian support of Iran, especially as Iran strives for nuclear capabilities, tensions between Iran's sponsor, Russia, and neighboring Saudi Arabia have grown stronger.

The 2016 agreement between the Obama administration and Iranian President Rouhani was supposed to dissipate the Iranian nuclear threat; however, the Saudi rivalry remained.

Despite the tension between Russia and Saudi Arabia, increasing Russian export to the West has sparked the idea in some OPEC countries of adding the Russian giant to the cartel as a full member—a move that would increase the strength and influence of the organization. Although this fantastic idea is used as somewhat of a threat by OPEC and Russia, such a merging of powers is unlikely to take place in the near future, perhaps due to OPEC members' concern that Russia as a member would become "a cartel within a cartel." Nonetheless, Russia reserves its right to observer status in OPEC, a position that stands at the heart of constant rumors, speculations, and conspiracies regarding Russian-OPEC relations.

"New" Russia

In the rapidly changing geopolitics of the last couple of decades, relationships between Russia and the former Soviet countries of the CIS have seen significant highs and lows. Some CIS countries have already emerged as independent oil producers, while others remain dependent on Russian oil and gas. A few of the former USSR states have even joined the NATO alliance, moving ever farther from their past Soviet heritage. Others pursue an independent affiliation in one form or another with the European Union and the United States, stirring up old disputes from the times of the Cold War and the inter-bloc struggle.

Tensions between Russia and its former satellite states grew stronger during 2007–2009. One example was in January and February of 2008 when Russia cut off the gas supply to Ukraine and left the country freezing in the Eastern European winter. Another was the outbreak of war in Georgia in the summer of 2008, and yet another gas supply cut in the winter of 2009 with the renewal of tensions between Russia and Ukraine, which resulted in yet the cease of Russian gas flow to Ukraine and created a gas shortage in the Balkan states and in some Western European countries.

Whatever the dispute between Russia and its former states may be—whether it is Georgia and Ukraine joining NATO, separatists against Russian loyalists, or a seemingly simple and straightforward economic dispute regarding debts and prices of Russian gas—it is obvious how the security of energy sources is a common issue, and that no country should ever rely on a single source of energy.

In what may be the largest and most direct confrontation between East and West since the dissolution of the USSR, in March of 2014 Russia annexed Crimea in a move some consider to be "new Russia's" leader Putin paving the way to regaining Russia's superpower position. Shortly after the Russian invasion into Ukraine left the world stunned, various sanctions were consequently imposed on Russia, peaking with Russia being voted out of the G8, which is now the G7. As of late 2016, Western political support of Ukraine has brought the situation to a standstill of constant aggressions.

While the fall of the Iron Curtain may have resolved certain issues, new ones arose in their place; some now revolve around energy and its supply. Soviet communism may have been overcome, but the "new Russia" with Putin's strong leadership has clearly identified the power of energy and the importance of securing its position as an energy superpower.

In October of 2014, Lithuania opened its first independent LNG terminal, and so did Poland in late 2015. The terminals will eventually reduce these countries' dire dependence on Russian gas while challenging other issues related to security of supply and Baltic States geopolitics.

III. PRICING

11. WHAT'S IN A BARREL:
THE ENERGY, THE VALUE, THE GREED

———————◆———————

Oil Barrel

The price of oil is obviously a derivative of the barrel's oil content, its quality, its source, how far away it comes from and the energy it brings. So what then is this "barrel" that has become a source of hysteria and panic in recent years?

The barrel by definition is a basic unit of measurement in the oil industry for production and supply, trade, and related energy activity. For energy products other than oil, the unit of measurement is BOE, which stands for "Barrel of Oil Equivalent."

The birth of the oil industry, created the need to transport crude oil from its production facilities in Pennsylvania to local refineries and markets, and later on to ports and across the seas to export markets. There were no pipes, so all available storage and transportation facilities were recruited.

Wooden barrels that were used mainly for transporting other liquids and goods, like wine and even fishes, became the common means of transporting oil as well. In the early 1870s, the standard barrel volume was defined as 42 gallons, 159 litters, which at a standard temperature of 15 degrees Celsius, weighs 306 pounds or 139 kilograms. Later on Standard Oil started to produce tin barrels painted blue.

The color has come to be identified with the company and is now actually inherent in the oil industry jargon worldwide: **bbl**, i.e., **blue** barrel. In later years the word "barrel" became common for oil. The price of oil is determined by the barrel, so oil consumption, oil reserves, and trade are all measured in barrels. For other purposes, the convenient measure is metric ton (MT) of crude oil, where one metric ton (MT) of crude oil equals 7.33 bbl.

The first product transported in barrels was crude oil, and then kerosene, which was used for illumination. Crude oil, as its name suggests, is the basic and primary product produced from underground and under the sea. Crude oil is a viscous liquid, a liquid mixture of several hydrocarbon or carbonates containing naphtha, paraffin, asphalt, gas, sulfur, nitrogen, oxygen, and metals. Its color is often dark brown to black, but it can also tend to look yellow and green. Crude oil varies greatly from source to source, by its composition, shape, and chemical properties as well as its viscosity and specific gravity. Its basic quality dictates the final quality and amount of products one can distil from that specific crude; besides that, the equation also relates to environmental quality requirements such as low sulfur or lead-free.

The Energy

Crude oil is complex and contains over a thousand ingredients and elements. Its quality is determined mainly by its density (mass per unit of volume at a given temperature), calorific value and sulfur content. When refined, the most well-known useful materials produced are gasoline, kerosene, diesel fuel, gas (primarily methane, propane, and butane), bitumen, naphtha, and lubricant oils. During the refining process of crude oil, liquid is heated to a temperature of 370–400 degrees Celsius, until it is separated into its different products. These products are subject to further chemical process to produce other products.

Another effective refining process is *cracking*, the latest been hydrogen cracking, which enables the production of more of the desired clean products by changing the crude's chemical structure. This process separates molecules of hydrocarbon under high pressure and at high temperatures. Sulfur, nitrogen, and oxygen, and other less-desirable elements are separated during the refining process. There are also other technologies for refining.

In the early history of refining, the expensive gasoline was only 20 percent of a barrel, but over the years with advanced process, nearly 50% of a barrel is gasoline. The U.S. Department of Energy publish refinery data that, on average, out of a barrel's 42 gallons, 19.4 gallons of gasoline produced—about 46%, (compared to 11 gallons, or 26% in early refinery days); about 24% of diesel; about 10% of jet fuel (kerosene), and smaller amounts of liquid gas (mainly propane and butane). Other heavy remains of the refining process as asphalt and other heavy dense liquid is used as heavy oil for shipping and industry, and, together with other remains or byproducts, is used as industrial petrochemical feedstock and raw material for plastics, fibers, fabrics, and a wide range of consumer products and lubricants.

Important for safety handling of the different products are the "Ignition point" where fuels will ignite by themselves (diesel at 210° Celsius, kerosene at 220° and gasoline at 250°); and "Flushing point" where the related vapor gases ignite.

These temperatures are low; hence release and vapor gasses of either gasoline, diesel, or kerosene are dangerous. Gasoline flash already at minus 45°, and kerosene at plus 40°. Mazut will flash at plus 66°.

Another point is the environmental pollution throughout the production supply chain. Shipping for example brings big risk, as seen with the Exxon Valdez disaster in Alaska, in March 1989. The Exxon oil tanker ran aground when sailed from the Valdez oil port in Alaska with a cargo of over 1 million barrels, creating the world's worst man-made environmental pollution (more on it in Chapter 17).

Other huge environmental disaster occurred in the Gulf of Mexico in April 2010 with the BP drilling rig Deepwater Horizon explosion. A huge oil spill that will cost BP a $20bn settlement, as granted by a federal judge in New Orleans, resolving years of litigation over this oil spill. The settlement will cover first environmental damages and other claims by the five Gulf States and local governments and will be paid out over a period of 16 years.

The Value

Since its early history, oil price was affected mainly by the demand and supply basic economic rule, but price fluctuations were always part of it—especially in times of crisis. The first crises led to the collapse of oil prices from $10 a barrel in January 1861 to $0.10 at the end of that year. Facing growing supply to three million barrels a year in 1862, up from 0.5 million barrels in 1860, without adequate demand for it. Price recovered a year later with increased usage of oil lamps. That year, oil prices have risen and reached $7.25 a barrel, only to go back down to $2.40 in the second half of that decade. This story indicates a trend to continue and hit the markets despite technology, communication, and the formation of modern markets.

If we search for a formula of oil prices, resulting of the production costs plus a reasonable profit, it will not be found. But we will find that international crises and certain market manipulation will be the case behind price instability. Deployment rumors or speculations are more to be found. A new factor found in the last decade was "Traders Fear," this "fear" originated in rumor, weather forecast or other pure speculation or trend, meant always a price rise. We never heard any objection for it. No one was trying to challenge or present a different approach to it.

The exploration and production cost should be the basic of oil price, but it turns out that the cost of producing not necessarily relates to oil. US dollar exchange rates, weather, politics—all became a part of the black box formula for oil prices.

Oil trade refers mainly to two oil types: the West Texas Intermediate, WTI, and the Brent, originated in the North Sea. The Brent gained the position of energy benchmark and indexation price—as with some gas supply contracts, where the price of gas related to oil prices under certain formula and indexation.

For example, some of Japan's gas supply contracts had been related for years to the Brent under certain indexation known as Brent percentage. "Brent 14" means that the gas under that contract pays 14% of the Brent barrel price. In practice, for $100 a barrel, Japan's gas price will be $14 per MMBtu of gas. (Btu is a standard energy unit that stands for British thermal unit—it quantifies and measures the heat required to raise the temperature of 1 pound of water by 1 Fahrenheit degree. A useful exchange reference would be 1 Bcf—billion cubic feet = 1 trillion Btu; and 1 MMBtu = 1,000 cbf—cubic feet of gas). These contracts exposed Japan's gas supply to disastrous price risk which had nothing to do with the economics of long-term supply that Japan and any of the consumer needs. In July 2008, when oil price peaked—so did the gas prices for Japan—breaking the $20 per MMBtu: a price that affected other LNG buyers, but mainly South East Asia buyers.

Gas at $18–20 per MMBtu became the sweat dream of all the gas suppliers in the world. During 2008, American buyers paid, according to their Henry Hub index, $8.86 per MMBtu, and Japan's 2008 average was $12.56 (spiked from $7.73 in 2007, and up from $4.27 in 2002). The US gas price was very high during that decade, reflecting other market structure failures and relating also to the Hurricane Katrina damages of August 2005.

This price differences from the United States market to the European market and South East Asia / Far East markets always brought into consideration the total dependency of countries in that region on imported oil. Hence a basic relation or formula refers to it as "Oil Parity"—the direct "value" conversion from oil to gas became also a factor: how much energy an oil barrel contains in relation to gas.

As one oil barrel contains 5.457 MMBtu, so the benchmark for gas vs. oil can be marked in such ratio. For oil at $50 bbl, gas benchmark would be 9.16. In practice, there are many other factors that change it to different levels (more on that in Chapter 18).

During the years there was certain difference between the WTI to Brent price. The difference was for quality, availability, proximity to major markets, and storage capacity. There was a small gap of about a couple of dollars in favor of the Brent. In recent years, a gap of more than $10 and close to $20 in favor of the Brent developed—a clear proof that the higher oil price is the wider the gap can develop. Interesting to note that in 2009 and 2010 they were almost identical, with $61.67 and $61.92, and in 2010 $79.50 and $79.50. In 2015, as oil prices decreased, the Brent averaged $52.39 and the WTI at $48.71. The year 2016 ended with the WTI at $53.72 and the Brent at $56.82. Marking the needed correction, we pointed at during the years 2015–2016, from $37.04 WTI and $37.28 for the Brent in the first trading day of 2016.

Will early 2017 price be inked as a floor price for the near and medium term? At our Independent Energy Security Agency (IESA) we believe it should be so.

As gas prices tend to relate to oil prices (not always, and not always at the oil / gas parity of about 1:6 ratio), it is impressive to see also how gas prices recovered during 2016, the Henry Hub—from $2.32/MMBtu in the first trading day of 2016, to $3.72/MMBtu on the last trading day of the year—making little over 40% recovery with its price as compared to the nearly 50% recovery oil price achieved.

In the decade of the Iran-Iraq war and the years followed the first Gulf War, oil prices dropped below the $20 price. $20 a barrel is an important benchmark, since this was the oil price average in 1990, the year of the Iraqi invasion to Kuwait. In 1998, the oil barrel neared the $10 mark while the average for that year was $12.72; the lowest price since 1979 and far too low by any criteria and economic base needed for market stability.

In such low level, exploration and production became hard to finance, and risks the future security of supply.

The 1998 oil price crisis, in which prices dropped dangerously low, is the most important crises to avoid. The common reason for it was *oil oversupply*; a surplus blamed on OPEC members, caused by overproduction and exceeding the quotas allowed by the organization.

This was a crisis caused by lack of control and order, resulting from utter lack of coordination between the producing and the consuming countries, between supply and demand. A crisis that may inflict financial ruin on any country dependent on oil and gas revenues.

In 1999, oil prices began to climb, crossing the $16 a barrel line, and returning to their mid-1990s average level. During the years 1986 to 1999, excluding 1990 and 1998, oil price maintained a relative stable level; with an average price of $15.70 a barrel. Although lower than OPEC's target price, this level still allowed significant revenues and continued investments in future development.

Some attributed the 1999 price increase to the economic soar in the West, the *dot-com* bubble, and the growing demands in China and India. During 2000, oil price peaked at $26 a barrel, high enough to satisfy the hunger and greed of all parties. This relatively high price in over a decade took the market by surprise, but was met by the strong global economy of that time, which was more than able to pay it without a blink of an eye.

The consensus in the industry in the early 2000s was that once oil prices reach the $30 price, oil sands production will become economic. And so did Canada, increasing its daily oil production from 3 million barrels a day in 2005, to 4.385 million barrels a day in 2015, taking its total proven oil reserves to more than triple since 1995 to 2015— and placing Canada at the third place after Venezuela and Saudi Arabia reserves.

This is how Canada became an oil exporter as it produces almost double of what it consumes as an energy-independent country. A remarkable change in North America oil supply happened in 2007, as Canada became the leading oil supplier to the United States, using for the first time in history the reverse flow pipeline of crude to Oklahoma.

In a survey I made in 2002, between several independent producers and few consumers, trying to learn what price level would be sufficient, the few who answered mentioned $15–$18, and $20–$23 when OPEC changed its target price to $25–$28 in the spring of 2002.

The Greed

If we search for the definition of "pricing" in a dictionary or a decent economics book, it will define the production cost, with certain profit or mark up.

What is considered as a reasonable profit? If we learn in basic economics that the purpose of a business is maximizing its profit for the shareholders, then profit is not likely to cause any regulator or other market force to intervene.

However an excessive one, or one achieved by certain manipulation will get the authorities' attention. This excessive margin can be made in a non-balanced market when the demand exceeds the supply, or in a market where there is no control. This is where the anti-trust laws were born, to control Standard Oil so many years ago, in such a case.

Hence one can argue how disappointing it is to find, half a century later, another cartel named OPEC, which dictates price level, quotas to be produced, and control a market. More on that in the next chapter.

The Crises

The modern history of oil after World War II faced several crises, most of them originated in the Middle East wars and unrests. These crises were drastic, immediate, and brought unambiguous rise in oil price. Started in 1951 in Iran: *The first oil crisis* occurred in 1951, when Prime Minister Mossadegh nationalized the Anglo-Persian Oil Company.

The second oil crisis, the 1956 Suez crisis, as President Nasser of Egypt nationalized the Suez Canal.

The third oil crisis, the 1967 six-day war and the closure of the Suez Canal.

The fourth oil crisis, the 1973 October war as the Syrian and Egyptian armies opened a war with Israel. It developed into the oil embargo and oil price to quadruple from below 3 dollars to $12, inking the terms economic-political weapon and terrorizing the oil industry and world economy.

The fifth oil crisis, 1979–1981: the Islamic revolution in Iran.

The sixth oil crisis, the 1990 Iraq invasion to Kuwait and the First Gulf War.

During the 1980s and 1990s, oil prices dropped and soared in what seemed without any direction or control. In 1999, oil prices began to recover, then dropped after the 2001 September 11 attacks, to continue its uptrend as forces were sent again to the Persian Gulf in 2003 for the Second gulf War, a war on terrorism which has seen few Middle East old states collapse into a chaos, while oil prices soared.

But the last decade price crises did not come as a result of any shortage of oil, nor of a real threat for it. In fact there was no energy crisis.

A certain "agenda" or "consensus" allowed oil to peak at $147 a barrel in July 2008. *The crisis of 2008* should be named the "NYMEX Crisis." A price crisis that occurred far away from the Middle East, India, or China—who were blamed for it.

So many questions arise, such as what price to reflect reasonable profit and balanced market which will cover the production costs, and also secure future explorations that will have to be carried out further and deeper than where they are now. What is the price to secure and maintain strong growth and development of an energy-thirsty world? Securing the strength of countries depends on oil and gas imports from dangerously rising prices as we have seen last decade, as well as securing stable income to the producers.

The Solution

A stable balanced price, to support also what Rockefeller coined as early as 1870—and as OPEC defines in its statue when founded in 1960—as "**Stability of Prices**." Stability which is equally important for the consumers, as for the producers.

What effect does the NYMEX open transparent trade have, if prices can be inflated and manipulated that high?

What does a British consumer enjoy when he or she pays nearly two pounds a litter of gasoline, while "his" or "her" oil company, British Petroleum, reports profit of billions? What should an American consumer think when he or she pays nearly $4 a gallon, while the American major oil companies report tens of billions of dollars profit.

Once oil prices rose and went out of control in the mid of the last decade, no floor price was set or leveled to a certain reasonable bench mark. It is evident the fact that none of the producers feared from price collapse.

In late 2014 as prices slid again and continued sliding to a dangerous deep low during 2015 and early 2016, it gave again a reminder of how important it is to maintain stable prices. We would not rule out, and in fact we recommend a pricing regime that has certain floor and cap limits.

In our *Independent Energy Security Agency*, we draw an energy security model based on 3 main pillars – Geopolitics, Price and Supply; that builds the energy security GPS. A stable long-term price should be achieved; hence it is not surprising that we start to see some long-term supply contracts of oil and gas, some with 20 years validity. This is part of the **Energy Future** we aim at.

Yet the barrel remains the best show in town!

12. OPEC – THE PROBLEM OR THE SOLUTION?

————————◆————————

The Magnificent 12

Do OPEC and its 12 members (14 as of 2016, with the return of Indonesia, and Gabon who joined in July 2016) mark the extreme line of oil producers in terms of greed and control of supply? Or is OPEC the solution for a stable oil market? Is it a powerless organization in terms of controlling oil prices, just as they portrayed themselves during the 2008 crisis? Or the one able to dictate prices?

Whatever the answer is, OPEC is a cartel—one of the toughest in the world economy. An organization that was the first to use oil as a weapon, by imposing an oil embargo and manipulating market forces. It is a cartel that no one has managed to overcome, as it continues to influence and threaten the oil market. Its biannual meeting has become the horror show event of the industry; regardless of the market situation—that meeting will get the central stage, the central threat.

OPEC, the Organization of the Petroleum Exporting Countries, inaugurated in Baghdad, Iraq, in September 1960, by Iran, Iraq, Kuwait, Saudi Arabia, and Venezuela, with its major goal to increase the low royalties they had from the oil majors. By 1971, six new members joined: Indonesia (who left in 2009), Qatar, Libya, United Arab Emirates (U A E.), Algeria, and Nigeria. In 1973, Ecuador joined, but left a few years later, just to rejoin later on. Angola joined in 2007 and the latest member, Gabon, joined in July 2016. Gabon holds 0.1% of the world oil proven reserves, but managed to join the big boys club.

OPEC members understood their position as developing countries which have the added value, or a main asset of oil. Oil so needed and wanted in the rest of the world. OPEC's statute states that *"the mission of the Organization of the Petroleum Exporting Countries is to coordinate and unify the petroleum policies of its Member Countries and ensure the stabilization of oil markets in order to secure an efficient, economic and regular supply of petroleum to consumers, a steady income to producers and a fair return on capital for those investing in the petroleum industry."*

Well said, we all agree.

A Solution or Threat

The organization strength looks much beyond its actual market share, reduced from about 50% in the early 1970s to about 30% at present. However, there is no argument that the organization has fantastic influence over the oil market, which allows it to take advantage of any situation for its own self-serving goals.

Regardless of their announcements from time to time that they have no control on the market, OPEC production capacity and its alleged control over its members' "quotas" becomes a main argument.

Consumers constantly plead with OPEC to increase their production in order to stabilize prices; however, OPEC replies that there is enough oil in the market, and refuses to accept blame for high oil prices. Sometimes after such an announcement, there will be another OPEC official who will say that OPEC might consider again to decrease or increase its production in order to maintain stable prices. Occasionally, they will mention that there is no physical shortage of oil in the market, which most of the time is true.

This manipulative behavior by OPEC was clearly visible during President Bush's visit to Saudi Arabia in May 2008. His plea to increase production received the same OPEC public relations statement: that there was no shortage of oil in the market.

No one during that period tried to look for the reasons of price fluctuation also in their backyard—in the New York Mercantile Exchange, NYMEX. Neither had they looked at the quiet followers— **the non-OPEC countries, responsible for 70% of the world's oil supply**—to act differently and make the different sound balance needed, and not obey the OPEC decisions and price dictating.

The NOPEC countries' supply part was never blamed or asked to be more responsive. Apparently, it was very convenient for too many world players and interests to leave OPEC at the front.

The Power

The OPEC cartel used to dictate oil prices, which it introduced in its semiannual meetings. In accordance with the price target they set, they would dictate production *quotas* to its members.

In March 2002, just 6 months after the September 11 terrorist attacks, OPEC announced their target price at $25–28 a barrel. It was during this time that the United States, like most of the Western world, was still leaking the wounds suffered by this jihadists terror attack. The OPEC announcement was straight-forward and tough: "**We gave the world 6 months to recover. . . . The world can pay more for the oil it consumes. . . .**"

Despite the absurdity of this statement at that time, it was met with no criticism. Soon after that, by early April 2002, oil prices climbed above the $24 a barrel to end at an average of $23.18 for that year. The 2003 average price was $26.96: The OPEC announcement succeeded in raising the prices! In fact, since March 2002, OPEC has never had to announce a floor price.

Unlike most of OPEC members, Qatar developed its strong positive position during years of quite efficient work. It is encouraging to see how Qatar provides stability and security for the supply of its gas and also some oil. Qatar produced (2016 BP data) 1.898 Million bbl/d in 2015, and with local consumption of only 0.324 Million bbls/d, it export about 1.5 Million bbl/d. Yet, Qatar is under potential threat by Iran, just like Saudi Arabia—a fact that places them at a favorite American support position in that region.

Some statistics: During the last 3 decades, OPEC members increased **their proven reserves** by more investment in explorations. In 1980, OPEC countries held 66% of oil-proven reserves. In the year 2000, OPEC controlled 77.9% of proven oil reserves, with Saudi Arabia alone at 25%. In 2016 it reached 71.5%.

However, in terms of **daily production**, OPEC faced a sharp decline—in 1965, OPEC produced 45% of the world production, which was 31.8 million barrels a day at the time. In 1973, OPEC members produced 53% of the total production; in 1978, 47.6% out of a total world production of 66.3 million barrels a day. In 1980, OPEC's share was reduced to 43.5% of the world production.

In 1990, OPEC's market share was reduced to 38.3%, but in 1992 went up again to 40.5%, which we can probably relate to the new order in the Persian Gulf after the 1st Gulf War. During the decade of 1996–2006, OPEC's market share increased again from 41.7% in 1996 to 43.6% in 2006. In 2008, it soared to 44.8%.

In 2015, OPEC countries produced 42.7% of the world total production, being 39.358 Mbbls/d of the total 92.15 Mbbls/d world production. If we deduct their self-consumption at about 12% of the world consumption, we will find that their share of world supply is less than 30%—what is left for them to export. Compared to a decade earlier, in 2005, OPEC's share was 42.86% of the 81.896 Mbbls/d world production, accumulating to 35.104 Mbbls/d.

In a world that advances fast to minimize its emissions, toward decarbonization where possible; with some countries aiming at minimizing or even banning its usage by 2050, proven reserves is no longer an asset. Definitely not a threat.

The following graph represents the data above and combines OPEC's total production and consumption. What should be especially noticed is the balance of OPEC's available export—a lesser threat than the 42.7% production.

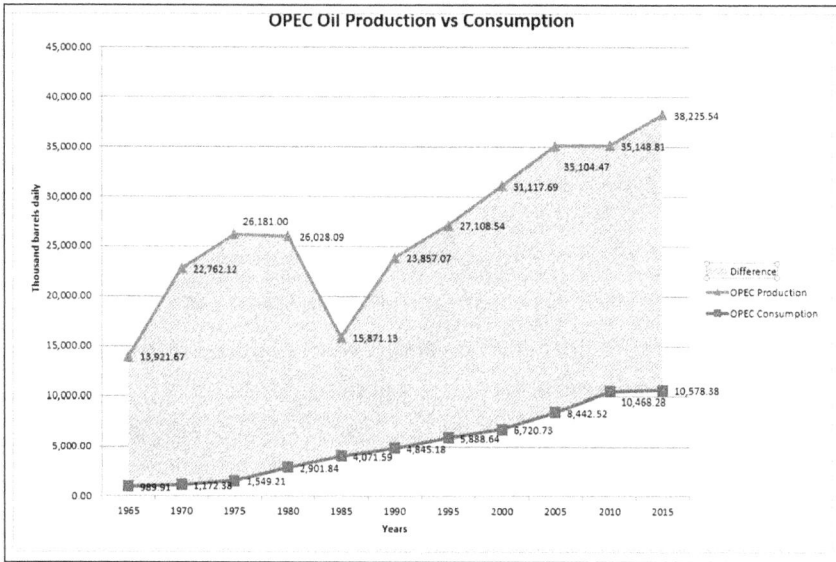

OPEC Oil Production vs Consumption

* Note the "available zone" shadowed—what OPEC offers

OPEC's website is rich with information, data and history; following is some information related to the year 2008, the peak of the oil price crisis (*with 2016 comparison data):

	Population (Millions) (*2016*)	GDP in US $	Oil & Gas export share / Billion $	Daily Oil Production Mbbls	Gas production In Bcm / Export	Refine capacity M bbls/d	GDP in US $ (*2016*)
Nigeria	151.54 * 177*	1,415	76.83/97%	2.017	32.83/20.55	0.445	**2,262**
Saudi Arabia	24.82 * 31*	19,405	304.36/93%	9.168	80.44/0.00	2.135	**19,902**
Iran	71.29 * 80*	4,837	108.47/82%	4.056	116.30/4.25	1.474	**5,120**
Algeria	33.88 * 41*	4,712	77.29/61%	1.356	86.51/59.67	0.523	**3,949**
Qatar	00.86 * 2.5*	106,610	55.96/70%	0.843	76.98/56.78	0.080	**152,509**
Venezuela	27.94 * 31*	11,464	83.17/93%	3.118	20.75/0.00	1.749	**9,257**

*Note that, for other references using the CIA Factbook, different data on GDP were published. For this chapter I am using the OPEC website data.

The enormous cash reserves built with some of OPEC members allowed another threat to appear: the usage of currency reserves as an economic weapon, emphasized, for instance, with the threats of Iran's Ahmadinejad to shift global oil trade to the European currency, as constantly was heard from Teheran since 2005 and along the sanctions period—a move that may weaken the US currency at certain point of time. Interesting enough is Iran's announcements in early 2016 that it will no longer accept US dollars for future oil trade, but Euros.

The huge petrodollars cash revenues were not used to fight poverty or illiteracy, neither the low living standards in some of the member countries. Neither any attempt to use them to solve any other central problems within its members or their neighboring countries.

Floor and cap, The OPEC way

An important point is the floor and cap prices: this is an absolute key for the organization's uncompromising policy, in fact that was one of the founding criteria: to maintain adequate income. This was always a standing position to fight for. It always came with a certain cap, allowing for a margin of a couple of dollars to the announced floor price. A price range no one challenges, but always magnifies it, dictating the fate of the oil and gas industry, our fate as consumers. The "expectations" and "forecasts" of OPEC's floor/cap by world players gave the power to the ministers to influence and manipulate.

When oil price continued its climb after the market ignored the 2004–2005 price crises (see Chapter 13, "The 2004–2005 crisis"), OPEC never had to set a floor price. Even by the end of 2006, when a certain positive lower price trend appeared with oil prices sliding back toward $50, they just had to speak or release a certain general saying, to redirect the market "rumors" and some new "expectations" of OPEC to set another price. I wonder how the phrase "Justice done by others" meet the scenario here. However, certainly no justice—but greed.

On two occasions during 2006 a possible price decline to the $50 level awoke the lions to gather and block the downturn direction started by mid-September. In mid-November and December the NYMEX oil prices dropped to the lowest level in 17 months, with the sharpest daily change of $2.50 down to $56.26 a barrel. It took less than a week to get the price back to the $60 level. 2006 ended at $65.14 (compared to 2005, which ended at the Brent average of $54.52 and 2007 at $72.39(.

In July 2006 the G-8 leaders met in St. Petersburg, where they expressed a polite concern over high energy prices. Earlier that year an important notice by the chairman of British Petroleum that the world did not like high energy prices, and certainly did not wish to get squeezed by high prices was maybe the only voice heard around, from such level and position.

As the Obama administration entered the White House in January 2009, the president announced his policy to release the burden of foreign oil that finances terror. The new Secretary of State, Hillary Clinton, said in a special discussion on the issue of energy security, that OPEC proved that an energy cartel is a dangerous cartel. It might be one of the first public announcements to name OPEC as a cartel.

Only few statements of leaders, finance, and energy ministers were heard, none was heard from the entities that their role is to keep an eye to avoid any such crisis; nor from regulating entities that must act to stop a greedy speculative price crisis.

A massive determined attendance of the leader's different tune was never heard from energy ministers or from utilities and large transportation companies. For example, a call to the non-OPEC countries to support a different price regime. It is just oil—and we are ready to pay just for oil, not to cover any other market intention and speculation.

In February 2008, oil crossed the $100 barrier, going only up, continuing on to May 2008 and crossing the $130 barrier—to be welcome with warm media voices that the $150 and $200 prices was imminent. The rest of the story in Chapter 14.

In late 2008, as oil price dropped, official statements were heard that $50 a barrel was comfortable enough and could definitely be a floor price. OPEC's clear sound for $50 should have done the job for a change to all of us, as it represented an acceptable level for the producers. There were other voices saying that $50 a barrel might stop future E&P activity.

They all forgot the Saudis' wish to have $30 a barrel in 2003, just 5 years earlier.

The Gas Cartel

Another concern related to OPEC is (or better to say now, *was*) the possible formation of an OPEC gas cartel, with Russia, Iran, and Qatar—having 48.6% of the world total proved natural gas reserves—getting together to create an influential entity to control the gas supply, as the magic they did with oil.

In fact, the gas exporters had since May 2001 their Gas Exporting Countries Forum – GECF. Established in Tehran with their first Ministerial Meeting attended by the governments of Iran, Algeria, Brunei, Indonesia, Iran, Malaysia, Oman, Qatar, the Russian Federation, Turkmenistan—and Norway as an observer. During this meeting, it was agreed that the aims of the forum would be to foster the concept of mutuality of interests among producers, between producers and consumers and between governments and energy-related industries; to provide a platform for research; and to promote a stable and transparent energy market.

Apparently a no harm organization, once they concentrate in some internal issues like "harmonizing in the long run the relations between gas producers and consumers," as can be seen in their website www.gecf.org/about/history.aspx.

This quiet organization, called "Forum," held their yearly meetings without any effect or related public relations on the market, until the year 2008 brought some other ideas, as Russia became the thruster power to promote this forum to an influential "gas alliance" with the leaders of Iran and Qatar. The official announcement came in December

2008, placing the capital of the gas alliance dubbed as the "Gas Troika" in Doha, Qatar.

The approaching "gas revolution" with other versatile world spread suppliers, strengthened by certain media ignorance of the forum, brought their second gas summit held in Moscow by July 2013 to issue their "Moscow Declaration," in which member countries affirmed to strengthen the GECF, enhance global scale coordination to protect the interest of the GECF, preserve principles of international trade as well as uphold the fundamental role of long-term gas contracts, and continue to *support gas pricing based on oil/oil products indexation*. Apparently, price and oil indexation came up front. But once the non-OPEC countries had other solution for gas supply, with the dominancy shifting out of Qatar and Russia to other suppliers, the potential strength or threat of an OPEC gas diminished.

The final shot came with the US shale gas revolution, covering the United States local market needs at comfortable prices, and offering any export market a new and different price mechanism, based on the Henry Hub (US HH) price. Probably for the first time in the LNG history, that price was offered regardless of its destination, bringing a very strong positive boost to the international energy market in general, and LNG consumers in particular.

During 2016, the United States started to export American origin LNG under massive long-term supply contracts being signed between the new American suppliers and worldwide customers. The gas revolution finally took a great international departure.

Can we do without one of them?

Can the world oil and gas market survive without any one or more of OPEC's members—Iran or Venezuela, or even temporarily without Saudi Arabia?

Who needs whom more? Is the dependency "equal" in a way or in certain terms? And if so, what went wrong in the bilateral relationship between producers and consumers, between OPEC and the consumers, and again an important issue: between the majority of suppliers out of OPEC to the market.

Certain events in the last 30 years proved that the world can do without one or two of OPEC members' supply. During the 1980s, the 8-year-long war between Iran and Iraq took most of their oil out of the market. The same thing happened with the Iraqi oil after the first and the second Gulf wars. In fact, Iraq was taken out of the OPEC's twelve-country supply basket during those years. The same happened also during the sanctions over Libya and later over Iran, proving that no oil shortage happened. The consumers, and for sure the OECD countries can do without any oil import for 90 days.

If we take the worst case scenario of certain disruption in Saudi Arabia's 12 Million bbl/d supply, for any reason cutting the supply for a couple of weeks, or even a couple of months or more, this is a huge portion of oil that may threat certain countries' supply—however here is where the IEA and other strong entities and countries will have to take the responsibility and announce an emergency situation and dictate a solution before NYMEX traders rocket us toward the $200 scenario. This way, for a change, the crisis would be managed and not free-fall between NYMEX and OPEC.

Crisis management, the way it never happened in recent crises

It means that a governing leadership will announce clear and loud that there is enough oil in commercial stocks in many countries which may be backed by government reserves; and yes, they will announce, "we call to support Saudi Arabia measures to return back to normal order and supply," and will cover any temporary shortage.

If this is the case, or in a reverse scenario, where and when a consumer wants to ban a certain supplier, it will be announced and mapped in details who are this supplier's customer that will have an immediate cover and support from other countries.

So, no threat, no fears (at least for the consumers), if any OPEC member, or other supplier, is taken out of the market for a temporary period.

Boycott and Sanctions Effect

The boycott over Libya, although was not absolute and had limited effectiveness, brought Libya, after more than 20 years, to announce it abandoned the support of world terror, and its nuclear program, which its ruler managed to hide from Western intelligence services. All to allow the country to enjoy the petrodollars of its 1.1 million bbls/d export, shipped mainly across the very short Mediterranean route to Italy (about half of it), France and Spain.

The same thing applied to Iran and could continue to be implemented for a longer time. The world could do without Iran's oil when Iran was left in economic chaos, which led it to the nuclear agreement with the United States in January 2016.

Iran's position in the global oil and gas equation is much less vulnerable to the world than to Iran. Mainly due to its dependency on oil products import. Due to its nuclear program and threats over its neighbors and Israel, it faced international sanctions that started in December 2006 with the UN Security Council Resolution 1737 and was intensified until 2010. The European Union joined in July 2010, to ban technical assistance or the transfer of oil technologies to Iran. It also banned the activity of some Iranian banks and added names to the United Nations list of individuals banned from travelling. In 2011, it froze the assets of 243 Iranian entities and around 40 more individuals, who were banned from receiving visas to certain countries. In January 2012 the EU approved a ban on Iranian oil imports and froze assets of the Iranian Central Bank, and by October 2012 new sanctions targeted EU dealings with Iranian banks, shipping, and gas imports.

Upon the beginning of the sanctions, Iran produced 4.3 million bbls/d. With its own consumption of 1.7, some 2.6 million bbls/d were left for export, mainly to the following ten countries: Japan, China, India, South Korea, South Africa, Italy, France, Greece, the Netherlands, and Spain. Japan led with 523 thousand bbls/d, the Netherlands and Spain with less than 100,000 bbls/d. For South Africa and Greece, Iranian oil covered about a quarter of their oil import, for India 13%, and for the others about 10% of their oil import. No doubt that any of the above ten countries could totally ban the Iranian oil. Apparently it was only the USA that kept the total ban over Iranian oil, since 1979.

Besides the fact that oil export brought Iran 80% of its export revenues and 50% of its total budget, Iran could not supply enough gasoline for its citizens due to the lack of refinery capacity. In 2009, Iran imported 250,000 bbls/d of gasoline, while there was already a limitation of 32 gallons a month for vehicles. In the next decade its refinery capacity improved too little, over 1.7 Mbbls/d, with its consumption just a little above; so, between 2010–2014 its dependency on petroleum products decreased to 4,000 bbls/d (from 107,000 bbls/d in 2010).

Apparently, one of the largest world oil producers could not supply enough gasoline to its citizens. Maybe because they needed it to fuel their ambitious military nuclear program.

On gas production and export, Iran's position was even worth, and still is. In 2007, its gas production was a massive 111.9 Bcm, with local consumption of 111.8; and here is the reason for the disruption of the Iran gas supply to Turkey during those years, as Iran could not fulfill the supply contract volume it had signed with Turkey. By 2008 its export volume dropped by 30%, probably as it had to compensate on some oil products shortage with gas—while it had to increase its gas import to 2.7 Bcm, compared to 1.14 Bcm in 2007—and Iran seats on one of the world's largest gas reserve.

In 2016 it produced 202.4 Bcm of gas (an impressive increase over 10 years from its 2006 production of 111.5 Bcm), while it consumed 200.8 Bcm. In practice, Iran was left with 1.6 Bcm available for export to support its existing long-term export deal it had with Turkey. Iran exported 7.7 Bcm to Turkey and 0.7 Bcm to the Ukraine, gas it had to import (!): from Turkmenistan 6.7 Bcm, and 0.2 Bcm from Azerbaijan.

One of the direct consequences of the world sanctions on Iran was to block its planned LNG production and export program, just like its neighbor Qatar on the other side of the Gulf. Other developing programs had to be scrapped as the international sanctions intensified, among them the IPI gas pipeline supposed to bring gas from Iran to Pakistan and India over an impressive 2,775 kilometers. Too much for a country under sanctions.

Iran's dependence on oil is clear, while the market already proved to be immune of the Iran (and Iraq at the time) oil supply. Between the years 2010–2014, as the sanctions were in force, but not enforced, EU countries reduced their import of crude from Iran from 764,000 bbls/d, to 117,000 bbls/d in 2014. Asia Pacific countries reduced their Iran crude oil import from 1.36 Mbbls/d in 2010, to 992,000 bbls/d, before picking at 1.839 Mbbls/d at 2012.

By 2015, as the talks with the USA, the International Atomic Energy Agency, and the UN continued toward a solution where Iran adhered to the terms of the new nuclear agreement, Iran produced 4.031 Million bbls/d and consumed 1.947, leaving 2 Mbbls/d for export—was that a threat for an oil crisis? For sure not to a market of over 90 million barrels a day.

So for the question 'can we do without Iran?' or other oil supplier, the answer is YES we can.

The problem or the solution

No doubt that OPEC must be part of the solution. A part relevant to its 30% share of oil export. The non-OPEC countries' voice must balance OPEC's position and aggressive approach—this is crucial, and had to be implemented years ago.

A return of the OPEC floor and cap price regime might be a positive move, once it will be the outcome of a broader base task force of consumers, decision makers, organizations, and Government. Not a sole OPEC directive.

In our newly established and introduced Independent Energy Security Agency, *www.TheIESA.com*, we will build that task force.

So far to date, no one have challenged OPEC, but times change, and part of the Energy Future will be a rebalance of the major oil powers we can name as OPEC, USA, Russia, and Saudi Arabia, and yet also the other non-OPEC countries. None of them should have the dominancy that OPEC gained over history. Those days must be part of history.

There are more hope and practical solutions in **Energy Future**, than we had in the decade's long OPEC dominancy.

13. THE 2004–2005 CRISIS
PSYCHOLOGY AT THE OIL PRODUCER'S SERVICE

———————◆———————

By the rivers of Babylon

During the years 2004–2005, oil prices started to soar at a pace and volatility never seen before. Signs of crisis appeared, but no official entity defined it as such, or tried to stop it. It could have still been possible to prevent the expanding oil price bubble, but perhaps it was intentionally overlooked by entities which identified the opportunities presented by inflating prices. The crisis year of 2004–2005 was the ignition fuse to a decade long energy price crisis. Its shockwaves were sent further into the summer of 2008, before it crashed with all its might against the shores of the world economy.

Some attribute the earliest precursor of the crisis to the outbreak of the second Gulf War in March of 2003 and the chaos shrouding the Middle East region in the following years. The energy market responded with fluctuating oil prices, which in practice became a full explosive crisis. Increasing terrorism in the region, internal struggles between local Islamic factions, and the daily war waged against Western forces there intensified.

Upon the onset of the second Gulf War, Iraq had already been removed from OPEC's production portfolio. Moreover, Iraq's share of OPEC's production was small even prior to the war, and was managed under the supervision of the *Food-for-Oil* plan, allowing Iraq to sell its oil only in exchange for food and medical supplies for its citizens. This plan was imposed on Iraq after the first Gulf War of 1991, and enforced by the international coalition forces.

A Gentle Balance

The onset of the crisis can be pinpointed to September 2004, when, for the first time in history, oil prices crossed the $50 barrel mark. Even the Saudis, who had long been wishing for $30 barrel price, were surprised to see price rocket that high.

The global recession of the early 2000s, resulting from the dot-com bubble, and the terrorist attacks on the United States on September 11, 2001, had brought oil prices down to an average of $24.44 a barrel in 2001. In early 2002, OPEC began calling for increased oil prices, announcing that the world could pay more for the oil it consumed.

By April of 2002, oil prices began to climb, rising higher the closer a second Gulf War seemed. When the war opened in March 2003, oil price increased to above the $30 a barrel mark. The impending war in Iraq was expected, along with its declared goals, to lower oil prices as well, upon the stabilization of a new democratic regime in Iraq. On the other hand, a heavy concern raised that oil prices might never return to their former lower level.

A Psychological Barrier

In the early 2000s, oil prices above the $30 barrel mark were considered either apocalyptic or altogether impossible, thus setting a psychological barrier around that level. Supporters of the moderate line claimed that a price increase to the $30–40 level would result in such oversupply that prices would crash, since the market would become saturated. Others claimed that the world had become so unpredictable, and the oil industry so sensitive, that prices could only soar, as increasing demands in China and India would disrupt the gentle balance between supply and demand, consumption, and available production.

2002 ended at an average price of $25.02 for Brent oil, which was higher than the 2001 average of $24.44. The $30 bar, temporarily cracked in January of 2003, as preparations for the second Gulf War were underway, was breached beyond repair by the end of that year, which yet ended with an average price of $26.96.

In January of 2004, the U.S. Energy Information Administration (EIA) published in its weekly inventory report that a surprising low level of crude oil inventory was about to be experienced; the lowest since 1982, with only 269 million barrels. In such a low inventory level, the EIA issued a warning of limited regional shortages that might occur. Oil prices reacted with an increase: from a $30 level in the beginning of 2004, to a year average price of $38.27 for Brent, and $41.49 for the Texas oil.

Out of Control

During 2004, events of a global scale had cast a cumulative shadow over the oil industry and trade: constant terrorism in Western-invaded Iraq; tribal riots in OPEC member Nigeria; a new President in Venezuela who did not hide his aversion to the West; hurricane season hitting the Gulf of Mexico. It became clear that it was only a matter of time, until the $50 barrier would be breached.

While previous crises might have resulted from concrete threats to the world oil supply, this time, as oil prices crossed the $50 mark, no such reason could be found. Perhaps for the first time, the events were triggered by the "fears and concerns" of traders, that were expressed so loud in the media.

One prominent example for that could be found in a CNN report from September of 2004, in which a group of Nigerian rebels were shown riding on a couple of rubber boats in the Niger River, waving AK-47s. This rebel group, led by the Mujahid Dokubo Asari, identified as "The Niger Delta People's Volunteer Force," blamed foreign oil companies in Nigeria of collaborating with the Nigerian government in the alleged genocide of the Delta residents, and pledged to open war against the government, starting from the first of October 2004.

Eventually, a handful of local armed rebels were successful in twisting the arms of an entire industry. News of the events conjured memories of past oil shocks assisted by psychological human behavior arguments, sending oil price to cross the $50 bar line for the first time in the history of oil trade.

Although the $50 line was crossed in September of 2004 only for a short period, soaring prices returned with a vengeance following the enormous devastation caused by the hurricane Katrina that hit the Gulf of Mexico in August of 2005. The destruction throughout the US southern coastline, from Alabama to Texas, and especially in New Orleans, took a massive toll on the American oil and gas production facilities in the Gulf of Mexico, cutting down production and supply to the US market by half, and sending oil and gas prices up. Financially, this was the largest natural disaster in US history, with damages estimated at over 100 billion dollars.

As prices, driven by local events and global fears, soared beyond prediction, expectation and reason, a fearsome realization became quite clear: **oil prices had gone out of control.**

Profit Taking

When investigating the events of 2004–2005 (in fact 1 year between September 2004 to August 2005) leading to the crisis, one can definitely observe the lack of control over market and prices. One increase followed another, always so well explained and excused: from raging terrorism in some corner of the world, to acts of God and nature. Even springtime in the US had been blamed for rising prices, as it marked the beginning of the travel season, increasing fuel demands.

Once prices rose, they hardly ever returned back to the previous levels when the immediate cause for the raise was over.

If by any chance prices decreased, it was nearly always a short-term decline due to traders cashing out on their speculative predictions; what the market calls "On profit-taking. . . ."

Perpetually rising price curves were a unique phenomenon at that time, never seen before in previous oil crises. Was there no entity to restrain the market? Were OPEC countries right when they claimed to have no control over soaring prices?

In October 2004, oil prices peaked to $55.17, and decreased by the end of that year to the $40 level. Earlier forecasts of certain analysts (forecasts that are always fed by the onset of a trend), outlined $70 and $100 a barrel as feasible prices for that year.

Contrary to that, at the end of 2004, the EIA published in its annual report a forecast for price reduction until the end of the decade to the $25 per barrel level, and $35 in 2025.

Forecasts of other official entities mentioned $30–31 a barrel by the end of the decade. In an interview to the *OGJ* (Oil and Gas Journal) in November 2004, the chairman of *BP* (British Petroleum), John Browne, claimed that, despite the $50 spike, he saw a market supporting a $30 price level. Moreover, he stated that his company took into account in its exploration and production estimates a price of $20 a barrel. Yet he summarized saying that prices might increase in the event of a significant change in consumption that will exceed the possible increase in production.

Added Fear Value

So what went wrong with this market? What brings entire economies to their knees when they have such a versatile range of sources, suppliers, and producers to choose from and with whom to bargain? Why is everyone so willing to pay any price asked, knowing well that the industry is long controlled by means of cartelization and fear-mongering?

Self-served and greed driven oil price manipulations most always result in contributing to global inflation and cause turmoil in the entire commodities market.

In January 2004, crude oil was traded in the $30–33 a barrel price level. Such a price represented an *added fear value* of the second Gulf War and rampant global terrorism; the latter's effect on prices is already known in the industry as *Terror Premium*.

That year, airlines and shipping companies around the world imposed a *fuel surcharge*, to be paid by the consumers and that remains in different levels since then. It was accepted by all of us. In early 2004 *Continental Airlines* increased the fuel surcharge to 6 cents a kilogram in domestic flights and 15 cents on its international routes. This was explained by jet fuel prices having a dramatic increase in October 2003; an increase of about twenty percent according to the company. The price for a gallon of jet fuel in December of 2002 was 75 cents, compared with 87 cents in December of 2003. For airlines, the expense on fuel is the second largest of its overall expenses.

For an airline in the scale of *Continental Airlines*, an increase of one cent in a gallon of jet fuel, accumulates to an annual expense of $180 million.

Dependency as a Crisis Catalyst

In February 2004, American secretary of Energy, Abraham Spencer, was asked about the United States' energy horizon in light of discouraging projections of an increased American dependency on imported oil and gas. Spencer confirmed what was already known at that time that over fifty percent of the oil consumed by the US was imported.

In light of this situation, the secretary pointed out that the US was already preparing itself for a future scenario in 20 to 25 years, when some 70% of oil and 25% of gas consumed in the United States would be imported.

By the late 2000s it had become very clear that breaking this addiction and dependency would require drastic measures to be taken, both in an active quest for better alternatives, and in backing this rehabilitation plan with a series of legislations and regulations. Such may include: leniency in granting liquid gas import licenses (during the crisis year, some forty new LNG import terminals were at various stages of planning and licensing), which would open new horizons for energy import to the US; putting to use the huge coal reserves in the US, while implementing a clean coal technology; increasing the use of highly efficient and safe nuclear energy solutions; and further development and application of fuel cells and hydrogen in the automobile industry.

The *unconventional* natural gas revolution, such as that produced from *shale gas*, has not been implemented yet, but had already been conceived and promoted among new energy sources to be developed.

When Daniel Yergin was asked in March of 2004 on future forecasts of the US oil market, he pointed at imported liquid natural gas as a key for more available energy within a stable price regime, as gas prices in the US continued to increase and had doubled between the late 1990s and 2004. However, extensive import of LNG to the US enhances and escalates the dependency of the American energy market on foreign sources, yet benefiting from varying sources, including new ones, such as Australia and Qatar.

Yergin pointed to another harsh truth, saying that compared with relatively limited dependency on import of about 30% of the energy needs during the 1973 energy crisis, it grew to a dependency of 60% in the early 2000s. This emphasizes how difficult it will be for the American administration to reach their important energy goal of secured supply at reasonable prices.

In an IEA report dated February 2004, it was stated that oil continued to be the dominant product of the energy portfolio of the leading industrialized countries "only due to the increasing use of transportation"—cars, airplanes and freight.

In residential energy consumption, a 40% decrease was achieved, compared with a 45% increase in oil consumption for transportation. This rise in oil consumption derived mainly from an increase in the number of vehicles on the roads; owning a car has become a new standard of living in the densely-populated metropolises of India and China.

OPEC's Role in the Crisis

Once again, in early March of 2004, close to the beginning of the second Gulf War oil prices peaked to $37 a barrel. The first quarter of 2004 closed with an average $35.25 for the Texas barrel; the highest in twenty five years.

By then, OPEC was still setting its price range at $22–28 per barrel; a price range reiterated by the Saudi oil Minister Ali El-Naimi, who stated that OPEC strived for a $25 price. In December of 2004, the OPEC countries called for a market level of $30 a barrel; *"$5 above the set $25 price level,"* as it was explained.

The aggressive (and perhaps destructive) role of OPEC in the oil pricing system was accelerated upon demand increase in 2004. During that year, the IEA published an updated forecast for 2004 predicting an increase in global consumption by 1.44 million barrels per day, compared with their previous forecast earlier that year, which had set that increase at 1.22 million bbl/d.

The revised forecast was published on the eve of the semiannual meeting of the OPEC Ministers in Vienna. And sure enough, this IEA publication had an immediate and severe impact on oil prices, as this expected rise in consumption was blown beyond any reasonable proportion to its relatively small change of 0.22 Mbbls/d. Despite this forecast of a relatively mild increase in demand, the next quarter's average price was $3.5 higher, and the following quarter averaged $10 higher than the first.

Oil consumption increased in 2004 by about 4.5% relative to 2003: 80.371 Mbbl/day compared to 76.916 Mbbl/day.

Disagreements and disputes between OPEC ministers, which commonly occur, seem to leak or be leaked to the media, where they attracted greater importance and proportions than it should have. Such news items are regularly accompanied by analysts of all sorts amplifying and magnifying every little piece of leaked information.

During the crisis year of 2004, the Saudi oil minister was publicly quoted as supporting the demands of his OPEC partners to cut back on production, saying that *"flowing additional oil to the market will have a destructive effect on everyone."* At the same time, the Saudis were blamed by other OPEC members, in a public news covered dispute, as the ones who are most interested in higher prices in order to increase their own revenues. In response to these allegations, Saudi officials were quoted as saying that *"only speculations are the basis of recent increase in oil prices."* Such contradicting messages conveyed by the world's oil suppliers, opening newscasts, and newspapers around the globe, can only spread dismay and confusion across the market.

The public debate amongst OPEC members ran its course, eventually serving its purpose of raising prices when in February of 2004 OPEC decided to implement a production cutback of one million barrels a day.

Oil Politics in the US

Hoping to prevent the planned production cutback, the American administration tried to apply pressure on Kuwait and the UAE, but failed in doing so. In Washington, as is always the case, Democrats blamed the Republican administration for failing to obtain cheaper oil from the producers. As fuel price in gas stations reached $1.63 a gallon in Houston by late March 2004, a very high price in American standards, Americans began protesting the steep price rise. However, as high as these oil prices were in 2004, they were still lower than in September 2005 and the summer of 2008.

2004 was an election year in the US, a year in which criticism had the power to replace administrations. In April of that year, a Saudi supporting player appeared in the White House, Prince Bandar Ibn Sultan, the Saudi ambassador to the US. Trying to pacify the American market, and perhaps more so President Bush's voters, the ambassador assured the American public that Saudi Arabia had a consistent policy against any oil shortage in all markets, and that the Saudis would refrain from destabilizing global economy with high energy prices.

Such statement by the ambassador came only a day after Saudi Arabia had voted in support of OPEC's decision to cut back production by an additional 4%, in order to prevent what the Saudis called "price crash as a result of oversupply."

The Saudi ambassador's statements had some effect on oil trade, as the market closed that day with price reducing by $1.49 to $34.27.

As prices rose, a longstanding debate in the US arose again as well, one which is mainly political in nature, though it may have practical effects on the market: the American strategic petroleum reserves, the SPR. This national emergency reserve was conceived in the aftermath of the 1973–1974 oil embargo, decided upon in late 1975 and begun being stored in 1977. The SPR holds reserve of about 700 million barrels, only permitted to be used by law to cover supply interruptions, but not for price control purposes.

Opinions were split in the question of whether tapping into the SPR during a time of dramatic price rises would indeed have a sweeping and effective result in reducing prices that might justify the use of the emergency reserve. Some argued that such a resort would only bring a local marginal effect, which would also be short-lived due to the necessity to refill the reserves.

Although left untouched during the price rises of 2004, the SPR was put to limited assistance in September of 2005, after the devastating hurricane "Katrina." The SPR proved very effective in reversing the increasing price trend during that crisis.

In April 2004, the EIA forecasts for the coming summer already warned that Americans would soon pay $1.76 a gallon for their gasoline.

Other even more bleak forecasts predicted a price of $2 a gallon that summer. Price levels of the previous summer, the one that followed the second Gulf War, were actually lower than the EIA forecast by about $0.20. The average fuel price in the summer of 2004 was about $1.50 per gallon.

Another disturbing information for the market was the fact that refining capacities in the United States, and the entire world for that matter, were almost maxed out. While demand peaked at a predicted 9.32 million bbl/d of fuel per day (2.2% increase from the previous year), local production could only reach 8.46 million bbl/d, and the remainder was therefore imported.

In the eyes of analysts and traders, when this is the case, any interruption to either supply or production, even the smallest one, would justify an overall global-scale price increase.

In Conclusion

2006 began on a calm note. It is possible that the crisis would have been resolved and oil prices stabilized, but after a short while, the rollercoaster went on its way again, this time, heading upwards only. It is important to present oil prices during the previous decade, and look for the reasons of those sharp increases and decreases.

During the 1990s, the average price for an oil barrel was $17.16.

The year 2000 led the turnaround for which the oil producers and large oil companies had been waiting, with the price beginning at the $23 per barrel level in January, increasing to $25 in February, $27 in March, slightly decreasing to $23–24 per barrel in April–May, and, in the summer of 2000, set a peak level of $27–28, which would last until October of that year. The dot-com and NASDAQ crisis pushed the barrel price down to a $22–23 level at the end of 2000.

In 2001, the average price was $24.98—a fair and reasonable price by all respects both for producers and consumers. It even met OPEC's target price.

A positive sign could be seen in the renewal of the *Chad-Cam* project by Exxon, which came to a halt upon the 1998–1999 price crash, and renewed in the early 2000s.

This was an ambitious and expensive project, where Exxon planned to invest $5 billion laying a pipeline from oil fields discovered in Chad to a loading port in Cameroon. As part of this project, the company had also committed to investing greatly in the local population welfare.

Those who had failed to stop the price from soaring in September 2004, when it crossed the psychological fifty dollar barrier of the time, met the price shock following hurricane Katrina in August of 2005. Since then, a series of ups and downs, almost orchestrated to order have taken oil prices out of control.

In the energy industry, information itself is highly transparent and accessible to anyone, regularly made public by various official influential entities, such as the EIA's weekly report on US inventories, the API, and the IEA. This data, however, usually serves as a psychological weapon in the hands of analysts and traders in building up their predictions and forecasts, which mostly range from negative to apocalyptic in nature, thus modeling the market to fit their interests.

And so, this psychological warfare for energy prices rages on, globally waged on the battlefield of mass media. And as the public is constantly bombarded with self-serving information and manipulated data from across newspapers and TV screens, it's become too common and acceptable for news items to open with *"Traders are concerned . . ."* or *"Analysts predict. . . ."*

In fact, we should be concerned that greed, deception, and manipulation keep dictating the prices we pay for our energy. In ***Energy Future*** we will introduce and lead a different attitude, based on insights from passed crises.

14. THE 2008 CRISIS: PRICES BUBBLE EXPLODE

———————◆———————

The Open Shot

I started to write the first edition of this book (published in 2012), back in 2003, after what I recognized as the open shot for an oil price crisis. What started by an OPEC minister call to increase oil prices which I had read in the Houston Chronicle in March 2002, continued with the $50 price bar crossing at the end of 2004—explained by few Nigerian rebels' threat against their government. **I was hoping that bigger, stronger forces than my opinion would stop this speculative, greedy and evil process and would save us the entire 2008 crisis— but nothing helped.**

The speculative bubble grew stronger, feeding itself with self-boiled and well-done stories. Stories like kid's tales and legends, presented as serious studies and researches by analysts and some world respected agencies and entities—they were all influenced by the previous story tellers about the enormous demand for oil and gas in India and China that will soon consume us all.

The bubble grew fat and big, threatening the market—mainly the consumers— and serving all the other financial analysts and entities, NYMEX traders and major oil companies It seemed as part of a greater financial bubble, the one to explode loud in the autumn of 2008.

Against these forces, the consumers were left alone. Those who had the tools to fight the newborn crisis cooperated with its creators. Instead of working to lower the height of the flames, they all inflated it with more fuel—an expensive one. The speculative crisis entered the cycle of its own lies and statistical information, each contributing more and more to the bubble.

The oil price crisis of 2008 led and marched parallel to the cynical financial bubble, and was reflected in the prices of other commodities, goods, and food. The crisis was deteriorating and span to last longer than any crises in the past. It became more convenient and fruitful for too many parties to ignore it, than to think about the destructive consequences for the world economy and population. It dragged the prices of other commodities, including basic food as rice and corn, the backbone food for the world developing countries. A threat to the increasing poverty and hunger in parts of the world was the result of the greedy oil prices bubble.

In fact, there was not even one drop of oil shortages, nor was there one rice grain shortage to justify the price increase.

The panic that gripped the markets and the public, as the financial bubble rose and exploded, has demonstrated again the importance of price stability. It proved that governments and other economical entities that have to guard us from such events have all failed.

There were too many signs of social, economic, and political disorder that allows price rise. The greed set in this crisis had no boundaries, with the "copyright" reserved to OPEC and NYMEX. When Goldman Sachs went out with their $200 "warning" (welcome), no one out there dared to speak a different tune. No one was out there to warn us that the $200 is a doomsday "forecast" coming just as another argument to inflate more the speculations.

In September 2007, I expressed my concern of the continuous price rise to a senior oil media editor. It was not the first time we discussed this price crisis since 2005 or so. The gentleman attributed it to "market forces," although admitting that speculative forces that do not understand oil and energy are active here. He also claimed that all is done in a free transparent open market, however until a more transparent trading mechanism is in force, there is no substitute to this existing future trading of the NYMEX.

On Profit Taking

The year 2005 ended with the Brent average at $54.52. For the first time in the decades-long history of oil the $50 broke out as a yearly average. Seen for the first time in late 2004, many people in the industry assumed this price level as not possible, a psychological barrier, and certainly a high stake that would turn all available and non-available alternatives against oil. Some also predicted that Saudi Arabia, as the largest oil producer, would not allow that level to be reached. 2006 ended with an average of $65.14 a barrel. 2007 ended with an average of $72.20 a barrel.

Before we entered the crisis year of 2008, it is important to look at the last 4 decades, with their average decade price. Apparently the first 3 decades with comfortable average price level, for a world that experienced the 1973 and 1979 oil shocks.

The 1970s	$9.49 (and only $3.68 for the first 5 years)
The 1980s	$25.76
The 1990s	$18.33
The 2000s	$49.60
For 2010–2015	$93.74

By January 2, 2008, the first trading day for the year, the WTI Texas oil price was set at $99.67. By May 21, 2008 oil price crossed $130 a barrel. The media celebrated with predictions and headlines like "Oil crossed the $130, and soon will get to $150." Goldman-Sachs contributed their $200 prediction.

It was a clear reflection and the essence of a crisis, accompanied with panic titles. The editor of one of the most important oil industry magazines agreed with me that week that we were dealing with an emergency; however, no one called for a "cease-fire" nor named it a crisis.

In June 2008, the average Brent price was $132.32, with the WTI average at 133.88 (higher than the July 133.37), and the 2008 march (of stupidity) continued; on July 11, 2008, the Brent peaked at $143.68, with the spot price at 144.49 (EIA data) and began its descent; the WTI peaked on July 14th at 145.78. It was not clear who hit whom that time: did the market realize that there was no justification for these prices and no further rise was possible? Oil prices were always climbing for very strong explanations and predictions, so it was more likely that the ground would begin shaking under the NYMEX traders as they realized they missed the market.

Two months later they gained the nickname "Fraud Street."

Exploding as a bubble

The July 2008 closing price was $124.17; August, $115.55; September, $100.70; October, $68.10; November, $55.21; and the year ended at the price of $44.60 a barrel.

OPEC ministers, as well as other major players in the market have already pleaded to accept the $50 price as "bearable" for the near future. An opportunity to fix a new order of floor and cap prices might have been there waiting for the right initiative and leadership.

But the coming 3 years proved again the volatility and disorder of the market, as price climbed in a straight ascending line—pointing again higher and higher.

At the end of 2009, prices hovered around the $75 a barrel; so we could hear the Saudi's voice echo—in early December 2009—that the prices were great for everyone. 2009 closed with average of $61.67 a barrel and 2010 at $79.50.

Suddenly there was no huge demand in China or India. No "threat" of shortage. The destructive greed that grew out of thousands of traders on Fraud Street, exploded as a bubble.

Was the "cheap oil era over," as some journalists and papers wrote since June 2008? Or perhaps the parasitic greed and speculation that grew and dragged with it the other goods and food was over; apparently Goldman-Sachs sent other voices to the market in January 2009—which we might face a $20 barrel scenario.

They all forgot that $20 a barrel is dangerous just as $200 a barrel is. It is essential for the benefit of subsequent potential future crises, to understand the reasons and consequences of the 2008 crisis; the variety of reasons and wise explanations that appeared during 2008 and the years preceding it, to justify the price increase: from a refinery closure or a fire (that only in the small letters, or after further investigations you will find it is a refinery in Sicily, producing 22,000 bbl/d), that in the worth case scenario will affect the local community or regional customers for a relatively short time; the travel season in the United States became a common reason impending every spring in the US; weather changes expectations. They all became a threat to the global oil and gas industry. Another scholar-wise explanation lying in the heart of that consensus was the dollar rate of exchange against the European currency. Apparently our barrel became the financial tool to compensate the rate of exchange and currency rate risk; again for the consumers account.

The fact that the winter is cold and the summer is hot is intensified by speculation and "comments" that the coming winter will be colder than normal, or the coming summer will be warmer than normal. Some hints and threats of war are also among the likely NYMEX explanations—one of the pearls here was in summer 2008, when the Israeli minister of defense, Mr. Shaul Mofaz, mentioned, in a certain political debate in the Israeli parliament, the possibility of Israel striking the Iranian nuclear program. It contributed to a nice hefty price rise over that day in the NYMEX.

An interesting "fueling" argument about the flame was, and still is, is one of the most transparent tools of the EIA and API weekly reports of oil and gas inventory in the United States. It became a speculative gambling by analysts and traders in Wall Street, being developed into a phenomenon when for every due weekly report, there are traders' expectations/forecasts/threats/fears that the levels will be somewhat other than they are.

Any change of the "Wall Street Consensus" between the actual report and the predictions/hopes/consensus becomes an energy crisis by its creators.

A common description on news item on that will be as follows: ". . . commercial crude oil increased by 400,000 barrels to 337.8 million barrels. . . ." Then comes the punch line of commentators, analysts: "well below their expected 1 million barrels on Wall Street. . . ." The report continues: ". . . gasoline stocks fell 5.2 million barrels in September, to the level of 209.2 million barrels." But according to commentators and analysts, the consensus on Wall Street was an increase of 1.1 million barrels: "Other distillates stocks declined on 1.1 million barrels to a total of 170.7 million barrels," thus passing the Wall Street expectations for a drop of 100,000 barrels only.

Making this transparent information—an energy crisis, or price-rise argument, and certainly not what it is published for.

Unbearable and disturbing was that the same mechanism and terminology repeated itself by the second half of 2009: short memory by media and traders—in order to reinflate the same wrong arguments leading to the 2008 crisis.

The price increase of September–October 2009 came out of the above interpretation around the United States available stocks, explaining them as we were about to face a shortage of gasoline or other oil product. In the first report for October, a decline in the stock of crude oil of 1 million barrels out of 337.4 million barrels. Yes, again against Wall Street expectations for a rise of 2 million barrels.

However, gasoline stocks grew at 2.9 million barrels to 214.4 million, the amount of which was larger than the analysts' consensus—so nothing dramatically changed (in the stocks), but not in the same manipulated destructive mechanism.

Just a year passed from the 2008 bubble loud explosive.

To summarize the above "October 2009 crisis"—no shortage. On the contrary: there is an excess of total crude and products. When the commercial inventory of crude oil, gasoline and other distillates comes to 723.6 million barrels, which at the end of the day (or week of that report) changed in only 0.8 million bbls, out of 723.6 million barrels, there is only a minor change of 0.0011%.

This is the essence of the 2008 crisis: greed won, and it came back just over a year later with the same players who do not hesitate to return with the same tendentious interpretation. This is how the 2011–2014 high oil prices returned.

Burning Caucasus

In contrary to the speculative crises, the August 2008 Caucasus war was a real crisis, yet regional, caused by the Russia–Georgia war. Certain disputes and conflict of interests, part of them related to Georgia's role in bypassing the Russian gas grid of Central Asian gas to Europe, led to the Russian attack on its little former Soviet Union (FSU) neighbor. Among the first targets was the old important railway from the Caspian Sea oil town, Baku, to the Black Sea town of Batumi—where the large export oil terminals are. Just imagine if this war would have started six months earlier. WOW! What a napalm bomb would that be into the burning hot NYMEX market at the time—sending rocketing prices up and even above the $200 a barrel—YET without a reason to affect the global price level.

The August 2008 crashing oil price and the upcoming Wall Street collapse were just around the corner—and no one cared about that war. Same weather disruptions, same terror striking here and there—and oil prices just continued their descent, proving that all side effects on prices were just background noises that should not have had the effects we were used to be fed with.

It's striking evidence was the end of an October 2008 headline in the Oil and Gas daily "Market Watch" which said ". . . **prices continue to**

fall as the market ignores OPEC. . . ." A headline or even a comment we have never seen before, but which surely could help during the developing price rise since 2004.

Yes we learn! The insights of the 2008 price crisis

An important outcome must be implement that once a sign of a crisis of any magnitude is happening, all the attention must be brought to solve it without delay, before it reflects all over the world.

Thus, for example, any slight incident in Nigeria, Nigeria—and only Nigeria— should bear the charge for it. It should be the only party to suffer the loss. If some local gang of terrorists manages to set certain disorder there, because of government lack of control, the market should not raise the global oil price, but just be able to absorb a certain temporary loss of Nigerian oil.

Otherwise, the whole market pays more for the same oil, making all the suppliers beneficiaries of such a crisis; and the responsible party in practice gets the same revenues even if it sells less oil.

The very same attitude must be taken at any other size crisis anywhere with any supplier. Take the hurricane Katrina of 2005, placing the Gulf of Mexico in severe damages, including to the oil and gas industry. Yet the damage and loss of supply was regional in the USA. This large scale event should have placed it under the United States government immediate control, to be handled and cared as an "Emergency." A large scale federal assistance should get into action, including supply of oil out of the SPR, the Strategic Petroleum Reserve (as it happened later in the crisis stopping the sharp price rise that occurred). In the case of the USA, the SPR should be the safety cushion of such potential crisis, and in other places in the world it must be the IEA compulsory 90 days' reserve the one to be used—thus, eliminating the destructive economic effect of NYMEX traders, raising the oil and gas prices globally.

Yes—our energy must be Accessible, Affordable and Available; free of threats. Threats should be implemented only on the suppliers of such crises. We can do without any harming supplier, we can choose from whom we buy and from whom not to buy.

If at the end of October 2009, when oil prices climbed again and crossed the $80 benchmark, OPEC ministers were those who gathered to warn that speculation rather than any shortage brings again a price rise; we have a hopeful sign of an insight learnt out of the 2008 crisis.

This was a clear sign that oil has a certain floor and cap price, with a certain unwanted price-range even for the producers. In December 2009 the Saudi oil Minister mentioned that oil prices were at a "perfect" level, this was at a $75 level, a level that should have been set as a cap for a good deal of time—what the industry likes to refer to as "long-term."

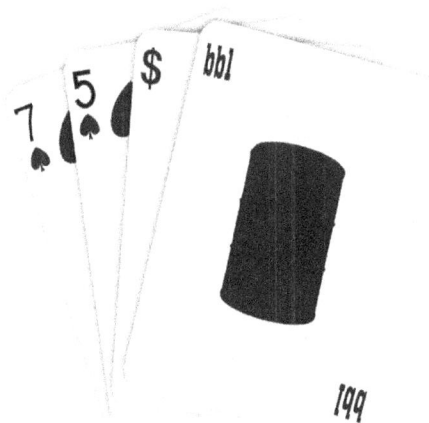

This was the opening page of this chapter
in the 2012 first edition of this book.

But the market, as a market, failed again to stabilize a potential long-term price regime, based on better relations between producers and consumers. Prices were set to rise to the level of $100 and above during too long time from 2010–2014, to be settled as a "consensus" level for the time. Just until the other side of the crisis came with sliding prices—the "dark side of a crisis. . . ."

The 2008 crisis "model" is the one to avoid, there are other means to follow in order to solve any developing crisis, before it turns into an energy crisis.

Our **Energy Future** can be secured by eliminating any developing crisis.

IV. Supply

15. EXPLORATION AND PRODUCTION

———◆———

E&P – Exploration and Production

As we know and understand, any barrel produced from our earth, and any molecule of gas consumed is not replaced. The oil and gas deposits started to form about 350 to 290 million years ago during the Carboniferous Period, which gets its name from the basic element in oil and gas: carbon. So it took hundreds of millions of years for the sediment of organisms to form from ashes, debris of ancient animals and woods to become the fossil fuels we know and consume.

This process, which takes thousands of generations, is a once-in-a-lifetime show as no substitute exists. Yet, the oil companies place in the center of their activity the "Replacement Rate" to measure their reserves: how much is left and how many new reservoirs they have found. The strength of the oil companies is their replacement ratio. Regardless of what they have sold and we have consumed in a given period; if their replacement ratio is positive, so is their strength.

Any oil and gas company reports in its annual balance sheet how successful they were in increasing their reserves. They also report the status of reservoirs in their hands, leaving some uncertainties as could be seen back in 2004 with the scandal of Shell's reserve reports, and the enigma of the Saudi Arabia reserves.

———

Upstream – from Deep Sea and Desert to Drive Our Energy Needs

The tool to achieve it is *E&P – Exploration and Production*. A sector of the oil and gas industry dubbed as "Upstream." This may be the most expensive and advanced part along the supply chain. The more oil consumed, the deeper and farther we will have to drill and explore for replacement.

Ever since the birth of the oil industry more than 150 years ago, E&P has developed and become an advanced industry that combines sophisticated technologies related to shipping, machinery, geology, oceanography, and chemistry in order to achieve its successful capabilities. The *Exploration* part of it developed itself into 2 Dimensions (2-D), 3-D, and in recent years to 4-D—related to how comprehensive it is by its ability to look deeper into the earth and below the oceans with certain number of dimensions or parameters.

The 3-D technique, which was introduced as early as 1963, opened the seas by introducing better seismic data processing, using more accurate techniques. Since its commercial introduction in 1975, it rapidly gained the majority of the seismic market share. The 3-D is using more dense arrays and arrays process to provide accurate and complete 3-dimensional pictures of the subsurface to display the image of the rock formations as deep as they are. It also covers it in shorter periods—what took a few seasons in the past now takes only one season work for a similar area. By bettering operation techniques, the 3-D also managed to reduce its costs and be widespread for initial explorations and not only to map existing or newly found reservoirs. However, it does not show what is in the 3-dimensional formation, so it still does not solve the initial problem of "what in that cavern"—hydro carbons or just hydro . . . water or air trapped there.

With other better modeling techniques, such as the 4-D, we can solve a certain uncertainty—frame it in "success percentage," i.e. "with so and so percentage to success, varying from 20% to 60% or so in recent target layers.

The E&P successfully reached ultra-deep water depth within the last couple of decades, which increased proven reserves and supply for the world. Be it 2-D, 3-D, or the revolutionary 4 dimensions (which adds imaginary computerized capabilities), this advanced exploration technology have assisted in cutting the time to reach the target layer or reservoir, wasting less on unsuccessful dry holes. It enables the oil companies to drill further and deeper; further into geographical zones difficult to get or work in and deeper into seas and oceans. The Chad development in the 1990s; the early 2000s' Sakhalin and Snohvit development in the Norwegian Sea at 72 north latitude are all examples of harsh environment locations enabled by progressive technological and explorative aspirations.

Exploration ends up with a dry hole or a successful drill that continues with appraisal drillings and mappings and evaluates the volume of the new reservoir. The next stage is the development and preparations for production. The deeper and further away the reservoir is, the more expensive it is to develop and more time it will take to reach the market.

After a final evaluation, a development program and budget is prepared against ensured market for the oil or gas of that specific new reservoir, taking it through a thorough process to its FEED (Front End Engineering Design) and FID (Final Investment Decision) once all parameters are lined up.

Yet one should note that the average time from discovery to production takes nearly 5 years. In some remote and complex regions it may take up to 10 years as happened with several leading projects. Sometimes with additional economic or political complexity, it may even take longer; or cancelled.

The Noble Energy and its partners in the "Tamar" field discovery in the East Mediterranean in January 2009 brought a similar challenge. Located 1,700 meters below sea level and further 3,200 meters below the seabed—a total of 4,877 meters or 16,000 feet; 50 miles offshore and 90 miles to its production platform. Appraisal drilling determined a reservoir of 10 Tcf (about 280 Bcm). Production commenced in March 2013—a record time—supplying gas to the Israeli grid.

Leviathan, discovered a year later close to Tamar, broke records by being the largest discovery in a decade, and was followed by the Block 12 discovery in Cyprus. Both still in an early stage of appraisals and development plans, more than 6 years after the discovery.

Courtesy Shell Photographic Service

The deep sea E&P has had more great achievements in the last two decades: offshore Angola, the Gulf of Mexico, deep sea Pre Salt off of Brazil, the East Mediterranean off Israel, Cyprus, and Egypt.

In the early days of oil discoveries and production, oil was not drilled, but collected from the earth's surface from locally existing traps. Then drillings were done where oil seeped to the surface. These first drillings did not always lead to oil production because no one knew what was below the surface. No one had any geological idea or understanding of the best locations to drill. It took some time for the technology and science to be able to look deeper into the ground, to understand better where oil and gas could be found.

As science developed, more accurate and deep drillings could be made. These days, any drilling done is based on a target mapped layer and is planned and budgeted to the last detail. Though even with all of the latest technology there is no 100% guarantee of success in this business.

This sector is a high-risk, high-capital professional playground.

The Majors' Major Task

Most of the upstream operation of Exploration and Production is done by the large oil and gas companies, the Majors and the NOC, the National Oil Companies. Most of these companies are fully integrated companies, involved in all parts of the oil and gas supply chain. They allocate a yearly, specific budget for E&P which is clearly seen in their budget books.

In 2003, ConocoPhillips, the world's largest independent E&P Company, had a variety of exploration and production operations of crude oil, oil sands, natural gas, and LNG around the world. This major oil company's efforts are to find huge reserves and plan large projects to continue its long-term activity. In 2003, the company had exploration operations in 25 countries over 5 continents, with production in 13 countries of 934,000 bbl/d (the world production was 79.3 million bbl/d), and 3.5 BCF of gas a day. ConocoPhillips' midstream and downstream operation of refineries and marketing oil covered 3 million bbl/day. It has fuel stations in 18 countries over 3 continents. ConocoPhillips has led E&P in Nigeria, built midstream pipeline in neighboring Cameroon. In Dubai, it has only production, while in Kazakhstan and Azerbaijan only explorations.

In Europe, the company is active in the North Sea. During that year the company had 25 drillings in the North Sea, including the new promising "Clare," north to the Shetland Island. In Nigeria, the company is active in supporting the supply for a new LNG plant. In Qatar, it has dominancy in the operation of existing and new drillings—as well as in Indonesia, Vietnam, and the Timor Sea; Russia and Central Asia.

Its offshore explorations are in ultra-deep water (over 2,000 meters depth), as well as shallow water of only 100-200 meters depth. Its global activity starts in North America, both in oil sands bitumen production in Canada and in efforts to enhance production of existing oil and gas fields in Alaska. In the Gulf of Mexico, the company has ultra-deep exploration and production with a rig in 4,700 feet of water. This remarkable achievement is to be applauded, because only a decade ago, Shell's "Mars" in 3,000 feet of water was the deepest well.

The company was also involved in several proposed LNG receiving terminals and in the design of the next generation LNG tanker—the Qatari Q-flex and Q-max, the largest LNG carriers built so far.

At that time the company was heavily involved in upstream operation in Venezuela, which was cut off by President Chavez when he nationalized the industry in May 2007.

During 2003 the major oil companies and industry players still set their budget at below $30 a barrel. The Saudis at the time already targeted $30 to support their Kingdom's budget. However, 2004 brought the end of a relatively stable three-year period, which averaged about $26 a barrel; and stability is crucial for the E&P industry.

To understand the instability effect on major E&P companies we can examine ConocoPhillips' 2014 data and budget, and how the price downturn was reflected upon the last quarter of 2014. The headline of the report confirms the importance of the E&P and the replacement discussed earlier in this chapter: "ConocoPhillips Reports Fourth-Quarter and Full-Year 2014 Results; Strong Reserve Replacement. The company operated in 27 countries, with $53 billion in annual revenue, employing 19,100 people (end of 2014). 2014 earnings were $6.9 billion, compared with 2013 earnings of $9.2 billion."

This is the result of the sharp weakening energy prices. The falling prices and revenue brought to light the following headline in the Oil and Gas Journal, just to be followed by others:

QTE . . .

- *ExxonMobil sees 2015 earnings fall 50%, cuts 2016 spending by 25%. ExxonMobil Corp. plans to reduce its capital and exploration expenditures in 2016 by 25% compared with that of 2015 to $23.2 billion.*

- *The company estimates earnings in 2015 totaled $16.2 billion, a 50% drop from the $32.5 billion earned in 2014. 2015 Capital and exploration expenditures were $31.1 billion, down 19% from the 2014 level.*

- *Fourth-quarter earnings were $2.8 billion, down 58% from $6.6 billion in fourth-quarter 2014.*

- *Full-year upstream earnings were $7.1 billion, down 75% from the $27.5 billion posted in 2014. ExxonMobil says lower realizations decreased earnings by $18.8 billion.*

- *The US upstream segment in 2015 reported a $1.1-billion loss while upstream earnings outside the US were $8.2 billion.*

- *Full-year production by the company total 4.1 million boe/d, up 3.2% year-over-year.*

- *ExxonMobil's downstream earnings of $6.6 billion in 2015 more than doubled that of 2014 due in large part to stronger margins. Chemical earnings were up slightly at $4.4 billion.*

. . . UNQTE

However it is important to note the "annual organic reserve replacement of 124%"; this is E&P! This represents year-over-year production growth of 4 percent with 1,532 million BOE (includes also gas and other energy products) out of total 89 million bbl/d produced that year globally.

ExxonMobil announced in 2012 it would invest 185 billion dollars during 2012–2016 in order to be ready to supply the anticipated demand for oil and gas in the coming decades. ExxonMobil predicted at the time 30% increase in demand by 2040 over 2010. As prices collapsed in late 2014 onward, the company, like others, reduced its investment, but remains to lead a strong growth.

Another important integrated major company is "British Gas," BG, with a quite similar upstream: worldwide borderless operations and investments. In some countries its integrated DNA shows operations along the supply chain from upstream to midstream and downstream. The company's upstream operations spread over 18 countries in 4 continents. In North America, there is sizeable concession acreage in Canada, of which 90% is not developed yet.

In Central and South America there are operations in Argentina, Bolivia, and Brazil. Brazil's upstream operation of BG commenced after it started to supply Bolivian gas to Brazil. In Central America the important Trinidad & Tobago LNG plant, in what remarkably developed in 1999 to become a strong LNG exporter, producing enough gas for the local market and enabling a very strong petrochemical industry to develop. This industry use natural gas as feed gas for ethylene production that has made Trinidad one of the largest ethylene producers in the world. Trinidad and Tobago BG-led LNG plants increased its production capacity from 5.32 MT in 2003 to 12.4 MT in 2006, to 16 MT production capacity of LNG by 2010, maintaining the 14–15 MT production through 2016.

In Africa, BG operates in 3 countries, among them Egypt, which produces LNG, as well as Tunisia and Mauritania. In Asia, BG operated in India, Thailand, and Kazakhstan. In the East Mediterranean off Gaza, gas was discovered close to the Noble's Yam Tethys, yet the prevailing geopolitical situation prevented them from producing this gas, therefore BG left the Gaza discoveries for the time being.

The E&P activity in Kazakhstan is challenging and exciting compared to the other regions, as it is in a harsh extreme environment, with temperatures varying from minus 40 to plus 40 degrees Celsius. In addition, it is difficult due to its limited access for export, depending on the Russian Gazprom pipelines to West Europe or through the Caspian Sea and west through the Caucasus to the Black Sea. Another option under development is one of the proposed Central Asia to Europe pipelines, which may be developed in the future. The huge "Karachaganak" field discovered by the Soviets back in 1979 started production in 1984. BG joined the Kazakh arena in 1992, where it participated and later became a partner in the huge "Kashagan" discovery of 2000.

Development for these two projects continues to this day, acting as proof that partnerships between major and local companies can assist in the development and supply to international markets. In 2012, the local Kazakhstan gas company joined the international companies there to form a partnership of five nations—with British BG and Italian ENI holding 29.25% each, the USA Chevron 18%, Russian Lukoil 13.5%, and Kazakhstan KMG with 10%.

To complete this global major E&P part, one must look at Shell. Since its early days in the industry, it is admirable how they continue their leading position into the 21st century. In the early 2000s, Shell operated in 36 countries with E&P operations; and in midstream and downstream in more than 90 countries around the globe. Shell, just like the other majors, emphasized the "Proven reserves replacement ratio," which, at that decade, was aimed at a minimum 100% for 2004–2008.

With more than 1.5 billion dollars E&P expenditure, the company demonstrated impressive results during 2003. In the early 2000s, Shell set an annual production target of 3.5–3.8 million bbl/d by 2005–2006, with a goal to increase it to 4 million bbl/d by 2009. In practice, Shell produced in the years 2009–2010 2% of the world's oil and 3% of the world's gas—taking the pole position in the US Fortune 500 companies by 2009.

Shell led the way in other important upstream sectors relating to LNG as well. Back in 2003, when the world LNG production was 125 MT a year, Shell produced 8% of it through global partnerships spreading from Malaysia to Nigeria, from Australia to Sakhalin, in Russia.

Further and Deeper

In 2011, Shell reached another LNG pioneer position when it was the first to order the construction of its newly developed floating liquefied natural gas (FLNG) technology for its offshore Prelude project in Australia. This multibillion-dollar project will bring the largest floating facility ever built, at 488 meters length and 74 meters width. It will weigh some 200,000 MT, displacing 600,000 MT of water.

The Prelude FLNG (Courtesy Shell)

The Shell FLNG facility is designed to produce 3.6 MT of LNG a year, and with the related LPG and other condensate total production will reach some 5 MT of products a year. Shell's definition of the Prelude FLNG: "We've developed a revolutionary floating LNG technology to access offshore gas fields otherwise too costly or difficult to develop."

A couple of other ultra-deep-water oil and gas development by Shell are the Gulf of Mexico's *Stones*, which will host the deepest production facility in the world in some 2,900 meters (9,500 feet) of water, and Malikai, Shell's latest deep-water project off of Malaysia, which strengthens the country's expertise in unlocking energy from beneath the ocean's depths.

The Perdido, which is the world's deepest offshore oil drilling and production platform, is moored in 2,450 meters (8,000 feet) water depth in the Gulf of Mexico, 200 miles off the Texas coast, and it produces 100, 000 BOE/day. Perdido started production in 2010 and opened up a new frontier in deep-water oil and gas recovery. The project shares the financial risks with Chevron and BP as major partners. Once again it is proof of the integrity and success of multinational projects, of cooperation and technology sharing between majors and service companies.

Unconventional Gas

Due to the energy-price crisis of 2002–2008, some upstream companies started to invest more in unconventional oil and gas sources spread all over the world, with large masses in North America. Among them the oil sands in Canada and the shale gas produced in the United States.

It brings the United States market a remarkable stability and security of supply; one that will spread all over the world. **Low and stable gas prices are achievable** thanks to that huge supply flow, some already describe it as *gas glut*—meaning oversupply. An oversupply we trust can be controlled and managed to a stable slight oversupply and stable price regime.

In our model of energy security we conclude that there is better some oversupply than shortage, or certain threat of shortage. More on that in Chapter 18.

Offshore

The trigger to explore further in the North Sea and the Gulf of Mexico was the 1973 oil crisis. Apparently, marine seismic surveys were easier than land surveys because the only obstacle was sea conditions, since the seismic equipment and technology better penetrate the sea and sand below than land, as sea water gives better conductivity than the earth.

But the exploration and production drillings are much more challenging, complex, and expensive. In some areas with difficult ocean conditions it might even prevent development and production.

The first offshore subsea well was in 17-meter (50 feet) water depth, offshore the US Gulf, back in 1960. It took 40 years to cross the 10,000 feet water depth challenge of more than 300 atmospheric pressure. The deep offshore technology, experience, and achievements allow the producers to increase their "horizon" deep in new frontiers.

The near shallow offshore successful projects triggered more explorations far and deep offshore. In 1978, Shell was the first to reach and breach the 1,000 feet of water in their Gulf of Mexico "Cognac" project in 1,025 feet of water. It went deeper to some 5,000 meters below the ocean's surface—where the seismic survey pointed at a potential reservoir.

More drillings followed and it took the industry more than a decade to surpass that depth. This was for the Gulf of Mexico "Mars" field in 2,940 feet of water. Then, in 1999, the largest reservoir—called "Thunder Horse"—was discovered. The challenges to develop and produce this field paved the way to more efficient and cost-effective technology for working in deep water environment. The reservoir lies below the seabed, from 4,265 meter to 5,790 meters. This depth creates extreme temperature and pressure, at 88–132 Celsius and high pressure up to 1,255 bars. All drillings and production equipment had to be redesigned to allow more and more of such drillings to be done. It took 10 years from its discovery to reach the 250,000 bbl/d production target

Barrel and Budget

The American Energy Information Administration, EIA, published in January 2008 statistics on exploration and production, quantifying the "lifting" costs— the actual extraction cost of crude oil from its reservoirs to the surface. They describe it from $4.00 in Africa, to $8.30 in Canada and an average of $6.83 in the US. This data referred at the time to the year 2006, and mentioned that it was already 23% higher than in 2005. In fact it reflected the *Price Crisis* of the years 2004–2005 (see Chapter 13). It advised also that total E&P costs varied from $5.26 per barrel in Saudi Arabia, to $63.71 in the Gulf of Mexico.

Supporting factors to the increased lifting costs were also the rise in the price of raw materials, increasing the cost of production rigs and other related commodities, services, and equipment between the years 2004–2006.

By early 2015, the falling prices overshadowed the industry's long-term planning as most of the oil and gas companies based now their budget on the $100 a barrel price that the market held quite steady for nearly 4 years till the last quarter of 2014. The uncertainties of energy prices affect the progression of some projects. The more challenging and expensive a project is, the more likely it will be put aside. Toward the end of 2015, more and more companies announced reduction in planned expenditure on E&P, including redundancy of manpower.

Yet the growing future demand for oil and gas will require more onshore and offshore exploration and production. The operation will have to become more efficient and cost-effective to allow the E&P to support the market growth under better supply and price regime, adapting themselves to the *Energy Future*. By early 2017, with oil price smiling up above the $50 a barrel, some optimism is back to the E&P

companies, looking to secure operation at the $50–$60 level for the near future.

Drill, Dill, Drill!

"Drill, drill, drill" was the message of the oil and gas industry during the crisis years of 2005–2008. This is what the industry leaders kept calling for, and what I have heard in so many energy conferences and meetings held with top executives. Apparently it happened quicker than anyone could imagine, bringing the supply glut, but definitely proving the strength of the E&P industry. Now the mission is to control this growing supply and harness it to one of the three energy security pillars we describe in our energy security model, under the Supply Pillar— stable and safe, with more than enough supply.

There are also huge risks involved to men and the environment as evidenced in the BP Deepwater Horizon explosion in April 2010. 11 people were killed and the US Gulf suffered one of the worlds' largest environmental disasters. It took 4 years and cost $14 billion to restore and clean the area. This spill shed some light on the risks of the offshore E&P.

In December 2015 PennWell's *Offshore* magazine selected 5 top 2015 offshore projects, based on best use of innovation, production methods, technology application, resolution challenges, safety, environmental protection, and project execution across the globe. They all had to overcome the low income from production, and managed to do so. It was also impressive to learn that 2 of the 5 projects adopted the "design one, build two" practice of economy of scale.

Three of them located in the Gulf of Mexico, a solid proof of the United States efforts of becoming energy independent with remarkable capacity for export.

The Venezuelan "Perla" project is proof that Central America has returned to the market; a positive sign that regime and foreign politics can be changed. Another Norwegian Sea project strengthened the depleting North Sea, challenging the dependency of Europe on import.

It is important to note the ENI late summer 2015 gas discovery, estimated at 30 Tcf, off the Egyptian Nile Delta. This long-awaited discovery was a Godsend to the Egyptian government as it helped to reboost the regional E&P activity, while Egypt still has to import LNG to overcome local gas shortage.

The multibillion 2015 merger of Shell and BG might be the result of falling prices, or a planned move toward stronger global E&P capacity, stronger integrated mega Major oil and Gas being able to better support the world's New Energy Era.

As we close this book for printing by the summer of 2017, and oil prices hovering around and below the $50, it is encouraging to see how the E&P continues across the globe.

The more oil and gas that will be found and produced, the more our **Energy Future** will be stronger and long lasting.

16. GREEN GOLD – RENEWABLES AND ALTERNATIVES

_____◆_____

Decarbonization of Energy

The continuous growth of world population and the intense economic expansion of developed and developing countries are among the major causes of the increasing demand for energy and the continuous alarming release of developed and greenhouse gases and other pollutants related to fossil fuels. This increasing demand is the cause for the urgent need of "**Decarbonization of Energy**." It requires evolution from black gold to green gold. **Fossils and beyond**—or **Beyond Fossils**.

The multibillion-dollar question is what lies in the future of energy, fossil fuels, renewables, and alternatives. How the human society will drive its future in the light and the shadow of the universe environment security. What price will energy be in 30, 50 and 100 years ahead? Will there be enough for all? What energy form will lead the future?

Will the more than 1 billion people living without electricity with many agrees that it must be renewable today finally gain access to it? And how the world growing population will drive their energy needs and feed themselves in future generations to come.

The role of alternatives and renewables is important in the future growth of the needed energy supply basket.

There is a worldwide understanding that fossil fuels are the main cause for our earth, soil, and air pollution, as well as global warming.

_____

This notion was further substantiated and agreed upon in the 6th **World Climate Summit in Paris**, in December 2015, by nearly 200 nations. The convention emphasized the need for cleaner fuels by securing a legally binding global climate agreement to curb carbon emissions.

Curbing carbon emissions will be achieved by renewable energy and alternative energy together with energy efficiency and innovative/ creative energy conservation mechanisms. In this chapter we will list the most important of these different "energies" already available, along with others that are still to be developed. They all must be clean, economical, and environmentally friendly, as well as socially accepted = sustainable.

President Obama was quoted back in 2013 saying, "So the question now is whether we will have the courage to act before it's too late, and how we answer will have a profound impact on the world that we leave behind."

Dr. Jim Yong Kim, president of the World Bank, reinforces this theory by stating that, "Taking action now will not only solve the problem of protecting the planet, but it will be a tremendous boost for economies. . . ."

How can this new energy compete with available fossil fuels, especially as oil prices continue to float low? What incentive do we have to develop and use other fuels that are much more expensive to produce than available fossils?

It is certain that the 21st century technology must create the right means of science and technology to make these fuels affordable and competitive.

It is important to note how the oil-and-gas-rich nations of the Gulf Cooperation Council (GCC) developed interest in sustainable and renewable energy sources in recent years, in what may be seen as paradoxical. They based the International Renewable Energy Agency (IRENA), headquartered in the United Arab Emirates, in what seems as proper preparations for the **energy future— beyond fossils.**

Saudi Arabia for example, plans to have huge capacity of renewable power production by 2032. The magnitude of these plans is for 41,000 MW of solar power, 9,000 MW of wind, 3,000 MW waste to energy, and 1,000 MW from geothermal.

If this tremendous boost will occur, as experts in the field predict, then why alternative fuels are not more prevalent in society? Why is the implementation of alternative fuel production so slow?

Some world programs, like the EU 2020, aim to see the EU reduce its greenhouse gas emissions by at least 20%, increase the share of renewable energy to at least 20% of consumption, and achieve energy savings of 20% or more; all by the year 2020. The EU countries must also achieve a 10% share of renewable energy in their transport sector. Other countries follow similar programs; however, these programs are still not sufficient, not in wider use yet.

So what are these alternative and renewable fuels that must be **Sustainable Energy**—non polluted energy, produced economically and socially under fair terms and conditions?

1. **Renewable Energy** – energy produced from the sun, wind, water, ocean waves, geothermal and biomass.

2. **Alternative Energy** – energy forms to replace the fossil fuels, including nuclear and fusion.

3. **Energy Storage** – Other forms of energy that might be considered as renewables or alternatives by the public, but in fact are different types of energy storage like hydrogen, fuel cells, hydro pumped storage, batteries.

4. **Energy Preservation and Energy Efficiency** - It's as simple as closing the lights behind us, and being more efficient (mechanically), to achieve the same or better work, power, travel range, and light with same or less energy.

Looking at the next 20–25 years, the IEA forecasts an average increased demand for energy of 25–40%. Even the lower forecast of

25%, according to ExxonMobil Corp.'s *2016 Outlook for Energy,* is large enough to encourage careful planning and more usage of resources other than fossil fuels. ExxonMobil's *Outlook for Energy* projects that carbon-based fuels will continue to meet about three quarters of global energy needs through 2040. It is consistent with other credible projections, including those made by the International Energy Agency. The outlook shows **a shift toward lower-carbon fuels** in the coming decades, which, in combination with efficiency gains, will lead to a gradual decline in energy-related carbon dioxide emissions. Other experts, however, say that it may yet be too conservative in terms of GHG (greenhouse gas) emission mitigation

Take Chevron's attitude and view of the role of renewables: "At Chevron, we recognize the world needs all the energy we can develop, in many potential forms. That's why we're investing in a broad portfolio of energy resources, with $40 billion budgeted in 2014 for capital and exploratory projects. We're finding and developing conventional and new sources of oil and gas. We're using energy more efficiently. **We're investing in renewables and the next generation of energy sources.**" Chevron recognizes that the growing part of the increasing demand must come out of renewables and alternatives.

1. Renewable Energy – The renewables are energy sources besides fossil fuels, which mother-nature or agriculture (as is the case for some biofuels) grant us.

The *sun* is the major global energy source. Besides its direct contribution to solar energy, it creates wind by the uneven heat and gradients that drive the air from high pressure to low pressure areas, and affect weather.

Solar Energy: the sun is a true nature power, and is available just when and where it shines. How to harness solar beams' energy to fulfill society's day-to-day usage attracts scientific curiosity. Today, solar energy is used mainly for power production: to create electricity on large scale projects, or just for home and industry use. However, while different technologies are used, there is still much more to be done, as its efficiency is among the lowest of the renewables.

Smooth and direct conversion of solar energy into electrical, chemical, or thermal energy is recognized as the renewable option with the highest practical potential.

As with other available renewable sources, there are limitations and technical challenges to make it widely used. Beside the different types of solar panels, those that use the heat of sun to activate electrons for producing electricity, the major solar farms mainly reflect concentrated heat, to produce heat that boils water to run steam turbines. Huge investments during the last 3 decades have produced some technologies to a certain mature stage of development. It is impressive to see projects or programs like the "Desertec," which planned to supply 15% of Europe's electricity needs from North Africa by 2050.

Unfortunately this project may stay on the drawing board due to North Africa regional geopolitical turmoil, and reduced interest from its leading commercial partners in Europe.

In one other large scale solar technique, long troughs of U-shaped mirrors focus sunlight on the center of oil pipes. The hot oil then boils water to steam that generate electricity. Another technique use moveable mirrors to focus the sun's rays on a collector tower, where a receiver sits. Molten salt flows through the receiver and is further heated to drive a steam turbine that runs a generator. Large-scale solar technologies are also very expensive and require a lot of land to collect the sun's energy at rates useful and efficient for mass production

Photovoltaic solar cells can convert sunlight into electricity and are currently dominating solar cell technology. The technology is based on crystalline silicon cells that have been continuously advancing in its efficiency and cost of production over the last 4 decades. At favorable locations, crystalline silicon solar cells can produce electricity from sunlight at a comparable price to that generated from fossil fuels.

Between 2006 and 2012, the cost of these photovoltaic panels fell by around 65%, partly as a result of a glut of solar cells on the market. Waning government subsidies for solar installations have made staying in the business even harder by lowering the demand for solar power, and the recent 2015–2016 falling energy prices will not add further appetite for further investments in the panels.

Other newer solar cell technologies promise even lower cost solar power, including solar cells based on thin-film vapor deposited semiconductors such as CdTe or copper indium gallium (di) selenide (CIGS). An additional newly developed solar cell uses a solution-processed or vapor-deposited organic thin film, organic semiconductors, or organic-inorganic hybrid composites.

Most recently, there has been an unexpected breakthrough and rapid evolution of highly efficient solid-state hybrid solar cells based on organometal trihalide perovskite materials.

The progress in photovoltaic technology points to the prospect of producing solar cells with low cost and high efficiency, and to make solar power one of the least expensive and most sustainable energy sources, yet as for other renewables, certain advanced storage technologies and devices are a must.

Despite the drawbacks, solar energy use has surged at about 20 percent a year over the past 15 years, thanks to rapidly falling prices and gains in efficiency. Japan, Germany, China, and the United States are major markets for solar cells. In terms of photovoltaics installed capacity, Germany is the world's number one.

To summarize this, solar energy is the most abundant energy resource on earth—173,000 terawatts of solar energy strikes the Earth continuously. That's more than 10,000 times the world's total energy use. It is necessary to note the tremendous growth in the United States, China, and other countries' solar industry because they help pave the way to a cleaner, more sustainable energy future.

Wind Energy: Over the last 20 years, wind energy has rapidly expanded from an emerging energy source into a mature, mainstream, competitive, reliable, and well-established global power mean.

Based on a unique collaboration between research, environment and industry, improvements in performance and reliability have helped to make wind energy one of the most well established sources of renewable power. Wind power has seen an average growth in total installed capacity of over 25% per year worldwide over the last 15 years, resulting in a total installed capacity of 285 GW by the end of 2012. That covers 2.6 % of global electricity. This achievement has only been possible due to continuous development, up-scaling, and maturing of the technology that is facilitated by the parallel development of research-based design tools, standards, and procedures.

Great opportunities, but also great challenges still remain for the industry. Wind power needs to compete with conventional generation sources on a cost basis and therefore must be established and operate as efficiently as possible.

It is impressive to see a great technological and production improvements that bring to production larger wind turbine generators (WTG), with standard capacity of 1.5–2.5MW, increasing to 5, 6, and 10MW turbines. A variety of producers offer a large range of turbines tailored to specific customer needs, at almost any location. Onshore and offshore, hot and cold environment, any elevation, any wind conditions from low wind speed to gusting winds.

More information is available in the United States Department of Energy website, with the remarkable paper "Wind Vision: A New Era for Wind Power in the United States," which quantifies the economic, social, and environmental benefits of a robust wind energy future through 2050.

The U.S. Department of Energy website lists 10 factors to note on "how human civilizations have harnessed wind power for thousands of years," some of which are relevant and vital today.

Early forms of modern wind turbine technology were seen with the usage of windmills to crush grain or pump water. Wind turbines are consistently getting taller in order to reach stronger wind levels, thus producing more electricity. Most of the components of wind turbines installed in the United States are locally produced creating more than 73,000 jobs. The technical resource potential of the US coastal waters wind is enough to provide more than 4,000 gigawatts of electricity, or approximately four times the generating capacity of the current US electric power system.

The United States generates more wind energy than any other country except China, and wind has accounted for more than a third of all newly installed electricity generation capacity since 2007. The United States' wind power capacity reached more than 65.8 gigawatts by the end of 2014. That's enough electricity to power more than 17.5 million homes annually—and represents nearly a 25-fold increase in capacity since 2000.

Wind energy is affordable, with prices for power contracts signed in 2014 for what the utility pays to buy power from a wind farm, as low as 2.35 cents per kilowatt-hour in some areas of the country. This is the lowest price ever recorded by the Department of Energy.

By 2050, the United States will have the potential to avoid the emission of more than 12.3 gigatonnes of greenhouse gases by continuing to increase the amount of wind turbine generation.

More detailed information on the technical, economic, and historical aspects of the wind power industry is also available in the Danish Wind Industry Association (DWIA) website.

The Danish DWIA agenda is quite similar to the one of the USA and looks as achievable. The agenda consists of developing wind energy to the point of being capable of supplying 20% of the total Danish energy consumption in 2030, projecting 100% renewable energy system by 2050. This achievement would maintain Denmark's position as home of the most competitive wind industry in the world. However large-scale wind integration is a great challenge for countries with ambitious wind targets, even for Denmark.

Hydro Energy: Hydro energy uses water turbines and generators for electricity production. Water dams concentrate water to flow strong enough to turn the turbines, and are widespread in countries that have the gift of abundant and strong water sources. The top world producers are China with 23.8% of total hydro electricity produced, Canada, and Brazil with 10.1% each, the United States with 7.5%, Russia with 4.7%, India with 3.7%, and Norway with 3.3% of the world production, which gives Norway 96.1% of its total electricity generation. In Brazil, hydro energy is responsible for 68.6% of its electricity generation, though in the last few years, it has been affected by bad droughts that reduced the hydropower production (thus increasing gas import). Venezuela achieves 67.8% of its electricity needs via hydro energy, while Canada generates 60.1% of its domestic electricity by hydropower. Russia and China achieve about 17% each. (Information based on the IEA.)

It is clear that hydropower is remarkably important for few countries, and recently new technology has been developed, making hydropower more appealing to a wider range of countries. However, large-scale hydropower plants are not considered environmentally friendly and not encouraged everywhere.

Marine Energy: Although mainly experimental, marine energy, which includes wave, tidal, and offshore wind, offers a significant opportunity for maritime nations to develop new and sustainable energy resources. The 1970s saw significant early international research. The UK, Norway, Portugal, and Japan all participated. This early research established the formal rigor required to underpin a new industry. Despite early research being curtailed by limited funding, the United Kingdom has taken radical steps to encourage the development of a new energy industry through innovative funding mechanisms to encourage pre-commercial development. Research has been encouraged in UK Universities through radical programs of funding, which has led to new studies in the ecological implications of development. Scotland has seen the creation of the European Marine Energy Centre (EMEC) in Orkney, which allows the testing of full scale wave and tidal current energy technology in representative conditions. Devices installed at EMEC can export energy into the local grid while being closely monitored for their hydrodynamic and electrical performance, yet at experimental scale.

Geothermal: Geothermal power generation is a well-established form of commercial renewable energy. One of its important characteristics is a high load factor, which means that each MW of capacity produces significantly more electricity during a year than a MW of wind or solar capacity.

Geothermal energy has been used for thousands of years in some countries for cooking and heating. It is simply power derived from the earth's internal heat. This thermal energy is contained in the rock and fluids beneath the Earth's crust. It can be found in all layers of the crust, from shallow ground to below the surface, to the extremely hot molten rock called magma.

These underground reservoirs of steam and hot water can be tapped to generate electricity or to heat and cool buildings directly.

A geothermal heat pump system can take advantage of the constant temperature of the upper three meters of the earth's surface to heat a home in the winter, while extracting heat from the building and transferring it back to the relatively cooler ground in the summer.

Geothermal flow is harnessed to generate almost clean, renewable energy. It produces and supplies renewable power around the clock and emits little or no greenhouse gases, leaving a very small environmental footprint. In the United States, the largest geothermal producer in the world, the U.S. Department of Energy is committed to responsibly developing, demonstrating, and deploying innovative technologies to support the continued expansion of the geothermal industry across the country.

The unique geological conditions required for geothermal power means that development has been concentrated in a relatively small number of countries, little over 20. Yet, its capacity grew by 5.7% (677 MW) in 2014, to reach 12.6 GW. The largest additions to its capacity were in Kenya (338 MW), which produces 32% of the world's total geothermal energy, and Turkey (141 MW). The United States has the largest geothermal capacity at over 3.5 GW (28% of the world total), followed by the Philippines (1.9 GW), Indonesia (1.4 GW), and New Zealand (1.0 GW).

Overall the geothermal share of global power generation remains very small (0.3%), but in certain countries it plays a significant role of power production, like Kenya (32%), Iceland (30%), El Salvador (25%), and New Zealand (17%).

The name of the game, as in other renewables, remains in efficiency and affordability—together with energy storage capability and capacity.

Bio Fuels, Bio Mass: The term *biofuels* is mostly used to refer to alternative substitutes for petrol, diesel, or aircraft fuels. Some biofuels are created by fermenting crops such as sugarcane and corn. This creates natural ethanol, which can be mixed with petrol to create a sort of hybrid biofuel that can be used in any petrol powered vehicle. Other varieties exist; yet they vary significantly.

Some examples are that of biodiesel, which is created by growing crops that contain high amounts of natural oil and then refining a more compatible bio diesel through a process of hydrogenation. This substitute can be mixed with mineral diesel and then used in any diesel-powered automobile.

Some gasoline in the United States is blended with a biofuel—ethanol. This is the same stuff as in alcoholic drinks, except that it's made from corn that has been heavily processed.

There are various ways of making biofuels, but they generally use chemical reactions, fermentation, and heat, to break down the starches, sugars, and other molecules in plants. The leftover products are then refined to produce fuel. Brazil has used this renewable fuel for decades, as it turned sugarcane into ethanol after the 1973 oil shock. By 1985, 90% of the vehicles produced in Brazil could be fueled with the locally produced renewable fuel.

During the mid-1990, with the decline of oil prices, it became less attractive, and increased again in the 2000s as oil prices climbed. It definitely reduced Brazil dependency on imported fuels.

It is important to understand that, although it has existed for years, its technology is still not mature enough. Been an agriculture product, it certainly contributed to higher corn prices as the 2008 price crises peaked and affected most of the commodities. Its efficiency is also quite low and its refining process demands the use of too much energy. Higher corrosive effect on engines is an issue, while it also increases the usage of fertilizers growing it—thus it becomes less sustainable.

Although its use has become more widespread, objections and criticism have arisen as some side effects on agriculture and ecology have been revealed.

As with other alternatives and renewables, its production process must be improved technically and economically in order to maintain and possibly increase its share in the secured energy basket we need to have in our **Energy Future.**

2. Alternative Energy

The Alternative fuels are those that by definition are due to replace the fossil fuels. Among them the most prevalent is **nuclear power**.

In 2015 the total nuclear-based power production share of the world primary energy was 4.4%, growing by 1.3% during 2016 (net growth in China only); while total renewables was 6.7% (6.0% in 2014). Nuclear is slowly recovering from the impact of the Fukushima incident of March 2011, in which a tsunami that swept the coastal region caused the Fukushima nuclear power plant to collapse. Japanese nuclear power output ceased in 2014 as the country's last operating reactor was taken off line.

World Production still remains nearly 10% below the 2006 peak. Gains in South Korea, China, and Russia more than offset the declines in Japan and the EU.

Despite being the only country to have suffered the devastating effects of nuclear weapons in wartime, Japan embraced the peaceful use of nuclear technology to provide a substantial portion of its electricity. However, public sentiment shifted drastically and there were wide public protests calling for nuclear power to be abandoned. The balance between this populist sentiment and the continuation of reliable and affordable electricity supplies is being worked out politically.

Unlike many other world nations, Japan's shortage of minerals and energy dependence for over 90% of its primary energy needs placed it in a unique desire to develop alternatives. Its first commercial nuclear power generator was introduced in 1966. This vulnerability became critical and a national strategic priority after the 1973 oil shock.

Early in 2011, nuclear energy accounted for almost 30% of the country's total electricity production. There were plans to increase this to 41% by 2017, and 50% by 2030. Nuclear power has been expected to play an even bigger role in Japan's future. The Japan Atomic Energy Agency (JAEA) modeled a 54% reduction in CO_2 emissions (from 2000 levels) by 2050 leading on to a 90% reduction by 2100. This would lead to nuclear energy contributing about 60% of its primary energy in 2100 (compared with 10% in 2008), a further 10% from renewables (increasing out of 5%), and 30% fossil fuels (reduced from 85%). This would mean that nuclear energy contributed with 51% of the emission reduction: 38% from power generation and 13% from hydrogen production and process heat.

This was in line with an earlier decision, in June 2010, to increase energy self-sufficiency to 70% by 2030, for both energy security and CO_2 emission reduction. It envisaged deepening strategic relationships with energy-producing countries.

However, following the Fukushima accident, in 2011 the government sought to greatly reduce the role of nuclear power. In 2012, a new government was elected. In 2014 the new government adopted the 4th Basic (or Strategic) Energy Plan, with a 20-year perspective, and declared that *nuclear energy is a key base-load power source* and would continue to utilized it safely to achieve stable and affordable energy supply and fight global warming. Consumption in 2010 was about 1,000 TWh; and as Japan's nuclear capacity was progressively shut following Fukushima, its energy basket changed accordingly. Preliminary IEA figures indicate that in 2014 Japan generated 1,025 TWh gross-337 TWh from coal, 413 TWh from gas (up from 300 TWh in 2010), nothing from nuclear (288 TWh in 2010), 114 TWh from oil (up from 94 TWh in 2010). Renewables' contribution in 2014 was small: 87 TWh from hydro, solar 24 TWh, wind 5 TWh, geothermal 2.6 TWh, biomass & waste 42 TWh.

In February 2015 the prime minister said that 80% of Japan's oil and 20% of its natural gas came from the Persian Gulf through the Strait of Hormuz. In April 2015 the government announced that it wants the base-load sources to provide 60% of the power by 2030, with about one-third of it being provide by nuclear.

This will also result in energy costs reduced by JPY 2.4 trillion (USD 20.0 billion) per year compared with the 2015 40% base-load scenario.

According to a 2011 government report, generation costs per kWh were JPY 9 for nuclear, JPY 10 for wind, and JPY 30 for solar. In 2014, the estimates were nuclear JPY 10.1, coal JPY 12.3, LNG JPY 13.7, solar (non-residential) JPY 24.3.

So, as listed above, the economic incentive is very high—JPY 3.6 trillion ($30 billion) is being spent on imported fuel each year to compensate for idle reactors, shading an existing policy that had saved Japan from spending ¥33 trillion ($276 billion) on import. The prospect now is aimed at increasing its share up to 60% of its primary energy needs. As of early 2016, 43 reactors were operable and potentially able to restart; 24 of these were in the process of restart approvals. The first two restarted in August and October 2015.

Beside a potential devastating effect of a nuclear power plant accident, the dependency on uranium is also a factor. A quarter of its known reserves are in Australia, and another quarter in Kazakhstan and Russia. South Africa and Canada each have 8%, the United States has 6%, and smaller reserves exist in Brazil, Niger, Nigeria, Jordan, Azerbaijan, Mongolia, India, and China.

Nuclear waste is also an issue, and in the last decade the potential terror effect was added. Many fear that radical terrorists will have access to a nuclear bomb, or will use a "dirty Bomb," which is based on some nuclear waste or elements.

The United States is leading the world production with 32.6%. France is second in world nuclear production with 74.7% of its electricity being of nuclear origin, and holding 17.0% of the world's nuclear energy production. Russia produces 7.6%, and China produces 6.6% of the world's total production.

With this in mind, we can say very clearly that nuclear energy has an important long-term role and importance in many countries' energy basket. In 2013, forty years after the major 1973 oil crisis, nuclear contribution to electricity generation was up to 10.6% from the 1973 3.3% share.

3. Energy Storage – Hydrogen, Compression, and other storage facilities such as pumped storage.

Among several scenarios, hydrogen is the most promising energy carrier to satisfy the required conditions for the ideal fuel. It is the cleanest fuel and has a heating value three times higher than petroleum. While it seems to be the ideal means of transport, the necessary storage of hydrogen presents several issues, mainly related to safety.

Efficient practical means of storing hydrogen are key challenges for the implementation of hydrogen as a universal energy carrier.

Novel material solutions are required to store sufficient amounts of hydrogen in terms of gravimetric and volumetric densities, at suitable thermodynamic and kinetic conditions. In addition, simulations can give insight into the behavior of hydrogen storage tanks based on novel materials and allow for optimization of the tank design to meet the desired application property profile.

Being in use in the defense industry for many years, both in missiles and submarines, hydrogen and the required fuel cell technology are proven and available, but still in the early days of commercialization. Yet, the production and storage of hydrogen is challenging, and this solution is still far from being commercially beneficial to our society.

Interesting to note is the IEA *Technology Roadmap for Fuel Cells and Hydrogen in the year 2050*,[2] published in 2015. It describes the hydrogen as a flexible energy carrier that can be effectively transformed into any form of energy for divers' energy end-use applications, i.e. not only for transport as thought, but also for domestic and power. It lays key steps to develop it, harnessing the full technological and economic strength of its members (OECD) with detailed roadmap.

It is impressive also to note the Toyota commercial introduction of its hydrogen driven car, the Mirai, which Toyota dubbed it "The Future. Available Now."[3]

4. Energy Preservation and Energy Efficiency

Considered to be the "hanging fruits of energy," *preservation* and *efficiency* are among the promising green powers. Some say we can save up to 50% off our daily consumption using several means of preservations, from switching off unnecessary lights, using more efficient lighting equipment which is already available, using more environmentally friendly cars.

---

2   https://www.iea.org/publications/freepublications/publication/Technology RoadmapHydrogenandFuelCells.pdf

3   https://ssl.toyota.com/mirai/fcv.html

In a recent energy conference, some marketing managers of leading gas station distribution chains said they are more concerned about the new generation of small and efficient cars that turn 1 liter of gasoline to 20 kilometers of driving, than all the other renewables available today.

Low or negative cost in energy savings can be achieved by filling gaps in energy efficiency investments. An energy efficiency gap refers to the difference between levels of investment in energy efficiency that appear to be cost-effective based on engineering-economic analysis and the lower levels actually occurring. The low market adoption of energy-efficient technologies, coupled with unrealized potential, implies that significant amounts of energy could be saved through investments in energy efficiency.

For many years, energy efficiency was not treated as the cheapest fuel in the energy sector. Today, this situation is changing. This net-negative cost fuel will never run out due to the following three factors: (1) limited and potentially increasingly expensive fossil fuels; (2) new governmental policies on energy and climate change, which always encourage investments in cleaner energy; (3) new energy-efficient technologies, products, equipment, and financial mechanisms.

As such, the actual potential of energy efficiency as a fuel will grow, while becoming more affordable.

A new field called "**Energy Future**" mentions, besides renewables and alternatives, the mission to reduce energy consumption and preserve individuals and organizations' energy consumption that create economic and ecologic challenges concerning societies as a whole. Energy from technological breakthroughs to improve energy production and improve energy efficiency in all sectors of modern society is a must.

It is most encouraging to see that the two top leading energy consuming countries, the United States and China, are to increase their renewables usage as summarized in the BP Statistical review of 2014 "The rapid growth of renewable power generation continued in 2014, with an increase of 12%." Traditionally, Europe and Japan have been the leaders in renewable development, due to generous government incentives, **but now the US and China have moved to the front with significant investments in wind capacity in particular**.

The renewable energy industry is rapidly gaining importance in terms of contribution to economic activity and employment. Yet, despite high growth rates, renewable energy still represents only a small fraction of today's global energy consumption.

In 2015, renewable electricity generation (excluding hydro) accounted for 6.7% of the global electricity generation. Renewables however, are starting to play a significant role in the growth of electricity production, growing in 2015 by 15.2%—with an average 15.9% yearly growth in the last decade.

Renewable energy sources, in power generation as well as transport, continued to increase, reaching a record 3.0% of global energy consumption, up from 0.9% a decade ago.

These sources are already playing an important role in some countries. Denmark leads, with 57% of power coming from renewables, followed by Portugal, with 30%, 26% in Spain, 24% in Italy, 23% in Germany, and 18% in the UK.

Fundamental Transition, Fundamental Necessity

This huge energy sector is in fundamental transition. The finite conventional fossil fuels are under scrutiny because of their negative environmental impacts and social cost. Nuclear power might be prohibited because of its disastrous radioactive contaminations, which endanger life on Earth for future generations. Transport is revolutionized by new fuels. Buildings become energy self-sufficient.

See below a slide made by TRI-ZEN, for a presentation in the LNG Bunker Summit held in Amsterdam in 2015:

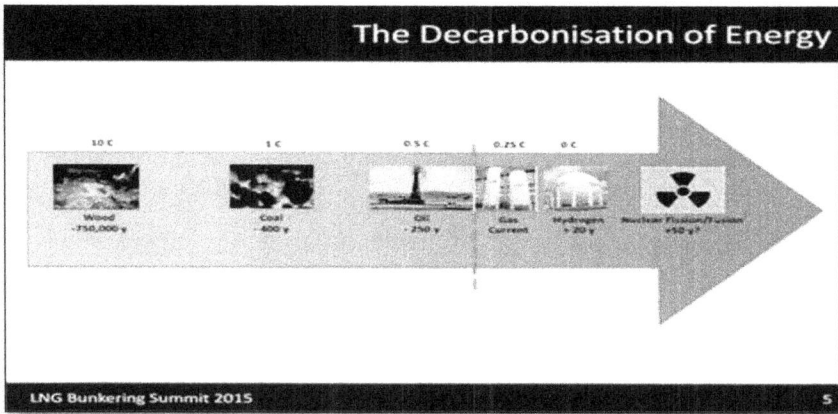

The Decarbonisation of Energy

LNG Bunkering Summit 2015

However, it would be important for us to add to this equation the growing important role of renewables in the future, besides the hydrogen and the nuclear power mentioned above.

In our model for energy security, the renewables and alternatives have an important role under the Supply Pillar (GPS for energy security consists of Geopolitics, Price and Supply), the renewables and alternatives must also serve as available, affordable and accessible. As it is more of advanced technology, it can relatively easy spread all over the world and decrease the dependency on fossils, while contributing to better security of the environment. Solid, safe, and globally spread, it will also add a huge number of jobs across the world, as it will challenge both scientific and technological scholars, engineers, and workers.

In the United States in 2015, electric power made up 39% of the total primary energy consumption, with transportation making up another 28%—and both major sectors have huge potential to shift to renewables and alternatives.

However, as primary energy looks easier to adapt to renewables and alternatives, while for transport, liquid fuel seems the "fuel of choice," and definitely the one easy to continue to use. But still enormous efforts are invested to shift it also to cleaner environmental friendly fuels. Price-wise it will have to be affordable, and compete with fossils at current levels of $50–$60 a barrel.

In 2016, oil remained the world's leading fuel at a third of the global energy consumption, while the world energy mix is shifting toward lower carbon fuels, mainly gas, thanks to the gas revolution.

It is important to note, in a report from the government of Japan made in April 2014, under the header "Strategic Energy Plan," how Japan's government stresses its need for reliable stable energy sources, and how they plan to shift it until 2030 to a "70% self-motivating energy ratio." Important to this chapter, and also for Chapter 19, "Energy Security" is what drives Japan to build this plan = its total dependency on fossil fuel import, which it described as even worth than in the Oil Shock of 1973, and the TEPCO Fukushima nuclear plant disaster that brought the insight of human engineering and safety measures limitations.

The report clearly mentioned the threat on its fossil fuel supply, and how important renewables and alternative energy is to Japan's energy, economic and viable life. On page 21, it defines the goal: "to establish a stable energy-supply-demand structure in Japan it is important to identify the characteristics of the respective supply chains if individual energy sources clarify the energy source' position in the supply-demand structure and indicate policy directions *so that their strength can be exercised to complement each other's weakness.*" And this is exactly what we clearly define in our GPS model—under the supply pillar: available and affordable supply of both fossils and alternatives.

The report continued and classified the sources for **Primary** and **Secondary** energy structure; and for the "**primary energy**" it lists them by the following order: 1. Renewable energy; 2. Nuclear power; 3. Coal; 4. Natural Gas; 5. Oil; 6. LP Gas.

For the Renewable energy the order is as follows: 1. solar power, 2. Wind Power, 3. Geothermal energy, 4. Hydropower, 5. Woody Biomass and its related Bio fuels

For the Secondary energy the report lists it by a different order, and defines the "Secondary energy" whereby end-users consume energy— mainly electricity and heat; and point at the 2 most important layers for it: 1. Maximum efficiency and 2. Hydrogen: the utilization of the "hydrogen Society," as the report names it. Yet, quite a time to reach it, but the government of Japan promotes investment and more R&D to make a practical realization of this technology in order of feasibility. The important part of it is to secure safety handling, production, and storage.[4]

The 21st century, will have to be the "**century of reduced emissions**," and not the "**century of oil**" as the 20th century was.

Some renewables have the potential of bringing energy security to any country in the globe, which makes it even more important for the world to invest and develop any means of the renewables and alternatives.

In our "**Energy Future – Fossils and Beyond**," an important attention is given to the "**Beyond Fossils**," yet a total "Decarbonization" era may be still quite far away.

---

4 http://www.enecho.meti.go.jp/en/category/others/basic_plan/pdf/4th_strategic_energy_plan.pdf

17. SHIPPING AND TRANSPORTATION, SIZE DOES MATTER

———◆———

"What do we need ships for?" the lecturer asked during the opening lecture of a London University course on Maritime Transportation which I attended in 1986. Among the different answers the new students give there is always a student that will mention oil and oil products. Is there any other way to ship 300,000 tons of crude oil from Saudi Arabia to Rotterdam, or from Valdez in Alaska to a Houston refinery? And how else can you ship corn, wheat, and other grains from the world's largest granary—the United States Mid-West region to other parts of the world where it is being supplied, or other commodities at any volume from any loading port to any entry port.

Thus, shipping is a derived demand, as it is necessary and is simply the most practical, economic time-proven solution to ship commodities and other goods across the oceans and seas. Different dry and wet commodities form the largest volumes to be carried in ships, among them are oil and oil products, natural gas and other gasses supplied and traded worldwide with specialized tankers. The massive growth in demand for energy products triggers large demand for shipping, so more and more tankers of different sizes and types have been built to serve the international oil, gas, and coal trade.

———

Oil Tankers

The demand for oil tankers started back in the 2nd half of the 19th century. At the time, oil was used only for illumination. American producers and other oil merchants wanted to supply oil to Europe and the Far East, or Russian oil via the Black Sea to the Far East.

The introduction of oil tankers allowed the international oil trade to develop and expand rapidly. The first American oil tanker to cross the Atlantic Ocean was the "Elizabeth Watts," in 1861. The ship was actually a standard cargo vessel carrying oil in barrels, as was common at the time. Within 5 more years a purpose built tanker was designed and built to carry oil in liquid bulk. Oil tankers were then built in the Caspian Sea, serving the Russian Empire needs of oil coming from Baku, carried through the Caspian Sea to the Volga delta port of Astrakhan and inland via Volga River and the inner waterways system. Soon more ocean going oil tankers were built and entered service, to carry oil also to the Far East.

A significant step was the Shell oil tankers that were built in England to carry Russian oil from the Black Sea via the Suez Canal to the Far East, which started in 1892 with the breakthrough sailing of the Murex (see Chapter 1).

During the 20th-century World Wars, oil tankers' strategic role in supplying American oil to the European and Far East fronts was significant in supporting the forces as they fought their way to victory.

As oil tankers were introduced, they quickly grew in size, which allowed for even larger shipments. In 1967, the closure of the Suez Canal triggered the design and building of larger oil tankers. The VLCC and the ULCC came to site, carrying two million oil barrels and more. The VLCC, Very Large Crude Carrier, has a carrying capacity of about 300,000 metric tons (MT) equivalent to 2 million barrels of oil. The ULCC, Ultra Large Crude Carrier, 500,000 tons.

The Murex (dwt 5,010), portrayed above, was the first tanker of the Shell Transport and Trading Company Ltd. It was built by W.M. Gray & Co. Ltd., West Hartlepool, in 1892. Flag: British. The maiden voyage of the Murex took her through the Suez Canal (August 1892). She was purchased from the Shell Transport & Trading Company in 1907, and torpedoed and sunk in the Mediterranean on December 22, 1916.

Both types were built in order to compensate for the longer voyage from the Persian Gulf to Europe and North America, around the Cape of Good Hope, in South Africa.

However, only few ULCCs were built initially as they were too complex to operate within the ports of the time due to their huge size. Thus, the VLCC became the main vehicle for oil transport. The VLCCs often sail from major origin oil load ports to destination ports where the main refineries are: the gates for its consumers. Other routes are to major hubs, where the oil is then reloaded on smaller shuttle tankers for further distribution to smaller ports. For a typical VLCC, a voyage from the Persian Gulf to Rotterdam around the Cape of Good Hope takes about 32 days to cover the 10,800 Nautical Miles NM, about 10 days longer than via the Suez Canal. Tokyo, 6,300 NM away will take 19 days to reach. It will get to Houston after a 36-day voyage covering the 12,000 NM range.

Other major size categories we ought to know are the Aframax size tankers, which hold about 100,000 tons, and the Suezmax, that carry 150,000 tons—equal to one million barrels. Both types are also in use to carry crude from major origin ports to destinations where VLCCs are too large to call, and also as shuttle tankers where needed. The Aframax is dubbed AFRA, which stands for Average Freight Rate Assessment, which is a system created in 1954 by Shell Oil to standardize shipping contracts. Its carrying capacity of about 750,000 barrels made it popular due to versatility and convenient accessibility to many oil ports in the world.

Shuttle tankers are also very important as in some places they are the only means to connect offshore production platforms to refineries or larger ocean-going tankers, like in the North Sea where they bring in crude from different smaller production rigs and FPSO – Floating Production Storage and Offloading, used for that purpose. Other common operation is "lightering" off larger ocean-going oil tankers, like VLCC or Aframax, to allow deliveries to local smaller ports.

A VLCC tanker

An interesting role for the shuttle tankers occurred during the 8-years long Iran-Iraq war in the 1980s. Oil shuttle tankers carried oil from the northern part of the Persian Gulf to its southern part where ocean-going VLCCs waited for them, avoiding the war risk in the northern region of the Gulf. Large fleets of shuttle tankers carried out that task for Iran and Iraq, while their air forces practiced shooting air-to-surface missiles at its enemy tankers. The goal was simple: hit and harm their vital economic route to the petrodollars required to feed their war efforts.

Despite the evolution of oil tankers size, the technology and design remained as conservative as shipping is. They were built as single hull with one "side skin" structure just like a big barrel, with standard propulsion and speed; but faced in the last 20 years major challenges that can be attributed to environment—preventing sea pollution in case of an accident damaging its hull. Other changes dealt with the propulsion technology and bunkering, for better economic and less pollution.

The major change in tankers design came to fruition after the Exxon Valdez oil spill of March 1984. The spill constituted an ecological disaster, showing that with any effective modern technology in hand, the human factor is often the most dangerous and destructive agent.

As a result of this accident, tankers were forced to be redesigned and built to different safety standards. Compulsory double hull and double skin were introduced, and the whole tanker fleets had to divert within certain limited time, as single hull tankers phased out and were slowly banned from major ports. The transition was not a major technical or conceptual change. It just required building additional skin at an extra cost, compared to the previous tankers.

Other important changes are in the propulsion, aimed at better speed/consumption and transition to less polluted fuels, mainly LNG as fuel of choice, which is entering slowly in this conservative industry, and might achieve wider usage in the coming future.

The large fleet of "Dirty" (for crude oil), and "Clean" (for oil products) tankers continue to sail across the seven seas carrying oil and its products around the world.

Listed below are the current major crude-oil export tanker trade routes:

– Middle East Persian Gulf to Southeast Asia and the Far East;

– Russian ports to Europe and Japan;

- West Africa (mainly Nigeria, Cameroon and Angola) to Europe, United States and Southeast Asia;

- Central and South America (mostly Venezuela and Brazil) to Southeast Asia.

In 2016, total crude shipped by tankers amounted to 39.7 million bbl/d out of the daily total production of 91.67 million bbl/d.

Gas tankers – compressed, cooled and liquefied

In contrast with the conservative oil tankers' design and structure, the gas carriers offer a different approach. Liquid gas, with its extreme cooled or pressurized cargo, requires special treatment and handling due to the nature of its origin gaseous state and behavior. The density and characters of liquid gas is different.

Technologies for both compressed and cooled gasses exist and have been working safely for decades now, with the cooling method being more commonly used. When natural gas CH4 is cooled down to minus 162 degrees Celsius to form liquefied natural gas (LNG), the process "shrinks" 600 cubic meters of natural gas to form 1 cubic meter of LNG, allowing it to be shipped economically from any deserted geographical location it is produced, to its markets. Access to markets on the other side of the world that cannot be connected via pipeline, became a reality due to LNG advancements.

LNG tankers are built under different technology and require special metallurgical care to handle a minus 162 degree liquid cargo. The LNG tankers use a Cryogenic metallurgical technology with special steel alloys (mainly 9% Nickel) or Aluminum that will not become brittle from the extreme cold.

When Algeria discovered its first 50 Tcf (1,400 Bcm) huge gas field in 1956, neither subsea pipes nor LNG technology was being developed yet for commercial application. Thus, Algeria introduced the commercial LNG system—liquefaction facilities and related LNG tankers that were at that stage experimental in a way. What started as an experimental gas shipment from Algeria to England with the 27,400 cubic meters capacity (m^3) "Methane Princess" LNG tanker, developed into an advanced production and shipping technology that was necessary to support this new energy supply chain.

The growing volume of LNG production required more LNG tankers to allow the trade to develop. When Brunei joined the LNG market after Shell discovered gas there in 1968, it ordered seven 75,000 m^3 capacity tankers from a French shipyard to support its sales agreement with Japan, which started in late 1972. In 1969 the US based El Paso gas company signed a Sale and Purchase Agreement (SPA) with the Algerian company "Sonatrach," which required nine LNG carriers of 125,000 m^3 capacity to serve the trans-Atlantic route from Algeria to the United States East Coast terminal in Boston.

The 125,000 m^3 size became the industry standard for some time, until the next size "standard" of 145,000 m^3 was introduced in the early 1980s, to cover increased LNG supply contracts. These tankers were then taken by size during the mid-2000s with the Conoco-designed LNG fleet for the Qatari ambitious export project of 77 million tons of LNG a year, representing 31% of global LNG production at the time.

A fleet of Q-Flex and Q-Max LNG tankers have a cargo capacity of 210,000 m^3 to 217,000 m^3 with each Q-Flex vessel, and 263,000 to 266,000 m^3 with each Q-Max vessel. By economy of scale, Qatar has reduced the cost of transportation by 30 to 35 %, giving the nation a powerful competitive advantage. A significant LNG fleet was built for Qatar to meet this goal in early 2011. The first of the 54 tankers of a strong fleet of larger than ever LNG tankers was delivered in 2007: the Q-flex "Al Gattara," which then joined the first Q-max, "Rasheeda," of 266,000 m^3, delivered in August 2010.

LNG tankers are very expensive to build. They cost more than twice the price of a VLCC oil tanker of the same size. During the second half of last decade, with the energy price crisis, there was strong demand for tankers. An average 140,000 m^3 LNG tanker price climbed from about $150 million in 2003 to $200 million in 2006 and $250 million in 2008.

With the coming financial crisis and collapse of the oil bubble in 2008, the industry entered 2 years of slowdown. Delays in new production plants and reduced demand for gas sent some ships to "layup," where they had to stay and wait for market revival. Thus, the price to build a tanker dropped below the $200 million mark. As the market stabilized and improved in 2010, demand increased and charter hire soared as ships were re-employed. The March 2011 tsunami in Japan raised the demand for LNG in Japan and LNG shipping dramatically, as any available LNG cargo was directed to Japan.

More orders for LNG tankers started to be booked in 2011 with about 40 new buildings ordered, compared to only few in 2010. Prices climbed again to the $200 million level, with a wave of orders that continued during 2014 and 2015. Some orders were "speculative orders"—orders that are not covered with a shipping contract, leaving the new built vessel uncommitted. This is unusual for the very conservative LNG shipping, but brings a sign and expectation to massive future growth. Certain overcapacity already brought a drop in charter hire rates as uncommitted LNG tankers were delivered in 2015 and 2016.

During the early 2000s when it became apparent that the USA was about to face gas shortage due to a gap between local production and demand, the EIA advised that the gap could only be met by increasing LNG import. During that period, about 40 new LNG receiving terminals were at certain stages of planning process.

Australia also planned to supply the US market and in practice started doing so, bridging the long 12,000 NM route. One industry official described the arrival of the first Australian gas to the US East Coast LNG terminal as, "after seeing that, I will never say never again."

The future for LNG shipping is promising with new LNG production plants under construction. The predicted growth in the coming years is already 50% from the 2015 production level of 338.3 Bcm, of which the most, 238.6 Bcm, went to the Asia Pacific region, 55 Bcm to Europe, 20 Bcm to south America (Brazil, Argentina, and Chile), and only 10.3 to the United States. 2016 marked the early growth to 346.6 MT, which will continue to grow now rapidly as more projects mature and send their LNG to the market.

By early 2015 proposed liquefaction plans reached a capacity of 807 metric tons per year (MTPY), of which 272 MTPY in the USA, 327 MTPY in Canada, 70 MTPY in East Africa (mainly Mozambique), 40 MTPY in Russia, and 34 MTPY in Australia—with other Pacific, West Africa, East Mediterranean, and Middle East total of 43 MTPA—compared with the 2003 total production of 170 Bcm (125 MT – Million tons a year capacity). Little over a decade later, in 2015, LNG production almost doubled to a total of 338.3 Bcm of natural gas (247 MT of LNG) exported from 24 producing countries, to 19 importing countries.

The new LNG tanker fleet may have different size and propulsion systems with other technological advantages. It's new standard size will be around the 177,000 m^3; while the old steam turbine propulsions are mostly gone and have been replaced by engines that are more efficient, economical and environmentally friendly. Some of them will be fueled by LNG, while others will use advanced, revolutionary electric motors.

One of the main issues of LNG transport is the "boil-off" gas, which represents the loss of gas carried due to evaporation as temperature rises during the voyage. It is common for LNG tankers to be at sea for 14–21 days, so the ships were built to consume the boiled-off gas during their laden voyage. The boil-off gas became a disturbing issue as LNG price rose, and the buyers (receivers of the LNG cargo) demand to receive the full volume that was loaded. It was solved with the installation of a small liquefaction facility on those tankers.

In 2014, the LNG shipping industry celebrated 50 years with some 77,000 cargoes delivered safely. The first LNG shipments loaded in

Louisiana, on board the 5,000 m³ Methane Pioneer, for delivery to the UK. It followed with the 27,400 m³ Methane Princess that opened the commercial era and trade between Algeria and the UK in October 1964. One year later the trade from Algeria to the USA opened, and Boston became the first US city to receive LNG.

American LNG production from Alaska opened the trade to Japan and Asia in 1969, followed by Italy's first LNG import terminal.

In 1977, Abu Dhabi became the first Middle East LNG exporter to Japan, with a 125,000 m³ tanker. In 1980, Brunei LNG delivered its 1,000th cargo, and France opened its 3rd LNG receiving terminal.

In 1986 the 10,000th LNG cargo was delivered, and Korea received its first cargo. Within a decade Korea would become the world's second largest LNG importer. In 1987 the Zeebrugge terminal opened in Belgium, the sole LNG terminal in the North Continent for more than 20 years. By 1989, Australia exported its first LNG cargo. In 1990, Taiwan joined the club of LNG importers, poised to become one of the top 3 importing countries of LNG. Together with Japan and Taiwan they form the "JKT" countries—the top 3 LNG importers. In 1996 Qatar shipped its first cargo, and ten years later it became the top LNG exporter in the world. In 1997, the 25,000th cargo was delivered. By the year 2000, Oman became the 12th LNG exporter, and Greece opened its receiving terminal. These are just few milestones to note.

LNG Fast Track innovations

The fast track of LNG projects is an initiative based on shipping practice to bring gas to where it is required in shorter and more economical methods, different from the conservative existing land-based large investments of the LNG receiving terminals.

It introduced floating terminals in different shape, design, and sizes; initially using existing LNG tanker design with floating regasification technology on board it. Saving time, money, and land resources required for similar size land-based import terminals. These FSRU (Floating Storage Regasification Units) take a growing position in the industry, with terminals spread worldwide from Dubai to Argentina and from China to Egypt and Jordan; Pakistan and Lithuania. Bringing gas to where it is needed at a much shorter lead time and budget.

Hoegh FSRU Independence

The FSRU system innovation introduced a new method, solution, and opportunity of fast track to LNG import receiving terminals. The floating regasification has demonstrated how quickly innovative technologies can be adopted and accepted by the LNG industry. It has resulted in reduced costs for receiving terminals from about $1.2 billion to less than $400 million, with some converted and newly designed FSRU units costing only $150–250 million.

A Floating Storage Regasification Unit, which was introduced first by Excelerate Energy, in January 2005, was supposed to lead the way in the USA for more LNG terminals to come.

This solution was so practical and economical for other countries that it was introduced in Brazil in 2008, Argentina in 2008, and Dubai in 2010. The number of LNG importing countries grew from 11 in the year 2000 to 22 countries by 2010.

In 2011 Israel signed its FSRU contract to cover the shortage created by the blowup of the Egyptian gas pipe to Israel, creating overnight a severe gas shortage, and highlighting the wrong energy security planning and backup by the Israeli government. Thanks to its initial characteristic of fast track, the FSRU was delivered and connected within less than 2 years.

Same fast-track ideas were developed and introduced for production and export of gas with floating production plants of LNG, being designed and already ordered—which marks good growth potential in the industry. In May 2011, Shell sanctioned its Prelude FLNG, the first one to be built. As for Shell, anything which is not huge is not big enough, so the Shell Prelude FLNG was designed and is being built as the largest floating facility in the world. At 488 meters length, this mega FLNG is designed for a capacity similar to the early generation land-based LNG production plants (dubbed Trains), and it will be able to produce 3.6 million tons a year (MTPY) of LNG.

FLNG platforms have already been offered by different industry players in different sizes and production capacity, from 0.5 MTPY to 3.6 MTPY. It introduces revolutionary approach combining existing technology and experience of LNG tankers with LNG production train, into a floating LNG production train.

The idea behind it was to get to stranded gas sources which are spread through many regions of the world. If there are only 4 large-scale known reservoirs at the size of 50–100 Tcf, there are 73 fields the size of 5–50 Tcf offshore (among them the 4 discovered in the East Mediterranean—Tamar, Leviathan, Aphrodite, and the recent Al-Zohr off Egypt); 337 fields at the 1–5 Tcf size, and almost 347 at the size of 0.5–1 Tcf.

FLNG platforms might be the only solution to produce gas from these sources.

The FLNG is flexible to move to the next reservoir once the first one is depleted.

Other significant milestones to note are the Rotterdam land-based large terminal receiving its first cargo in September 2011, meaning Holland became the 26th LNG importing country, while Indonesia, one of the first LNG exporters, inaugurated its first floating receiving terminal in May 2012 to overcome the local shortage of gas, mainly due to distribution difficulties.

By May 2014, Papua New Guinea became the 20th LNG exporting country, and the total LNG tanker fleet reached 400 vessels. During 2015, Egypt introduced its first FSRU receiving terminal, and soon it will introduce a second unit to increase the required gas import capacity.

By early 2016, the LNG fleet stood at a record high of 449 existing tankers, and 168 on order. Its important role for the current ongoing gas revolution places the shipping industry at the center of this energy scene—as the new wave of available LNG supply is coming out to the market to redefine shipping trade. By January 2017, the total fleet grew only by 2 units to 619, including 141 on order; which shows certain equilibrium of this segment that is able to carry the current and expected medium term LNG shipping growth.

Shipping, as it has always been the case, will continue to be crucial and a necessary part of the international oil and gas trade in times of peace and war, and certainly the backbone of the day to day worldwide energy supply routes in the **Energy Future**.

18. THE GOLDEN AGE OF GAS, NATURAL GAS AND LNG—GAME-CHANGER!

---◆---

Golden Age of Gas

The term "Golden Age of Gas" came to existence in the last few years as increased amount of gas was discovered, and new technology was developed in the United States, producing natural gas from shale gas—unconventional gas.

As more gas became available, and the technology to liquefy it improved, it turned to economy of large scale production trains spreading to more places around the world. New liquefaction projects were initiated, some of them to enlarge existing plants, as more fields were developed in the producing countries like in Australia, while others will allow remote stranded gas reservoirs to be developed, exported, and monetized. However, the main volume will come out of the shale gas reservoirs in the United States, named the "Gas Revolution."

Natural gas is made out of hydrocarbon molecules, explored and produced from either onshore or offshore reservoirs, just like oil. It consists of methane $CH4$, with some related gasses like ethane C2H6, propane C3H8, and butane C4H10.

The organic compound contains only one "C" carbon molecule which minimizes the gas emissions left out when it is being burned to produce the energy we need. The other component is "H" (hydrogen); it exists also in our waters as H2O; and it is an interesting candidate to become one of the potential alternatives to fossil fuels.

The methane is the lesser polluted fossil fuel, producing 30% less emission than oil, and 50% less than coal. It will most probably serve as the world main fossil fuel in our passage to a less carbon environment,

The natural gas is much easier to produce than crude oil, and its internal pressure makes the production process easier. This process enables the utilization of up to 95% of a reservoir content. Similar to that of oil, the exploration for gas has gone through tremendous changes since 1963, with the introduction of 3-dimensional geology surveys. Better data processing tools results in a better definition of the prospect. The very strong computerized and imaginary capacity of 3-D and 4-D seismic technology enables more efficient, accurate surveys over larger areas than before. It enables penetration in remote areas, some of them offshore in deep sea. Better seismic leads to more successful exploration drilling results. In a way, the depths of earth and subsea have become more transparent to the geologists searching for oil and gas.

However, the exploration part of the upstream is still challenging, and even with the best processed data there are more "Dry Holes" than discoveries.

The world has recently been blessed with a rising flow of gas discoveries. When gas (or oil) is found, it still has a long and expensive process to go through before it is brought to the market. Only after several more appraisal drillings it will either be defined as a "commercial discovery" or declared as non-commercial. Either because it is too small to develop, or the gas found is not at the expected quality. The "commercial discovery" will then have to be developed with huge investments before being brought into the market. The deeper offshore or remote it is, the higher investment and time will be needed to develop it.

As a result of the 2002–2012 decade-long oil price crisis, the attention shifted to "unconventional gas" as an available source of energy. This is most notably shale gas in the United States, coal-bed methane (CBM), mainly found in Australia, and other unconventional gas sources that have been discovered recently or have been analyzed as a potential source for further future development.

Official information from different agencies quantified the unconventional gas reserves in 2011 as equal to the conventional gas reserves, with 6,622 Tcf of gas in 32 countries. In 2013, the EIA update data on shale gas reported 7,299 Tcf of gas in 41 countries, and in 2015 it reached 7,576 Tcf in 46 countries, while the conventional gas reserves stood at 6,600 Tcf in 2015. These new gas reserves are well spread worldwide with huge volumes also in Europe, China, and South Africa.

It is also notable that global conventional gas reserves discovered have grown by more than 50% during the last 20 years due to successful worldwide E&P.

The production of gas from the United States unconventional reserves also boosts employment, and in 2011 it contributed 9% of all new jobs, giving also a huge economic boost.

The rise of Qatar and Australia as the largest LNG suppliers during the last 10 years was due to huge demand forecasts in the United States, Europe, and Asia during the early 2000s. It brought a massive plan in the United States to build about 40 LNG import facilities to allow the import of LNG mainly from Qatar and Australia. American-based major oil and gas companies invested billions in Qatar and other world locations to secure LNG supply. It included Angola, Equatorial Guinea, Peru, Nigeria, and other countries.

With the partnership of Western companies, Russia also built its first LNG plant at Sakhalin, on its Pacific coast, which supplies gas mainly to Japan since 2008.

LNG – Liquefied Natural Gas

LNG became the key for more gas supply and for natural gas to reach any destination and market, regardless of its geographic location; regardless if a pipe grid is available or not.

Give it a port, or a shore line access, and you have access to international gas supply, connecting you to the international gas market.

LNG production and supply grew dramatically in the last decade, and recently celebrated 50 years of commercial shipping (see Chapter 17, "Shipping").

LNG is liquid methane, it liquefaction process becomes more available and scaled up to enjoy the benefit of economy of scale. Qatar brings the best example of expanding LNG production capacity and market so far; however within less than a decade to come, the LNG market will be changed dramatically; more suppliers, increasing volume from versatile geographic locations—from Russia's White Sea, to Mozambique; from Australia to North America.

The physical process of producing LNG is fascinating and brings the magic of "shrinking" about 600 cubic meters of natural gas NG to 1 cubic meter of LNG. Gas becomes liquid, a very chilled liquid.

Once produced and loaded on ocean going LNG tankers, it will cross any range to its destination, where the LNG will be discharged to storage tanks. From there the cooled-down liquid will be regassed and piped to the gas grid to its end-users.

The whole supply-chain parts linking the liquefied gas to its overseas markets must be made to withhold the minus 162 degrees Celsius liquid. This is cryogenic metallurgy, which makes all LNG equipment more expensive than other equipment used in energy production and supply.

Shale gas contribution, shale gas revolution

The shale gas is changing the future of the global gas supply, with new trade routes that will start soon. By 2025 the LNG trade routes will look much different from today. New wide supply routes will also link the United States and Canada to their worldwide buyers, together with other that will link additional new sources from Africa, Russia, and other new suppliers to existing and new buyers.

The *oil price crisis* of 2002–2008 brought a change to North America, just as the 1973 oil crisis brought a change at the time—pushing Europe to the North Sea, and the United States to the Gulf of Mexico.

Canada started the oil sand production that allowed it to become an oil exporter to the United States. Yet, the big revolution took shape in the United States with shale gas. Within just a few years, new and improved technology for fracking and horizontal drilling has brought a huge amount of gas to the market, making the United States self-sufficient with its gas needs and making it a gas supplier that will become a bridgehead to cover the global rising demand.

The so called "Gas Revolution" is changing the entire plans for North America's LNG receiving terminals, having them redesigned for LNG production and export. The United States and Canada will soon become top world LNG exporters. In early 2016, the LNG terminal in Louisiana shipped its first export cargo. Still earlier, other terminals had started to export existing LNG cargoes stored there, becoming storage and trading terminals; just like what happened in Europe in the last couple of years, making Spain the largest European LNG exporter.

The major discussion in the industry during the last decade was "Who will be the next Qatar?" It became clear during 2014 that the United States would be the one. The US has undergone a dramatic change from LNG importer to a major gas exporter that signs deals with customers worldwide. It is impressive to see that, as part of this process, different utilities (like EDF Portugal) and other major utilities—mainly Japanese—are playing a direct role in the gas revolution, becoming direct buyers and not allowing themselves to be dependent on any local supplier, just as EDF Portugal will bypass for its gas supply the local supplier Galp.

Golden Rules

The "Gas Revolution" brings the "Golden Age of Gas" as the IEA report described earlier in this decade. Recent estimates of proved and probable reserves of natural gas bring the industry to estimate further availability of natural gas for 250 years and more!

Exploiting the world's vast resources of unconventional natural gas holds the key to the golden age of gas, but for that to happen, governments, industry, and other players must work together to address legitimate public concerns about the associated environmental and social impacts. A May 2012 special *World Energy Outlook* report on unconventional gas, "*Golden Rules for a Golden Age of Gas*," by the International Energy Agency, presents a set of "Golden Rules" to meet those concerns.

"The technology and the know-how already exist for unconventional gas to be produced in an environmentally acceptable way," said IEA Executive Director Maria van der Hoeven. "But if the social and environmental impacts are not addressed properly, there is a very real possibility that public opposition to drilling for shale gas and other types of unconventional gas will halt the unconventional gas revolution in its tracks. The industry must win public confidence by demonstrating exemplary performance; governments must ensure that appropriate policies and regulatory regimes are in place."

The Golden Rules underline the importance of full transparency, measuring and monitoring of environmental impacts and engagement with local communities; careful choice of drilling sites and measures to prevent any leaks from wells into nearby aquifers; rigorous assessment and monitoring of water requirements and of wastewater; measures to target zero venting and minimal flaring of gas; and improved project planning and **regulatory control**.

"If this new industry is to prosper, it needs to earn and maintain its social license to operate," said IEA Chief Economist Fatih Birol, the report's chief author. Applying the Golden Rules could increase the cost of a typical shale-gas well by around 7%, but, it may in many cases be offset by lower operating costs. The report sets out two possible future trajectories for unconventional gas:

In a "Golden Rules Case," the application of these rules helps to underpin a brisk expansion of unconventional gas supply, which has far-reaching consequences:

- World production of unconventional gas, primarily shale gas, more than triples between 2010 and 2035 to 1.6 trillion cubic meters.
- The United States becomes a significant player in international gas markets, and China emerges as a major producer.
- New sources of supply help to keep prices down, stimulate investment and job creation in unconventional resource-rich countries, and generate faster growth in global gas demand, which rises by more than 50% between 2010 and 2035.

By contrast, in a "Low Unconventional Case," where no Golden Rules are in place, a lack of public acceptance means that unconventional gas production rises only slightly above current levels by 2035. Among the results:

- The competitive position of gas in the global fuel mix deteriorates amidst lower availability and higher prices, and the share of gas in energy use barely increases.
- Energy-related CO_2 emissions are higher compared with the Golden Rules Case, but in both cases emissions are well above the trajectory required to reach the globally agreed goal of limiting the temperature rise to $2^{\circ}C$.

The US shale gas

Other important promoting agency active in implementing the gas revolution is the American Gas Association (AGA), reporting since 2013 a robust growth in US gas reserves, thanks to the unconventional developments. Under the header **"Natural Gas: Rewriting Our Energy Future,"** it mentions that the abundance of clean natural gas provides an incredible opportunity to drive economic growth, while protecting the environment and boosting national energy security.

The US shale gas contribution is based on practice well-known since the late 1940s and has been used extensively since the 1950s. Recent innovations have been able to combine vertical and horizontal drilling with hydraulic fracturing to cost-effectively extract natural gas shale formations.

It continues to mention the importance of the largest 2 shale reservoirs, the Eagle Ford and Marcellus. Eagle Ford became to be the largest oil & gas development in the world based on capital invested. Almost $30 billion was spent developing the place in 2013, creating over 100,000 new jobs since 2012. It is located in South Texas, in depths between 4,000 and 14,000 feet. Its name is from the town Eagle Ford where the shale outcrops at the surface in clay.

Marcellus—shale formation of middle Devonian-age—low density organic rich carbonaceous shale occurs 9,000 feet below subsurface, cause greater pressure which results in higher production rates and higher methane proportions than related gas components or condensates.

It spreads beneath much of Ohio, West Virginia, Pennsylvania, and New York. Drilling started in 2004, and later on the horizontal drilling assisted in producing more out of it, with much lesser surface drilling rigs.

The shale developments is coming with some environmental concerns, well-covered in an IGU (International Gas Association) report from June 2012, opened by the statement, "To date, sharply contrasting opinions about the environmental impact of shale gas development has characterized the debate. Therefore, a rational, objective, fact-based discussion of the environmental concerns that can lead to operational and regulatory approaches that ensure that this resource is developed in an environmentally responsible manner is required."

It lists the process main stages, and covers each of them with the necessary risks and ways to minimise them to a practical continuing development that will contribute to the United States and world economy and security of supply.

According to the IGU report, the production process comprises six main steps:

- Site development and preparation with access roads and production facilities.
- Vertical drilling to the depth where shale formations exist.
- Drilling horizontally from the end of the vertical well to several directions
- Hydraulic fracturing of shale formations, using a fracturing fluid comprising about 99.5 per cent water and sand, plus 0.5 per cent chemical additives.
- Recycling and disposal of fluids used and natural water brought to the surface.
- Well completion and operation, the latter lasting up to a decade or more.

The report addresses each and every point, and refers to wide information bases, from government agencies to environmental entities; with no crucial conclusion.

Gas prices

Gas prices remain both a challenge and a crucial factor for further developments, production, and potential export. The US industry benchmark is the HH, the Henry Hub gas price, reflected by traders on the NYMEX. The question is whether HH is a $2.00 or $4.00 level, or its indexation to the Brent remains crucial—certainly in light of the huge price volatility in the last 15 years.

If a Brent indexation is the one to take, then at what ratio? The Brent 14% was too tough and destructive when oil "stabilized" at the $100–120 during 2010 to 2014, taking Japan's gas price to the $14 MMBtu level (with oil at $100 bbl).

Other indexations refer to certain basket of oil products, coal, and consumer index.

Others will consider the oil parity as a guideline to the dangerous heights of oil prices. It refers to energy comparison of a single oil barrel producing 5.8 MMBtu—thus a Brent bbl price divided by 5.8 = when oil at $100 is divided by 5.8 equals to 17.24 MMBtu. If we take the oil and gas prices in the last 15 years, we will see that Japan was exposed to it at its worst.

Year	Brent $/bbl	Oil Parity bbl/MMBtu	HH Henry Hub MMBtu	NBP MMBtu	LNG Japan MMBtu
2002	25.02	4.31	3.33	2.37	4.27
2007	72.39	12.48	6.95	6.01	7.73
2012	111.67	19.25	2.76	9.46	16.75
2014	98.95	17.06	4.35	8.25	16.33
2015	52.39	9.03	2.60	6.53	10.31
2016	43.74	7.54	2.51	4.56	6.89
first half 2017	51	8.9	3.11	5.58	7.72

There is a great debate amongst the producers over what the breakeven economic price is, but this is a question we leave beyond the scope of this book. With gas production lifting costs remaining at the low level at which advanced drilling and production technology allows, we trust prices can be maintained relatively low, to support worldwide growth of supply. This is what the combination of horizontal drillings and hydraulic fracturing (known as *fracking*) allows the needed change in unconventional E&P.

The AGA listed ExxonMobil Corp. as the largest US gas reserves holder, with more than 26 trillion cubic feet (Tcf), followed by Chesapeake Energy Corp., BP PLC, ConocoPhillips Co., and Anadarko Petroleum Corp.

"In fact, ExxonMobil's current reserves position is more than twice the second largest reserves holder," stated the AGA, emphasizing that seven of the ten largest US gas reserves holders are independent producers, while the remaining three are integrated multinational major oil and gas companies.

Related part of the gas revolution is the rise of US oil production, associated to the shale gas production. US crude oil production grew from 7.5 million bbls/day in 2010 to 10 million bbls/day in 2013, and peaked by 2015 to 12.7 million bbl/day, placing the United States as the world's top oil producer ahead of Saudi Arabia and Russia.

The gas revolution continues with its other related effects on international trade and geopolitics. It comes with some geopolitics effects and concerns. Like the lifting of the international sanctions on Iran, which may place it in future competition with Qatar's gas export. The early 2016 incidents between Turkey and Russia, when a Russian jet fighter was shot down by a Turkish jet, overshadowed the progress made in recently signed gas supply deals between the two countries. This fact, once again, highlighted the importance of "Transit Countries," in this case, the Turkey Bridge to Europe for Central Asian gas piping.

The New Energy Era

Shipping will again become a crucial part of this supply chain, as was recently demonstrated by the departure of the first USA ingenious (lower 48) LNG cargo, described under a header so fitted to the topic of this book: "**US LNG enters a _new era_**," by Mike Corkhill. "The departure of the first commissioning cargo from Cheniere Energy's Sabine Pass LNG terminal on February 24, 2016 marked the start of a new era for the global LNG market and for the domestic US gas industry. The shipment on board the 160,000m³ _Asia Vision_, bound for Brazil, is the first LNG export cargo from the continental US, the first processed from shale gas and the first loaded at a bi-directional terminal that can regasify LNG (for local use) and liquefy natural gas (for export)." In April 2017 it had already shipped its 100th LNG export shipment.

The LNG tanker _Asia Vision_ sailed 57 years after a trial LNG shipment—the first-ever seaborne cargo of LNG which was loaded at

Calcasieu Lake, just 50 km from Sabine Pass. Since then however, the United States has been a marginal supplier in the international LNG market, with its small export terminal at Kenai, Alaska, since 1969 dispatching cargoes to Japan—while now huge export projects are taking shape in North America.

'Low-carbon' world practice

The gas revolution must come with more gas applications from **NGV**, Natural Gas Vehicles, able to fuel natural gas simply at any gas station fed from the grid. **GTL**, Gas to Liquids, need also to become more economical and widespread. This is a technology to convert natural gas into high quality liquid petroleum products—quality equivalent to that of white distillates! Once this technology becomes economic and largely spread, it can challenge also the LNG; imagine GTL refineries being built at natural gas origin locations worldwide, and then being shipped as liquid petroleum in standard tankers.

It will bring much less polluted liquid fuels to be widely used as an alternative to the more polluting crude-oil refined gasolines, and ease the cost and complexity of LNG shipping on exported gas.

As we are just at the beginning of this gas revolution, we can only conclude now that the United States—just like other new suppliers and growing existing suppliers—will be a great partner and supporter of the **Energy Future** as the world reshapes its security of supply.

Gas is here to stay; it is here to grow and contribute to the "low-carbon" future.

19. ENERGY SECURITY – THE NEW ENERGY ERA, AN ERA TO LAST

————————◆————————

ENERGY SECURITY provides the security of supply of oil and gas, as well as other energy-related products. **Energy Security needs to be combined and merged into the global foreign policy and defense interests of each and every country in the world.**

The IEA defines energy security as an "uninterrupted availability of energy sources at an affordable price." Affordable price was not considered a factor until the 2008 oil price crisis.

The IEA was founded in response to the 1973 Oil Crisis. Its initial role was to help countries coordinate a collective response to *major disruptions in oil supply* through the release of emergency oil stocks. The participating countries work together to ensure reliable, affordable, and clean energy.

Note the *major disruptions in oil supply*: no reference or attitude was taken to potential sharp fluctuation in prices.

Some distinct developments have been shaping the *energy industry* (in "energy industry" we include the oil and gas industry as well as the different types of renewable and alternative energy), whereby price in our opinion should no longer get affected by irrelevant issues among them wars in the Middle East, market speculations like the "magnificent" stories on endless growth of demand in India and China that bring some to believe there is no limit for it.

————

A new energy paradigm that includes a diverse set of global energy sources utilizing available alternative fuels, renewable sources of energy, and energy efficiency and conservation measures can provide not only greater economic opportunities but also greater security of energy supply. It remains uncertain whether this marks the end of the energy crisis era as we know it in the last several decades since the early 1950s. What lays ahead is what we can consider as an opportunity to create better **Energy Future.**

Sustainable energy security can be achieved now and last for decades, ensuring the future security of supply for the world. As this book is being published, a unique opportunity that combines supply glut, accompanied with low energy prices, gives the perfect background for it—as it can be seen in the next chapter.

Yet the energy industry maintains its attractive position for investors, and for the major oil and gas players, to continue their investment in future E&P and other technologies the energy industry needs, though with reduced budgets.

It is well understood now that in our **Energy Future** a sustainable energy security can be achieved and has almost arrived. The energy future is almost here.

Is it the end of the Energy Crises Era? We cannot tell yet, but the world can certainly promote this change and name it *"The New Energy Era."*

If some analysts, trading houses, banks, and others that promoted the high energy prices scenario in the past, are saying now that "lower energy prices will contribute more to the global economy," then we certainly face a change.

Global Approach to Energy Security

It is important to know how leading countries, as well as major oil companies and organizations, define and treat their energy security. How do the United States, Japan, Singapore, the G8 countries, and the top oil and gas majors approach their energy security?

United States of America

The United States constitutes the single largest national economy, the preeminent military, diplomatic, and economic force of the world. With a large population of 324 million people by mid-2016, and high energy consumption per capita, the US is the largest energy market in the world. As such, the US market has become increasingly dependent on security of supply, which means that measures must be taken to assure it.

Large multinational corporations, governments on both the state and federal level, environmentalists, economists, and the public all have differing views on where the key to US energy security lies. Natural gas and fracking, offshore drilling and Arctic oil, and numerous other opportunities serve to bring the United States down the road to a secure future.

The United States was for years the 3rd largest crude oil producer in the world and managed to take now the pole position, leaving Saudi Arabia and Russia behind. It also has the largest world refining capacity of 18 million barrels a day, yet it must achieve both supply and environmental security.

The Obama administration claimed that the best strategy for ensuring the United States' energy security was an "all-of-the-above" strategy, with solar, natural gas, oil, biofuels, wind, nuclear, clean coal, and fuel efficiency listed as the main tenants. Ultimately, its stated path is to reduce American dependence on foreign oil, develop safe and responsible domestic oil and gas production, further develop and implement Carbon Capture and Sequestration technologies (Clean Coal), develop and implement Clean Energy Sources (renewables), and advance in energy efficient technology and usage patterns. Essentially, the federal strategy was an amalgamation of all that is available, favoring a path of independence, higher domestic production and renewable sources rather than international free market support.

The United States Energy Information Administration stated in 2013 that the United States had already surpassed Russia as the largest natural gas producer in the world, in 2011, and that by 2020 would surpass both Russia and Saudi Arabia to become the largest producer of oil (which in fact happened much earlier—in 2015). This increased production allowed the United States to enhance its path toward **energy independence**, achieving the production of more energy than imported in November of 2013 for the first time in years. From this point, the next target is to set itself as an oil exporter, just as it became an LNG exporter.

The possibility that the United States may become addicted to foreign energy beyond rehabilitation, and thus become utterly dependent on every producing country promoting its own interests, spells danger for the American economy. In a speech titled "Blueprint for a Secure Energy Future" held at Georgetown University in 2011, President Barack Obama put it best, saying:

"We cannot keep going from shock to trance on the issue of energy security, rushing to propose action when gas prices rise, then hitting the snooze button when they fall again . . . It is time to do what we can to secure our **energy future**."

In this respect, as President Trump entered the White House in January 2017, it looks as fossil fuels dominancy will set to be kept for several reasons that the new President already declared. What would **"America First"** bring to the United States heavy industry and energy industry?

The whole world is looking at the president's policy on energy as well as the international policy of Russia, Saudi Arabia, Iran, and South America—all lead to the final equation of energy security. In this respect, the pole position of oil and gas market between the United States and Saudi Arabia on the one hand and with Russia on the other hand. With both of them a fierce competition is developing on the same markets. For the gas markets, United States vs Russia mainly on the European market; and vs Qatar on other international markets for gas.

Japan

An interesting case study in energy security of a dependent country can be seen in Japan: its decision to pursue a different form of energy security. Japan is the third largest economy in world, as well as the second largest energy importer. Japan's population of 127 million people by mid-2016, had high energy consumption.

Japan turned to nuclear power as a method of assuring its access to clean electricity at a cheaper price than most other fuels, renewable or conventional. Despite Japan's lack of economically viable energy resources, nuclear power promised to reduce the drain of Japanese wealth for high level fuel imported, as well as to continue the efforts to meet emission standards from the Kyoto Protocol that Japan itself initiated.

The Japanese government amended their 2010 Energy Plan in 2014, to include a position to decrease Japan's dependency on nuclear power. Instead, it sought to find new, unconventional, and renewable sources of fuel, in an attempt to address various issues that have come due to the hurried nature of nuclear plant decommissioning.

The lack of alternative clean sources created the need for Japan to purchase large volumes of oil and gas from the Middle East, which, along with increased competition from industrializing countries for oil in markets, has deteriorated Japanese energy security as well as destroyed marked progress in the reduction of greenhouse gas emissions. An issue in which Japan had previously been a pioneer.

As the Japanese economy struggled to recover and maintain growth after leaving its economy's Lost Decade of the 1990s, its reliance on foreign energy supplies has grown and drained away the nation's wealth, as well as led Japan into growing trade deficits that further destabilized its economy.

Japan paid the highest prices for its gas import for years, all by means of LNG. Traditionally, Japan's gas price index for gas, which is based on a unique price mechanism, took into consideration its total dependence on LNG import, exposing Japan to pay the highest gas prices in the world—related to the JCC, Japan Crude Cocktail, or also

Japan Customs Cleared. For the past decades, international LNG trade in Asia has been based on the JCC price mechanism—a formula related to the Brent price with certain indexation. It has been around the "Brent 14" as it is typically dubbed; 14% of the Brent. For example, at an initial Brent price of $100 a barrel, the basic Japan LNG price is $14 per MMBtu plus the shipping cost. Just imagine the horror show of Brent at $150 or Brent at $200; and Japan's LNG price climbed to 21 or 28 $/MMBtu.

In 2002, with the NBP Europe gas index at 2.37 $/MMBtu, Japan paid $4.27.

In 2007, the NBP average was $6.01, and Japan paid 7.73 $/MMBtu.

In 2012, the NBP average was $9.46, and Japan paid $16.75, while the US Henry Hub averaged 2.76 $/MMBtu.

In the summer of 2015, as oil and gas prices fell and remained at the $50–60 level, LNG prices dropped to a record low for the last years, with the Henry Hub prices averaging 2.78 $/MMBtu during the first 3 quarters of 2015 and falling close to $2.10 by year-end and averaging $2.69; LNG in Europe NBP was little over $6, while in Japan was little over $7. The end of 2016 brought a remarkable improvement to the HH price to $3.59 in December—yet 2016 averaged $2.5.

This is a further evidence that price must be part of any energy security equation, regardless of any individual country's geographic position or its dependency on any certain commodity.

In fact the new LNG producers in the United States already offer a flat FOB export price! This brings great relief to Japan's LNG future prices.

Japan's ministry of economy, trade, and industry (www.meti.gov.jp) places at a top priority Japan's aim to aggressively promote energy conservation, while its main declared mission is to develop *"Japan's economy and industry by focusing on promoting economic vitality in private companies and smoothly advancing external economic relationships, and **to secure stable and efficient supply of energy** and mineral resources."*

In this respect, a 2014 Strategy Report they issued[5] shows in details Japan's government concern from world changing geopolitics, in particular the instability of the resource-supplying regions (as they name it) of the Middle East and North Africa. In addition, the report highlights a concern that in light of the United States energy independency it will soon have, the United States may have less interest in the Middle East, which will only contribute to worsen the situation there. It admits that "the energy supply network in which Japan is directly involved is never stable." The impact of the shale gas revolution takes an important part mainly for its effects on oil prices and on coal demand and prices. It mentioned the fact that by 2018 the United States will become net exporters of gas, and soon South America will also become energy independent—not affected by Middle East oil and gas. This will shift the center of gravity to South East Asia, where China's growing demand is challenging the region, and may have negative effect on potential price reduction for Japan, Korea, and Taiwan—which will still remain dependent on Middle East oil and gas.

European Union

The European Union represents a high number of OECD (Organization for Economic Cooperation and Development) countries, and one of the largest concentrated energy markets today. European demand has remained incredibly high, thus European nations have been ramping up the import of natural gas from Russia, increasing their dependency on the Russian gas. Their efforts to increase LNG import placed them in competition with the Asian markets' higher price offered to LNG producers.

There are, however, other options that remain for the Europeans to secure their energy supply, some of which will be detailed below. During the last years, more LNG terminals have been built in European

---

5   http://www.enecho.meti.go.jp/en/category/others/basic_plan/pdf/4th_strategic_energy_plan.pdf

countries to increase their access to LNG from different global sources. The key lies in versatile LNG sources, including those of new suppliers

This is the official "Five Pronged Plan" by the European Commission, outlining their Energy Security Strategy in a five-part plan that is reproduced by many other governmental organizations and committees around Europe and in other countries:

- Increasing energy efficiency and reaching the proposed 2030 energy and climate goals. Priorities in this area should focus on buildings and industry, which use 40% and 25% of total EU energy respectively. It is also important to help consumers lower their energy consumption.
- Increasing energy production in the EU and diversifying supplier countries and routes. This includes further deployment of renewables, sustainable production of fossil fuels, and nuclear energy.
- Speaking with one voice in external energy policy, including having EU countries inform the European Commission early on with regards to planned agreements with non-EU countries that may affect the EU's security of supply.
- Strengthening emergency and solidarity mechanisms and protecting critical infrastructure. This includes more coordination between EU countries to use existing storage facilities, develop reverse flows, conduct risk assessments, and put in place security of supply plans at regional and EU levels.

Europe's plan can be summarized in 5 words: Conserve, Diversify, Connect, Communicate, and Keep (reserves).

Huge plans for new gas pipelines from central Asia to Europe are on the agenda, and some plans have changed; however, all were meant to increase the security of supply to Europe.

A combined partnership of few countries within each of the proposed projects strengthened the projects, as could be seen with the original partners to the Nabucco pipeline (Bulgarian Energy Holding), Romanian Transgaz, Turkish Botas, Austrian OMV, German RWE, and Hungarian FGSZ—all working together to carry the Central Asian gas to Austria as the gateway to the European grids. In the last couple of years, other versions to the grand Nabucco have been suggested, as the Turkish Trans Anatolian Pipeline (TANAP) that takes shape these days, crossing 1,200 kilometers in Turkey to either continue via the Nabucco West or via other proposed pipeline like the Trans Adriatic Pipeline (TAP) that would route the gas via Greece, Albania, and across the Adriatic Sea to Italy.

The shareholders are Swiss AXPO (42.5%), Norwegian Statoil (42.5%), and German E.ON Ruhrgas (15%).

On the other hand, to complete the security of supply options, some of the EU countries have strengthened their supply by building LNG terminals and signing new long-term supply contract agreements to compete and backup the Russian gas, increasing dramatically their energy security.

As 2016 ended, it is interesting to see the success of the Russia to Germany "Nord Stream" systems in delivering more and more gas to Europe—delivery of more gas to Europe totals 43.8 Bcm out of its maximum capacity of 55 Bcm.

Most remarkable is the new LNG receiving terminal opened in October of 2014 in Klaipeda, Lithuania, marking the end of the Baltic state's reliance on gas supplied from Russia.

Klaipeda FSRU, Picture courtesy Hoegh LNG

The next LNG receiving terminal, opened in late 2015, is in no other than the ex-Soviet controlled Poland. More European LNG terminals will open soon in Sweden, Finland, Ireland, the UK east coast, in the Adriatic Sea, and possibly more in the Northern Aegean Greek coast.

Other LNG activity takes shape in the European coastal waters, mainly the LNG bunker for the shipping and more of the small-scale LNG distribution.

The gas diversity of supply will increase the security of supply to Europe.

Geopolitics is also at the center here, with the current tensions between East and West been raised to their highest level since the Cold War. The annexation of Crimea by the Russian Federation in March 2014 has created great uncertainty as to the long-term viability of the European energy strategy that relies on Russian cooperation, as some of the gas West Europe relies upon must flow through pipelines in Ukraine. The ongoing crisis in Ukraine symbolizes the gradual erosion of Europe's security architecture. Energy security is a very important part of it.

Singapore

An island nation off the southern tip of Malaysia, Singapore is one of the richest countries in the world by GDP per capita for its population of nearly 5.7 million. Singapore is an Asian Tiger economy that expanded rapidly as a center of trade, finance, and technology.

Active in oil trade since the late 19th century, Singapore has been long served as a hub for energy services, with oil re-export and refining making up 5% of the GDP of a city-state with no domestic natural oil and gas resources. As Singapore has relied almost entirely on energy imports for its existence, it has sought to develop new and innovative ways to secure its energy supply, while capitalizing on opportunities available in the energy industry.

The government of Singapore currently claims to be the largest bulk liquid logistics center (including LNG since 2013) in South East

Asia, a position it believes will bring large-scale growth as countries in the region switch to cleaner natural gas. The price decline helps this process, as developing countries in Asia seek to meet climate objectives and reduce their energy budgets. Singapore also believes it is perfectly positioned with: its chemical, semiconductor and energy industries, to serve as a leader in the research, development, industrialization, and implementation of the renewable energy sector that will fuel growth in coming years.

As Singapore seeks these long-term goals in energy security, its short-term strategy is distinctly similar to that of many other countries. Singapore will rely on open markets to provide steady supplies of oil and gas, it will implement measures to encourage competition in domestic electricity supply to decrease cost to consumers, all whilst reducing consumption to a more sustainable level.

The G8 countries

In Rome 2014, the G8 (or G7 due to Russia's expulsion due to the Ukrainian crisis), released its outline for the sustainable path toward energy security, detailed as follows:

1. Development of flexible, transparent and competitive energy markets, including gas markets.

2. Diversification of energy fuels, sources and routes, and encouragement of indigenous sources of energy supply.

3. Reducing greenhouse gas emissions and accelerating the transition to a low carbon economy as a key contribution to ensuring energy security.

4. Enhancing energy efficiency in demand, supply, and demand response management.

5. Promoting deployment of clean and sustainable energy technologies and continued investment in research and innovation.

6. Improving energy systems resilience by promoting infrastructure

modernization and supply and demand policies that help withstand systemic shocks.

7. Putting in place emergency response systems, including reserves and fuel substitution for importing countries, in case of major energy disruptions.

Global Energy Security

Apparently, the global energy security can be improved if more countries have a better attitude toward a more efficient supply of fossil fuels as well as better technology and economics of renewables and alternative fuels—all must be harnessed and summarized to an efficient and better **energy future**.

An important aspect of energy security (that we do not develop in this book) will be the cyber threats and hacking, which also require their tools for cyber security—due to the threats to energy installations and other parts along the supply chain, and their impact on the energy market.

Yet it is not enough, as it is not treated in one strong voice—in one global independent approach that will harness all or most parties in a united front to combine and utilize the best of the 3 pillars of energy security as defined in our *model for Energy Security*—securing stability of supply and prices, as well as the security of our environment.

Stay tuned, as we need your support for this initiative.

20. THE INDEPENDENT ENERGY SECURITY AGENCY

———————◆———————

In Chapter 19 we asked: **Is it the end of the Energy Crises Era?**—and we replied that we cannot tell yet, but certainly can promote and name it *"The New Energy Era."* A new energy era that will form the **Energy Future** can be achieved if some measures are taken, if a lot of efforts are invested to build it, and then work the necessary arrangements to maintain and control it.

A careful follow-up and surveillance of the market is a must to identify any potential market weakness or failure. Once we identify that a crisis is about to occur, a proper **crisis management** will be performed to make the difference from past oil crises by preventing the next oil crisis or oil shock.

Recent decades brought what we consider to be a "status quo" of constant energy crisis, but we have now the opportunity to create a different present and future. If the status quo makes the mirror of history—history of energy crises, caused mainly by geopolitics events—it is clear that the **geopolitics** is changing (not necessarily a positive change); but also the **supply** is changing and bringing hope and opportunities.

Opportunities to create a different long-term stable price regime and eliminate its volatility. Can we aim and set a limited "volatility" price regime? And at what level and what price of oil to make it feel comfortable at such a less volatile environment?

———

What should be the gas price reference? Local (United States HH), regional gas prices—NBP for Europe, another level for Asia, Brent-related, or other mechanism. By all means it must be defined at the same parameters of oil in terms of limited volatility and global reference.

With a wide-angle view, we do have the understanding and insights of the energy crises and energy security issues of over the last 50 years; lessons can be and should be learnt and implemented in our struggle to bring global **Sustainable Energy Security**.

This is where we introduce the Independent Energy Security Agency—the IESA model for energy security—based on three pillars:

- **Geopolitics** – the oil & gas industry is stronger than any geopolitical events and effects.
- **Price** – affordable with limited volatility.
- **Supply** – of both fossil and renewables/alternatives.

The Independent Energy Security Agency

The newly introduced **Independent Energy Security Agency (IESA)** will act to develop an independent approach to energy security, with better mechanism and price regime to secure its members their security of supply.

The Independent Energy Security Agency's mission is to become an international global agency that acts to achieve energy security by harnessing a large base of members and support along and across the energy supply chain.

As a public policy agency, we introduce an important agenda to be spread and accepted by our members, customers, and audience to **Explore, Advise, and Influence** the energy market.

Challenges ahead

Following is our modus operandi, but first we have to light and map the challenges, understand what should and can be done, then work to achieve it.

In the changing arena of energy, geopolitics, and environmental legislations, one should not forget that the energy industry is here to produce electricity for its different domestic and industrial applications, and fulfill the worlds' transportation needs. It has carried this mission for more than a century, and needs to continue this way.

But the priorities are changing, and so are the threats and challenges. Threats and challenges for many components of our life and energy supply chain.

As we entered the 21st century, the top priority is to maintain our Energy Security. It is a necessity for our economy, budget, defense forces, foreign policy, transportation and infrastructure that depends on energy.

In such a dynamic world there is no escape from facing the threats and tackling the challenges head on in order to reach a sustainable global Energy Security that will last for decades.

The route toward a solution, our model

With crisis after crisis, it is essential to recognize the difficulties ahead, to evaluate and look for a solution, then implement it. Take drastic acts and change the prevailing status quo to achieve better order and security of supply.

Our road-map brings 4 tools and steps to be taken as follows:

- **Team Work** – collaboration between producers, consumers, leading agencies, governments.

- **Different Tune** – use of an advanced information process system to contain available information and a better tool to process it in a way that it is available, transparent, and clear from manipulations—to assess better planning of a balanced market.

- **The Golden Age of Gas** – expanding the usage of gas by taking the advantage of the opportunities it provides to the market with huge diverse gas supply that will bring more countries to achieve security of supply and energy independence.

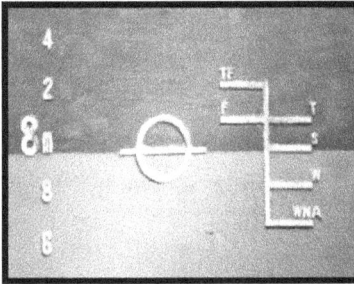

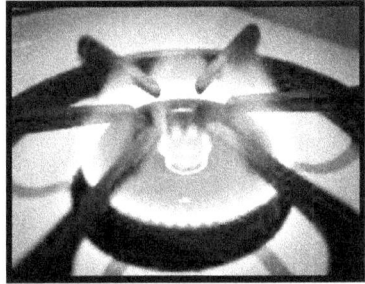

- **Market Control** – there is no escape from using the major tool of market regulation. Certain floor and cap mechanism is required to secure a stable long-term price, assuring the producers and consumers a strong economic base.

With this in our hands we proceed to our GPS – the 3-Pillar Model.

Our GPS model to navigate to the Energy Future is based on *Three Pillars of Energy Security*.

To ensure we implement these pillars, we introduced our private and independent Energy Security Agency. In our analysis of sources, prices, and geopolitics, we came to evaluate the similarities and differences of the 2008 oil price crisis and the 2014–2016 crisis, to conclude that where there is no market control, there is chaos; where there is information being manipulated, there is chaos; where there is no crisis management, there is chaos.

Recent crises were not assessed and managed properly, or not managed at all. A crisis management leadership could solve each of them much earlier, before it gets out of control.

In our struggle to achieve a global **Sustainable Energy Security**, we came to the following model which is based on *3 main pillars*, the **GPS,** to direct us to the safe destination of energy security:

Geopolitics	to allow our energy to be	*ACCESSIBLE*
Price	stable to support E&P and strong economy growth	*AFFORDABLE*
Supply	of both fossil and renewables & alternatives	*AVAILABLE*

ENERGY FUTURE
Achieving Energy Security In a Dynamic World

The Independent Energy Security Agency

Will promote and consult on Energy Security, based on our 3 pillars:

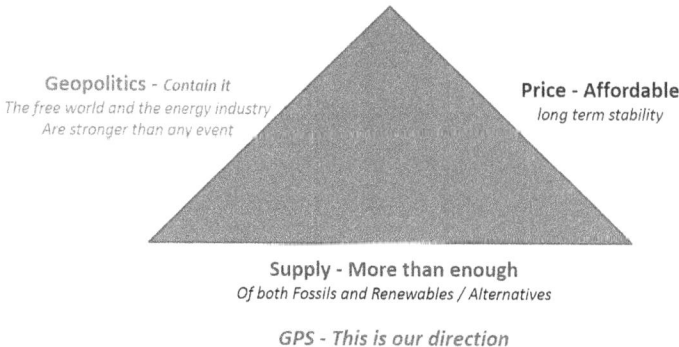

Geopolitics - *Contain it*
The free world and the energy industry
Are stronger than any event

Price - Affordable
long term stability

Supply - More than enough
Of both Fossils and Renewables / Alternatives

GPS - This is our direction

Geopolitics: The outcome of September 11 and the Arab Spring still affect the world, mainly the MENA countries (Middle East and North Africa).

The new "Oil Wars" (can be symbolic to "Cold War") of late 2014 till 2017 prove, just like the Iran Iraq war of the 1980s, that the market managed to work an uninterrupted supply at a low-price scenario. It means that the global economy and the energy industry can contain any geopolitical threat and event. This is what our **Geopolitics** pillar means.

Major **Geopolitics** influential powers like the United States, Russia, OPEC, and Saudi Arabia are able to manipulate and influence certain processes and occurrences. Neither of them gave their final word on this current crisis as this book was published in the summer of 2017.

Pricing: The Energy Security Agency will promote setting a cap and floor price structure, and certainly will raise our members' voice once a certain interruption occurs, or is about to happen. This will be the tool to serve a long-term security of supply, in a stable economic environment. Take the "pain" of speculations and volatility out of the market.

The oil-producing countries and mainly the petrodollar-oil-dependent producers are losing huge income; which is more crucial to the OPEC members and Russia than for others. Their **need of a long-term stable price mechanism** is strong just as the other party to this tango dance—the consumers' **need of a long-term stable price mechanism**.

As we hear some encouraging voices that describe the current low prices as serving better some economies, with good influence on the global economy, we can assume that we may be at a certain balanced equation point.

We can definitely state that the 2014–2016 price decline brings a unique opportunity to set a stable price regime for years to come.

Price will be a central point of activity for the ***Independent Energy Security Agency***. If the current (summer 2017) $50s level is hard to achieve, it means that we have a certain equilibrium now. It means that the $50 should serve as a benchmark, and might be considered as a floor price. Once a floor price agreed, or settled, it must come with a defined cap price, which will include proper definitions for its changes within the defined range.

Back in 2012, as the other cycle of too high energy price crisis hit the world with the oil prices yearly average at over $100.00, we published, in the first edition of this book, a call for a $75 barrel cap price. After five years, considering 2017, it seems a good target, and a top limit. Both floor and cap prices strongly represent benefits for all parties involved—over the short, medium, and long term.

Certain winter/summer allowance and few other relevant parameters are to be inserted in this paradigm.

***Supply** of both Fossil & Renewable*: The days shadowed by the Hubbert Curve are gone. There is enough oil and certainly enough gas to allow the required transition time to other sustainable energy solutions **beyond fossil.**

By all means, in the next 40 years and beyond we will have enough supply of fossil fuels and renewables, to bridge and allow a smooth transition to less carbon environment—decarbonization.

The 21st century high-tech industry will find suitable solutions and better utilization of other known sources, from nuclear fission to hydrogen and other creative alternatives, to make them available at a modest and affordable cost.

The strength of the oil and gas industry, or let's coin it differently by adding the renewables and alternatives to name it "**The Energy Industry**," has the ability to control and secure all of our energy needs for years to come—to make it accessible, affordable, and available.

Action items:

Join us to:

1. Explore	together
2. Advise	each other
3. Influence	the energy industry

We are here to serve you all—suppliers, consumers, oil majors, oil independent companies, governments, utilities, airlines, shipping companies, industrial companies, and corporate entities, as well as each individual, in order to achieve our mutual goal of better **Energy Future.**

[6]This model has been introduced by the author since August 2014 in a few international energy conferences, the last one in Inverness, on August 2017, where he chaired the Energy Security session (please, see the link below).

---

6 http://energy7.nscj.co.uk/sessions/Haifa.htm. A session worked according to the author's agenda: **ENERGY SECURITY – provides the security of supply of oil and gas, as well as other energy-related sources.** See also the appendixes with related articles and abstracts presented in this respect during the last years.

EPILOGUE

————————◆————————

2008 Versus the Present

The first real *oil crisis* that caused an oil shortage in major markets hit the world in 1973. Thirty-five years later, the 2008 *oil price crisis* took the industry through yet another price hike. Many joined the "festivities" of the thirty-fifth anniversary of the 1973 crisis: major energy companies, traders and capital market analysts, speculators, investors, steel producers, as well as shipyards, shipping companies, drillings and pipeline companies. All had much to gain from the 2008 spike in oil prices and took in extraordinary profits, while we all paid the price, and the celebrations raged on, despite warnings and predictions that the world economy would by no means be able to withstand such a price.

Another price crisis occurred in 2014, when the price of oil dropped below the $60 mark. This continued to deepen in 2015 and 2016, with the lowest prices in nearly a decade, at times falling below $40 per barrel, and in early 2016 to hover around the $30 level. The falling prices should have been considered a full-fledged *oil price crisis* as well. This phenomenon mirrored the crisis in 2008, when soaring prices were followed by a plummet at year's end.

The 2008 crisis was deeply rooted in the OPEC and NYMEX's market manipulations and self-serving supply and price regimes. But failure to learn from the 2008 crisis proved to be a direct catalyst for the crisis of 2010–2016.

The soaring prices of 2008 encouraged increased production aiming at selling more oil at higher prices, but apparently this brought prices down. This lack of long-term planning could only result in overproduction and a supply glut—surpluses rendered without demand, leading to a price crash: price peak and crash leading to another wave just two years after the 2008 crisis—a phenomenon that must and can be stopped.

Note that the average crude price during the years 2011–2014 was $107.41, certainly reflecting a price crisis level of a too high price, considering that even the year 2008 averaged $ 97.26.

Throughout 2015, oil prices continued their turbulent descent, hitting the $40 level in August 2015, followed by the threat of a new low of $20 per barrel in February of 2016 on the floor of the NYMEX. February 2016 opened at $31.62 for WTI and $34.24 for Brent, and recovered to a more balanced level between $45.83 for Brent, in May, and over $50 in June–July 2016, to end 2016 at $53.27 WTI, and $56.82 for the Brent.

In 2017, as this book was published, the opening price of the year by the first trading day, 3rd of January, was $52.33/bbl and $55.47/bbl for the Brent. Henry Hub gas opened at $3.33/MMBtu. It showed a good recovery from the 2016 open levels at $37.04 for WTI and $37.28 for the Brent, with 2.32 for HH gas. So, oil and gas had an impressive recovery during 2016 of nearly 50% for the oil and little over 40% for the gas. It certainly represents our **Energy Future** long-term needed price level, or at least its floor level, and this is a price we hear "the industry can live with."

The price of $30 per barrel or $130 is one and the same—a price crisis challenging world economies and further highlighting severe market failure and instability. Our **Energy Future** must be supported with affordable energy prices that dictate the need for a thorough structural change in today's energy supply and demand models, as well as energy security models.

The Silver Lining

It is encouraging to see that one of the results of the 2008 crisis was the utilization of newer, unconventional fossil resources: oil sands and oil shale. In North America, both Canada and the United States have become major producers of oil and gas from these sources.

Canada commercially produced oil from oil sands resulted in earning the title of the largest oil exporter to the United States since 2008, with 2.46 million bbl/d, passing the 2 other large exporters to the United States from South America and the Middle East. The United States itself soon followed suit with mass production of natural gas from shale gas. The enormous volume of gas produced from unconventional sources added to the world's proven gas reserves, the true importance of these new sources is, however, that once again they show that the energy industry is more resilient than the financial sector, and that the former can safely lead the world to a new energy era with secured supply.

In this new era of secure supply and abundant sources, the "hydrocarbon man" should be better able to find solutions to future energy needs that are cleaner, sustainable, and affordable.

"Explore and drill" has been the approach with the most success to date, as well as acquiring new alternative energy sources for years to come. It was highly encouraging to see that in a 2012 forecast, exploration and production (E&P) investments for the following five years planned at $330 billion worldwide.

However, this trend changed in 2015 as prices dropped, though even when prices are low, one should always remember that extensive investment in exploration and the development of new energy sources is the answer to our **energy future** needs. With some 35 percent more energy estimated to be required worldwide by 2030, a new approach became a must.

Paying the Price

The main message of our **Energy Future** is a social, political, and economic one. Consumers are being regularly extorted by industry giants from the oil majors to Saudi Arabia, Russia, the United States and the OPEC. Each exporter has its own different set of interests and political battles at heart.

The chain of greed and extortion runs throughout the industry, like a price snowball hurtling downhill toward the end-user, the consumers—domestic, industrial, power producers, who are always the ones left to pay the bill.

When examining where profits go at the end of this overpriced supply chain, one should look first and foremost at the huge revenue generated by major oil companies, year after year. From the largest giants of the industry to the last service provider, oil and energy-related companies report huge profits, regardless of whether the market is in a state of crisis.

ExxonMobil, for example, showed a constant increase in revenue and profit for years during the previous decade's price crises, peaking in 2008. In 2003, the company reported $21.51 billion in profit; this almost doubled in 2007, with a profit of $40.6 billion; a year later, the crisis year of 2008, ended with a record profit of $45.22 billion.

In the first half of 2015, ExxonMobil, facing a rollercoaster of unstable oil prices, saw a massive dive in its earnings. The company announced estimated earnings of $4.2 billion in the second quarter of 2015, compared with $8.8 billion during the same quarter of the previous year.

It is impressive to see that even though earnings cut by half within a year, the company's expenses and investments in oil and gas exploration declined by only 12 percent during the first half of 2015, compared with the same period in 2014. In 2015, ExxonMobil produced four million BOE (barrels of oil equivalent) per day—an increase of 139,000 bbl/d, or 3.6 percent—mainly from new developments in Angola, Canada, Indonesia, and the United States.

Nothing to Fear

It is necessary for consumers to realize that they must declare clearly and decisively to only pay what the energy they consume is worth, while still allowing oil producers to make a reasonable profit. Consumers must not fall for all the speculative scenarios of market shortages and unattainable demand. Producers should be the ones having fears and concerns—the fear of losing their precious petrodollar incomes.

Headlines in late 2008, such as **"Prices Fall as Market Ignores OPEC,"** allow consumers to recognize the single most important lesson that they must understand: There's nothing to fear.

Crisis management should be conducted with boldness and decisiveness; any fears of rebels and terrorists should be put aside. Al-Qaida in Afghanistan or Libya, ISIS in the deserts and oil fields of Iraq, Syria, or Libya again shouldn't matter. With this understanding, we will see the end of the energy crisis era.

Only a combination and integration of all existing, developing, and possible energy sources can bring electricity, heating, water, and energy to every corner of the world. After all, without energy, there can be no life.

In recent years, the world has seemed to ride an amazing wave of exploration and development of oil and gas sources that, along with unconventional gas, has significantly increased the world's proven reserves that, together with renewables and alternatives, strengthen the world energy security of supply and market stability—beneficial to both producers and consumers.

Energy Future – The New Energy Era

Many high-tech startup initiatives, technological entrepreneurs, and academic research institutes deal with alternative energy, along with energy preservation and efficiency. These endeavors will undoubtedly reach a breakthrough in the near future, which is a common target of all energy industry players. Calls for the total ban of fossil fuels are also on the agenda, but this seems less practical at this stage, and in the near future.

All possible methods of energy production, preservation, and efficiency of both fossil and non-fossil fuels will be part of the **energy future**, which will grant us all accessible and affordable energy.

A new energy era is the only possible outcome of everything discussed in this book. The energy industry, in particular the oil and gas industry, constitute the backbone of the world economy. Having been discovered in ancient times, flowing from the earth beneath us, fossil fuels have become the driving force of human life, and will remain as such in the coming future.

Oil and gas offer us the most attainable, economical, and relatively simple way to produce and utilize the energy society needs. Had these sources not begun to run dry, or their polluted nature been so destructive, the world would have been able to draw from them for as long as they are needed and as long as they exist and are available. But resources are in fact exhaustible, and as such, they require long-term planning, wise utilization, and preservation in preparation for years to come.

After reading this book, I trust the reader will understand that controlling energy sources, their supply, the development and use of alternatives and renewables, as well as the price we pay are what energy security is all about.

A certain balance between major players involved in the industry may well be the solution. It must come under some terms and condition of regulations by international regulators or other agreed entities. As it may be seen, the United States, Russia, Saudi Arabia, the OPEC (and non-OPEC as always), have yet to say their last word, and so must do the consumers.

A new statue is needed between producers and consumers, with a broad base of support from other players, to minimize the fluctuation of energy prices; while the need to set rules for floor and cap prices becomes a necessity.

As told and proved in this book, the world can produce the energy we need and will need in the future, and it can do that in an affordable price.

We remain with the understanding that disturbing geopolitical events happen just as wind, storms, and other weather phenomena happen—while the **energy industry** is much stronger than any or all of them—stronger to prevent any possible future oil crisis.

Our **Energy Future** is not fate, but choice. It is clear and secured, leading us to a **New Energy Era**, where the energy we need will be **Accessible, Affordable and Available**—and indelibly result in the global and unthreatened security of supply that we all need.

APPENDICES

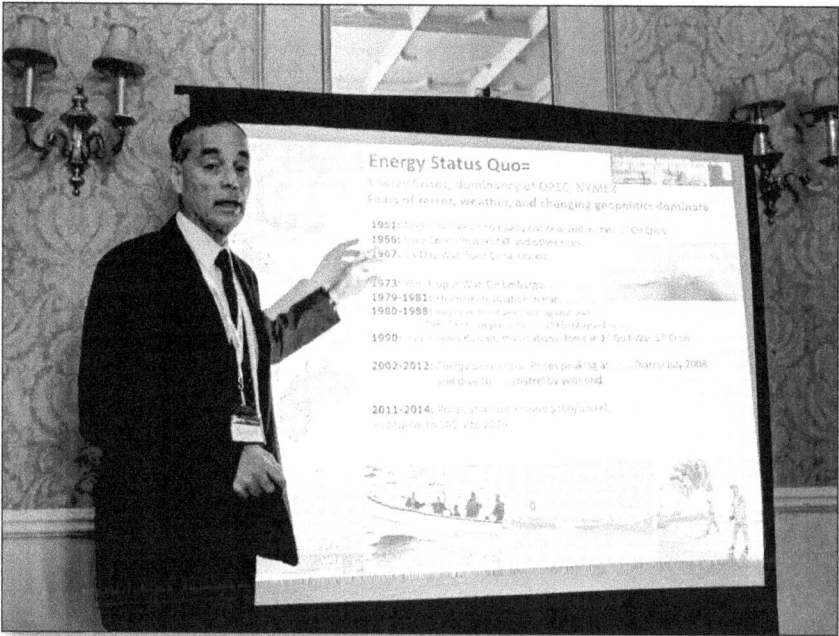

At the ECM 6 August 2016 – introducing the energy security model

Abstract from the ECM 6

Session 04: **ENERGY SECURITY**

Provides the security of supply of oil and gas as well as other energy related sources, among them renewables and alternatives.

IEA defines energy security as "an uninterrupted availability of energy sources at an affordable price." However, energy crises and other energy related (or not related) events brought sharp volatility of prices in recent decades. Most of it without any justification, as no shortage was experienced. If "Traders fears" caused prices to go up, how do they go down "on profit taking. . . ." With some important events taking shape in the industry, price may no longer be affected by irrelevant issues. Broader base of energy sources, spread worldwide and not controlled by any single power; together with better economic and available alternative fuels, renewables and energy conservation assist to provide the required Energy Security of supply.

Is it the end of the Energy Crises Era? We cannot tell yet but certainly can promote and name it *"The New Energy Era."* If analysts and trading houses, banks, and others that have promoted the high energy prices in the past, are saying that "lower energy prices will contribute more to the world economy," we did enter a new era. In this session, the following issues are addressed:

- Energy status quo – the mirror of history (energy crises)
- Changing geopolitics – risks
- Changing supply – hope
- Measures to be taken by both suppliers and consumers
- Potential market control and regulation, floor and cap prices?
- IEA and other world institutes' role in the changing "environment" and approach
- Oil from $110 to 80$ during the 3rd Quarter of 2014, ending at 56$ by December 2014 and continuing sliding during 2015— down to mid-30's USD/bbl in December 2015, which is the lowest in 9 years, and as we enter 2016, it continued to slide to the price level of 12–15 years ago!
- Does it create a potential long-term stable pricing regime, or the volatility continues? Can we aim and set a limited "volatility"

price regime? And at what level? Gas prices: regional gas prices or Brent related.

This session aims to provide attendees with a wide-angle view of Energy Security over the last 50 years; a lesson on how to implement them in our struggle to bring **Sustained Energy Security** to the world. It will introduce the NRGPrice model for energy security, based on 3 pillars:

- **Supply** – of both Fossil and Renewables/Alternatives
- **Price** – affordable and less volatile
- **Geopolitics** – the oil & gas industry is stronger than any geopolitics side effect

ACCESSIBLE, AFFORDABLE, AVAILABLE.

Session 04G, 17th August 2016, 9:30-11:15
Moderator: Dr. Henry Tan, University of Aberdeen, United Kingdom

The New Energy Era *(30 minutes) Abstract*
Moty Kuperberg
The International Energy Security Agency |
Dynamic Shipping Services, Haifa
Israel
Bio-sketch

Moty Kuperberg is a graduate of the Department of Middle East History at the University of Haifa (1984), and has a post graduate Diploma in Business Administration of Shipping from the City of London Polytechnic, 1988.

He lectures in national forums about natural gas and LNG (Liquid Natural Gas), in energy conferences, in the MA Energy Management and Policy program at the University of Haifa, and at the Israeli Institute of Energy and Environment http://www.energy.org.il

He has over twenty years of experience in the field of shipping, and is the head of the LNG and off-shore development project at Dynamic Shipping Services.

As part of his work in the company, he acts as a consultant for organizations, companies and governments around the world, assisting in the development of the energy sector and LNG projects. Among other things, he has carried out projects for the Government of Cyprus and the Turkish national gas company BOTAS.

He attends several leading international conferences and conventions on energy each year, giving him direct access to seniors from the global oil and gas industry.

An expert on the combined interrelationship between energy/geopolitics/pricing and how they combine to influence the creation of real and imaginary energy crises.

He is the recent author of an insightful book on the subject (so far published in Hebrew only) - see bottom of page in http://www.petroleumupstream.com/

Another related article by Moty appeared in the LNG Industry Journal, here http://www.lngindustry.com/magazines/issue.aspx?seo=LNG-industry&month=3&year=2012 – 'Small scale solutions', Moty Kuperberg, Dynamic Shipping Services, Israel, explains the benefits of using the small scale LNG feeder system to supply consumers spread over many destinations.

ENERGY FUTURE – FOSSILS AND BEYOND
THE NEW ENERGY ERA

Energy7
13-17 August 2017
Manchester, UK

Moty Kuperberg

Dynamic Shipping Services Haifa, Israel
The Independent Energy Security Agency

Abstract

The International Energy Agency (IEA) defines energy security as "uninterrupted availability of energy sources at an affordable price." However energy crises and other energy-related (or not related) events brought sharp volatility of prices over recent decades, mostly without any justification, since shortage of supply was not experienced.

Some distinct developments have been shaping the energy industry (namely the oil and gas, renewables and alternatives). A new energy paradigm that includes a diverse set of global energy sources utilizing available alternative fuels, renewable sources of energy, and energy efficiency and conservation measures can provide not only greater economic opportunities, but also greater security of energy supply. It remains uncertain whether this marks the end of the energy crisis era as we know it. What lies ahead is what we can consider a "New Energy Era."

To understand this new energy paradigm, the following topics will be discussed: history of the energy crises status quo, ever-changing geopolitics, its associated risks, the changing energy supply, the role of fossil fuels (mainly natural gas) in bridging to a less carbon world, and how 21st century technology can assist in this development—leading to the emergence of a new **energy future beyond fossil fuels.**

An energy security **GPS** framework is identified using three pillars: geopolitics, price, and supply and discussed as a means toward an accessible, available, and affordable **energy future**.

Keywords: energy, geopolitics, price, supply, fossils, renewables

Bibliography: Books

A leading book, must be the reference book for any reader at any level: The Prize, Daniel Yergin, Simon & Schuster, London, 1991

Answer to History. Pahlavi, M.R. New York: Stein and Day, 1980

Eisenhower at War, 1943-1945. Eisenhower, David. New York: Random House, 1986.

From Beirut to Jerusalem. Friedman, Thomas L. New York: 1989. Farrar, Straus and Giroux

Iran Between Two Revolutions. Abrahamian, E. Princeton, University Press, 1982

Looking Forward: An Autobiography. Bush, George, with Victor Gold. New York: Bantam, 1988.

Mission for My Country. Pahlavi, Mohammed Reza. New York: McGraw-Hill, 1961.

Modern Economics. J. Harvey. Macmillan London, 1985

Oil Markets: Past, Present, and Future. Yamani, Ahmed Zaki. Energy and Environmental Policy Center, Kennedy School of Government, Harvard University, September 1986.

Persian Gulf Oil in Middle East and International Conflicts. Abir, Mordechai. Jerusalem: The Hebrew University of Jerusalem, 1976.

Saudi Arabia in the Oil Era and Elites; Conflict and Collaboration. Abir, Mordechai. London: Croom Helm, 1988.

The European Community and the Middle East: The Polities of Ambiguity. Yaniv, Avner.

The Fall of the Shah. Hoveyda, F. London: Weidenfeld & Nicolson, 1980

The Petroleum Industry, A Nontechnical guide. Charles F. Conaway. PennWell Publishing Company, Tulsa, Oklahoma, 1999

The World Crisis. 4 vols. Churchill, Winston S. New York: Charles Scribner's Sons, 1983-29.

White House Years. Kissinger, Henry A. Boston: Little, Brown, 1979.

Years of Upheaval. Kissinger, Henry A. Boston: Little, Brown, 1982.

Useful links to oil companies and related entities

American Petroleum Institute: www.api.org

Bloomberg: https://www.bloomberg.com

British Petroleum: www.bp.com

Bunker World: www.bunkerworld.com

Chevron: www.chevron.com

The World Factbook, CIA: www.cia.gov

Conoco Phillips: www.conocophillips.com

World LNG Summit: www.cwclng.com

Australian Department of Defence: www.defence.gov.au

Dow Jones: www.dj.com

Singapore Economic Development Board: www.edb.gov.sg

The Economist: www.economist.com

The European Central Bank: www.ecb.int

Eco Energy: www.ecoenergy.co.il

Japanese Agency for Natural Resources of Energy: www.enecho.meti.go.jp

Energy Bulletin: www.energubulletin.net

Energy Future Australia: www.efa.com.au

Energy Information Administration, Department of Energy: www.eia.doe.gov

Energy Market Authority: www.ema.gov.sg

Europa: https://ec.europa.eu/

European Energy Forum: http://www.europeanenergyforum.eu/

Exxonmobil Perspectives: www.exxonmobilperspectives.com

CIA declassified documents (Freedom of Information Act): www.foia.cia.gov

International Energy Agency: www.iea.org

Australian Department of Industry: www.industry.gov.au

Japan Times: www.japantimes.co.jp

Middle East Review of International Affairs: http://meria.idc.ac.il

Ministry of Foreign Affairs of Japan: www.mofa.go.jp

National Geographic: http://www.nationalgeographic.com/

Offshore Magazine: www.offshore-mag.com

Oil and Gas Journal: www.ogj.com

Organization of Petroleum Exporting Countries: www.opec.org

Ormat Technologies: www.ormat.com
Re-Energy: http://www.re-energy.ca/
Renewable Energy World: www.renewableenergyworld.com
The Baker Institute Energy Forum: www.rice.edu/energy
Siew: www.siew.sg
Spiegel Online: www.spiegel.de
Techcorr: www.techcorr.com
The Guardian: www.theguardian.com www.themarker.com
Trade Winds: www.tradewinds.no
World Nuclear Association: www.world-nuclear.org

Additional references

http://www.chevron.com/globalissues/energypolicy/
http://www.conocophillips.com/newsroom/speeches-and-presentations/Pages/
    the-new-energy-landscape.aspx
http://www.defence.gov.au/ADC/Publications/Commanders/2012/08_SAP%20
    Linda%20McCann%20-%20Japan.pdf
http://ec.europa.eu/energy/en/topics/energy-strategy/energy-security-strategy
https://www.edb.gov.sg/content/edb/en/industries/industries/energy.html
http://www.efa.com.au/Library/cthEnergyWhitePaper.pdf
http://www.eia.gov/beta/international/?fips=wotc&trk=p3
https://www.ema.gov.sg/cmsmedia/News/Speech/539124d55780004062014_
    ACE_s_Opening_Remarks_for_Changing_the_Game_final_web.pdf
http://www.enecho.meti.go.jp/en/category/others/basic_plan/pdf/4th_strategic_
    energy_plan.pdf
http://europesenergyfuture.economist.com/balancing-act/
http://www.exxonmobilperspectives.com/2015/02/23/obama-administration-
    highlights-lng-export-benefits/
http://www.exxonmobilperspectives.com/2015/02/20/another-north-dakota-
    production-record-and-the-power-of-markets/
http://www.exxonmobilperspectives.com/2012/05/07/imports-exports-and-u-s-
    energy-security/
http://forumonenergy.com/2014/06/10/an-analysis-of-japans-4th-strategic-
    energy-plan/

http://www.iea.org/media/freepublications/security/
  EnergySupplySecurity2014_Japan.pdf

http://www.industry.gov.au/energy/Documents/Energy-Security/nesa/National-
  Energy-Security-Assessment-2011.pdf

http://www.japantimes.co.jp/news/2015/04/07/business/economy-business/ldp-
  proposes-future-energy-policy-heavy-on-nuclear-power/#.VZJwYfmqqko

http://www.siew.sg/docs/default-source/e-book/siew_energy_book2013.
  pdf?sfvrsn=2

http://www.techcorr.com/news/Articles/Article.cfm?ID=4954

http://www.theguardian.com/world/2015/apr/22/japan-moves-nearer-to-
  restarting-nuclear-reactors-after-court-gives-go-ahead

BP Statistical review up to the latest 2017 edition: http://www.bp.com/content/
  dam/bp/pdf/energy-economics/statistical-review-2016/bp-statistical-
  review-of-world-energy-2016-full-report.pdf (this is for 2016 data).

Following are a few of the important international energy conferences I have attended – which allowed direct meetings with top industry leaders—mainly LNG conferences—since 2003, among them:

CWC World LNG Summit since 2003 to 2015
http://www.thecwcgroup.com/events/

Euromed Cyprus - East Mediterranean offshore conferences 2013-2017
www.euromedoffshore.com

Different projects executed in the last 12 years on small scale LNG, as well as shipping project cargoes and heavy lift projects to the energy sector worldwide—which gave me the opportunity to see how the energy industry works and developed itself into the highest technological and economic frontiers.

Leading projects we handled included the master plan for the coastal LNG distribution for the Turkish gas company BOTAS, similar projects on other locations in the Mediterranean, Black Sea, European North Continent, the Caribbean, and South East Asia.

INDEX

www.ingramcontent.com/pod-product-compliance
Lightning Source LLC
Chambersburg PA
CBHW060332200326
41519CB00011BA/1907